THE CATHOLIC UNIVERSITY OF AMERICA
CANON LAW STUDIES
NO. 266

Documents Required for the Reception of Orders

A HISTORICAL SYNOPSIS AND COMMENTARY

BY

REV. JOSEPH JAMES QUINN, A.B., J.C.L.
Priest of the Archdiocese of New York

A DISSERTATION

Submitted to the Faculty of the School of Canon Law of the Catholic University of America in Partial Fulfillment of the Requirements for the Degree of Doctor of Canon Law

THE CATHOLIC UNIVERSITY OF AMERICA PRESS
WASHINGTON, D. C.
1948

Nihil Obstat:

JOANNES ROGG SCHMIDT, J.C.D.,
Censor Deputatus.

Washingtonii, D. C., die 5 Martii, 1948.

Imprimatur:

✠ FRANCISCUS CARDINAL SPELLMAN,
Archiepiscopus Neo-Eboracensis.

Neo Eboraci, die 5 Martii, 1948.

Printed by
THE PAULIST PRESS
401 West 59th Street
New York 19, N. Y.

51

TO MY MOTHER

AND

IN MEMORY OF

MY FATHER

TABLE OF CONTENTS

CHAPTER III

CHAPTER IV

PART TWO

CANONICAL COMMENTARY

CHAPTER V

CHAPTER VII

CHAPTER VIII

CHAPTER IX

FOREWORD

In the first recorded instruction regarding the conferral of Holy Orders, St. Paul warned Timothy: "Impose not hands lightly upon any man, neither be a partaker of other men's sins." [1] This warning has been echoed and re-echoed by the Church, the divinely appointed guardian of the sacraments, down through the succeeding centuries. Because she realizes so well the inestimable dignity of the priesthood, and because she knows so well the very serious harm that can be done to the cause of Christ through the admission of unworthy candidates to that lofty office, she has always endeavored to insure, as far as is humanly possible, the presence in the candidate of those qualities which she deems necessary.

To achieve this end the Church has used various means. At first the approbation of the faithful was asked before the candidate was admitted to the clerical state. With the growth of the Church this system became impractical, and so in time the responsibility for seeing to the candidate's fitness was placed primarily upon the bishop. To assist the bishop in this all-important task the Church from time to time enacted appropriate legislation. Among the requirements established by such laws was the presentation of documents by the candidate to prove his fitness.

In the early Church no mention is found of documents. In time, the permission to be ordained outside one's own diocese came to be expressed in writing, although this was not necessary from the general law of the Church. In the course of the centuries the nature of these dimissorial letters, as they were called, underwent a radical change. With the Council of Trent came legislation requiring testimonials on the part of every candidate, to be given further specification by the Constitution *Speculatores* of Pope Innocent XII. The latter document together with the subsequent decrees and decisions of the Sacred Congregations was the guiding norm in this matter prior to the Code. With the coming of the Code of Canon Law many of the requirements which were purely particular or merely a matter

[1] I Tim., V:22.

of practice became part of the universal law of the Church. Final specification was given to the law by the Instructions *Quam ingens* and *Quantum Religiones* of the Sacred Congregation of the Sacraments and the Sacred Congregation of Religious respectively.

It is the purpose of this dissertation to trace the history of the law in this matter and to outline the documents which must be obtained before the candidate may be promoted to orders. Many problems which concern ordination itself have been merely referred to in an effort to make the work as practical as possible for those who are concerned with these matters.

In conclusion, the writer wishes to express his gratitude to the Faculty of the School of Canon Law of the Catholic University of America for their help and direction, to the Right Reverend John M. Fearns, S.T.D., Rector of Saint Joseph's Seminary, Yonkers, New York, and to many other priests of the Archdiocese of New York for their aid and encouragement, and to all who aided in any way in its preparation. Most of all the writer wishes to express his gratitude to His Eminence Francis Cardinal Spellman, Archbishop of New York, for the opportunity to pursue graduate study in Canon Law.

Part One

Historical Synopsis

LEGISLATION OF THE FIRST TWELVE CENTURIES

Article I. From the First to the Fifth Century

When the purpose of the Church's laws which require certain documents for ordination is kept in mind, it is not surprising to find that in the early Church there were in general no such laws. Since in the early years of the Christian era, while the local Church was yet comparatively small, it was not difficult for a bishop to know thoroughly each candidate and his qualifications, such requirements were not necessary. With regard to those candidates who were to be ordained by a bishop who was not their own such was not true, and so for these certain regulations were set forth. From these has come, eventually, the present law of the Church with regard to dimissorial letters.

1. *The Necessity for Dimissorials*

The successors to the Apostles in the episcopate were definitely limited in the exercise of their jurisdiction. There were numerous reasons why such was the case. Among these was the desire to avoid the confusion and the quarrels which might very well result if a bishop were allowed to ordain indiscriminately candidates subject to some other bishop. A still greater reason was the exclusion from the ranks of the priesthood of unworthy men, which could not be done when the candidate was, for all practical purposes, a stranger to the bishop.[1] To this end popes and councils legislated that bishops were

[1] Reiffenstuel (1642-1703) summed up the situation very well: "Certum est, quod unusquisque non nisi a proprio Episcopo ordinandus, nullusque possit ordinare extraneum, nec etiam primam tonsuram huic conferre absque proprii Superioris licentia. . . . Et merito: tum ut dissensiones evitentur, quae suborire possent inter Episcopos, si unus alterius subditos, eodem ignorante, ac saepius invito, ordinare praesumeret. Tum ut obvietur malitiis hominum, atque indigni

not to enter the diocese of another bishop to ordain, nor were they to ordain candidates who were not their own subjects if the permission of the candidates' own bishop had not been given.[2]

Pope Innocent I (401-417), when writing to Victricius, Bishop of Rouen, forbade the ordination of men from other dioceses unless their proper bishops gave the requested permission.[3] It should be noted here that when the councils declared that the penalty for the violation of such precepts was invalidity of the ordination, what was really meant was what is known today as a suspension of the exercise of the orders received.[4]

From a great number of councils, held both in the East and in the West during this early period, there issued forth similar legisla-

et ignorantes ad sacros ordines non promoveantur, qui alioquin clericales ordines, quos a propriis episcopis forsan sibi jam denegatos dolent, aut ex certis impedimentis canonicis sibi denegandos fore merito verentur; ab extraneis episcopis, nullamque de ipsorum defectibus notitiam habentibus, in animarum suarum perniciem, et ecclesiastici ordinis dedecus, recipere praesumerent."—*Jus Canonicum Universum* (5 vols., Parisiis, 1864-1868), t. 1, in c. 4, X, *de tempore ordinationis et qualitate ordinandorum,* I, 11, n. 77; see also Moeder, *The Proper Bishop for Ordination and Dimissorial Letters,* The Catholic University of America Canon Law Studies, n. 95 (Washington, D. C.: The Catholic University of America, 1935), pp. 25-27 (hereafter cited *Proper Bishop for Ordination*).

[2] An exception to this rule existed in Africa, where the Bishop of Carthage had the right to ordain men for any Church in pro-consular Africa—III Carthage (397), c. 45—Mansi, *Sacrorum Conciliorum Nova et Amplissima Collectio* (53 vols. in 60, Parisiis, Arnhem, Lipsiae, 1907-1927), III, 809 (hereafter cited as Mansi). Cf. Hallier, *De Sacris Electionibus et Ordinationibus ex Antiquo et Novo Ecclesiae Usu (De Sacris Elect. et Ordin.)* (1860), Pars. II, sect. V, cap. III, art. IX, n. 2—Migne, *Theologia Cursus Completus* (Parisiis, 1863-1866), XXIV, 1209 (hereafter cited *MTC*).

[3] Mansi, III, 1032; Jaffé, *Regesta Pontificum Romanorum ab condita Ecclesia ad annum post Christum natum MCXCVIII* (2. ed., correctam et auctam auspiciis Gulielmi Wattenbach curaverunt Kaltenbrunner, Ewald, Loewenfeld, 2 vols. in 1, Lipsiae 1885-1888), n. 286 (hereafter cited Jaffé).

[4] Schroeder, *Disciplinary Decrees of the General Councils* (St. Louis: B. Herder Book Co., 1937), pp. 46-47, footnote 106; Thomassinus, *Vetus et Nova Ecclesiae Disciplina circa Beneficia et Beneficiarios* (10 vols., Moguntiaci, 1787), Pars II, lib. I, cap. IX, n. 1 (hereafter cited *Ecclesiae Disciplina*). Cf. also Hefele-Leclercq, *Histoire des Conciles* (10 vols. in 19, Paris: Letouzey et Ané, 1907-1938), I, Pars I, 604, who state that at least with regard to the Council of Nicaea (325), c. 16, the matter is not clear.

tion. The Council of Elvira, Spain (305), ordered that candidates were not to be ordained outside of the provinces in which they were baptized, on the grounds that the lives of such men were not sufficiently known to the ordaining bishop.[5] The Council of Nicaea, the first ecumenical council of the Church (325), ruled that, if anyone should attempt to ordain the subject of another without the consent of the candidate's own bishop, such an ordination was to be considered invalid.[6]

The Council of Antioch (341) enacted similar legislation, stating that a bishop was not to advance to the priesthood or to the diaconate those who were subjects of another bishop, except perhaps with the consent and advice of the bishop of that region.[7] The I Council of Carthage (348) legislated that a bishop was not to appropriate to himself, for the purposes of ordination, laymen from other places without the knowledge (*conscientia*) of their own bishop.[8] The legislation of the Council of Vannes (465), in western Gaul, is quite interesting in this matter. In that council it was decreed that bishops were not to promote to higher orders those who had been ordained clerics by other bishops, if they had not received the permission of those bishops.[9]

[5] C. 24—Bruns, *Canones Apostolorum et Conciliorum Saeculorum IV-VII* (2 vols., Berolini, 1839), II, 5 (hereafter cited Bruns). Cf. Mansi, II, 10.

[6] C. 16: "Si quis autem ad alium pertinentem audacter invadere, et in sua ecclesia ordinare tentaverit non consentiente episcopo, a quo discessit is, qui regulae mancipatur, ordinatio hujuscemodi irrita comprobetur."—Mansi, II, 682. Cf. c. 3, D. LXXI; Bruns, I, 18.

[7] C. 22: "Episcopus . . ., nec constituat presbyteros, aut diaconos alteri subjectos episcopo, nisi forte cum consilio et voluntate regionis episcopi."—Mansi, II, 1326; c. 7, C. IX, q. 2. The date of this council is controversial. Some hold the date given, viz. 341, others are of the opinion that it took place after the Council of Laodicaea, which was held sometime between 343 and 380, while still others hold that it took place in 332. Cf. Van Hove, *Commentarium Lovaniense in Codicem Iuris Canonici,* Vol. I, tomus I, *Prolegomena ad Codicem Iuris Canonici* (2. ed., Mechliniae-Romae: H. Dessain, 1945), pp. 143-144 (hereafter cited *Prolegomena*).

[8] C. 5: ". . . neque apud se retinere, nec laicum usurpare sibi de plebe aliena, ut eum ordinet sine conscientia ejus episcopi de cujus plebe est."—Bruns, I, 113; c. 6, D. LXXI.

[9] C. 10: "Episcopi quoque ab aliis episcopis ordinatos clericos sine permissu eorum a quibus fuerint ordinati promovere ad superiorem ordinem non prae-

Among the authors there was discussed at length the question whether this legislation, and that which followed this period, applied to all, lay as well as clerics, or merely to clerics. Thomassinus (1619-1695) was of the opinion that these laws were intended only for clerics. He pointed out the examples, given by many other authors also, of Origen (184/5-254), who although born in Alexandria was ordained in Palestine without the consent of his own bishop; of Jerome (ca. 342-420), born in Dalmatia, educated in Rome, and ordained by Paulinus, Bishop of Antioch (362-388); and of Augustine (354-430) as well as of others.[10]

Thomassinus stated that until the year 1000 the bishops of both the East and the West were able to confer tonsure and orders on subjects of another diocese, but were not permitted, as long as they had not obtained proper permission, to confer orders on one who had received tonsure or minor orders from another bishop.[11] Those who held this opinion pointed to the ordinations mentioned above, and also to the words of St. Augustine himself as expressed in a letter written in the year 401, in which he expressly indicated that this law applied only to clerics.[12] They also adduced many councils in

sumant, ne concordiam fraternam injuria illata contaminent."—Bruns, II, 144. For further pronouncements on this matter cf. Council of Sardica (343), cc. 18-19—Mansi, III, 29-30; Council of Turin (397), c. 7—Mansi, III, 862; IV Council of Carthage (398), c. 27—Mansi, III, 953; I Council of Orange (441), c. 8—Mansi, VI, 437; II Council of Arles (451), c. 13—Bruns, II, 132; Council of Angers (453), c. 15—Bruns, II, 138; I Council of Tours (461), c. 9—Bruns, II, 141.

[10] *Ecclesiae Disciplina*, Pars II, lib. I, cap. I, nn. 8-9. Cf. also Petra, *Commentaria ad Constitutiones Apostolicas* (5 vols. in 2, Venetiis, 1729), t. V, n. 63, p. 149.

[11] *Op. cit.*, Pars II, lib. I, cap. V, n. 12.

[12] *Epistola LXIV*: "Recense ergo concilium [Carthage, 398] . . . et ibi etiam invenimus de solis clericis fuisse statutum, non etiam de laicis, ut undecumque venientes non recipiantur in monasterium, non quia monasterii facta mentio est, sed quia sic institutum est, ut clericum alienum nemo suscipiat."—Migne, *Patrologiae Cursus Completus, Series Latina* (221 vols., Parisiis, 1844-1864), XXXIII, 233 (hereafter cited *MPL*); *Corpus Scriptorum Ecclesiasticorum Latinorum*, Editum Consilio et Impensis Academiae Litterarum Caesariae Vindobonensis, *Corpus Vindobonense* (Vindobonae, 1866—), XXXIV², 231 (cited *CSEL*).

which are found the words *alienum clericum, alienum ministrum,* and similar terms, which clearly pointed to the fact that these designations were intended merely for clerics.[13]

Hallier (1595-1659), on the other hand, stated that the law forbade bishops to ordain *ullos* without the consent of their own bishops.[14] Hinschius (1835-1898) in agreeing with him stated that from the very nature of the legislation and its purpose it was presupposed that the law applied to all, clerics and lay alike.[15]

It would have been indeed a glaring contradiction for the Church to be so strict about the place where people received Penance and the Holy Eucharist, so that they could not communicate away from home without commendatory letters from their bishop, and to be so liberal about the sacrament of Holy Orders, that lay candidates could receive ordination anywhere.[16] If there were councils which supported the view of Thomassinus, there were also councils which supported the contrary view, inasmuch as they made no distinction in their legislation and therefore, so it must be concluded, intended to legislate for all, not just for clerics.[17]

With regard to regulars and their ordination, legislation was very

[13] The I General Council of Nicaea (325), c. 16—Mansi, II, 10; Sardica (343), c. 19: "Alienum ministrum"—Mansi, III, 30; Turin (397), c. 7: "clericum alterius"—Mansi, III, 682; Telepta (Zella in Byzacium) (418), c. 7: "clericum alienum"—Mansi, IV, 380; Vannes (465), c. 10: "clericos"—Mansi, VI, 437, among others.

[14] *De Sacris Elect. et Ordin.*, Pars II, sect. V, cap. X, n. 1—*MTC*, XXIV, 1035.

[15] *System des katholischen Kirchenrechts* (4 vols., Berlin, 1869-1888), I, 86. Wernz (1842-1914) was of the same opinion on the question—*Ius Decretalium* (3. ed., 6 vols., Prati, 1913-1915), II, n. 26.

[16] McBride, *Incardination and Excardination of Seculars,* The Catholic University of America Canon Law Studies, n. 145 (Washington, D. C.: The Catholic University of America Press, 1941), p. 43 (hereafter cited *Incardination and Excardination*).

[17] Councils of Elvira (305), c. 24—Bruns, II, 5; Antioch (341), c. 22: "alteri subjectos episcopo"—Mansi, II, 1326; I Carthage (348): "laicum usurpare"—Bruns, I, 113; I Orange (441), c. 8—Bruns, II, 123; II Arles (451), c. 13—Bruns, II, 132.

scant. In the very early times these were not exempt from episcopal jurisdiction, and therefore even as regards the receiving of orders they were subject to the bishops. Hence it was not strange that the V Council of Carthage (398) established an excommunication for a bishop who illegitimately ordained a monk from a monastery situated in another diocese, and deposition for the monk who thus wrongfully acquiesced in his promotion to orders.[18]

2. *The Nature of Dimissorials*

In the legislation of these early councils, as a general rule, it was not expressly stated that this *licentia, consensus, conscientia* (and other terms used to express the same idea) had to be manifested in writing. It is believed by many, however, that writing was the ordinary means employed in the expressing of this consent. There is some justification for this in a letter of Saint Augustine, written in the year 404.[19]

In the early Church there were in use many types of letters. Lupus (1611-1681) listed many of these, including the *litterae pacificae,* the *litterae canonicae,* the *litterae commendatitiae,* and the *litterae dimissoriae* or *dimissoriales,* all of which have some import in the present study.[20] It is quite clear from a reading of the canons of the councils that many of these terms were used interchangeably. Even among the authors there was no complete agreement as to the precise meaning of each one. With regard to dimissorials, for the most part there is no doubt that these were letters given to a bishop for the sake of authorizing him to ordain a candidate who was a subject of the bishop who issued them. It must be stressed, however, that the meaning of the term as it is known today has, since antiquity, undergone a very great change. Then they were used not for sending a man to another bishop merely for ordination, the original bishop in the meantime continuing to maintain all rights over him, but rather for transferring the man to the diocese of the

[18] C. 13—Mansi, III, 971. Cf. Wernz, *Ius Decretalium,* II, n. 26.

[19] *Epistola LXXVIII*: "Sed cum promoveri in clericatu sive illic per me, sive alibi per litteras meas vehementissime conarentur . . ." *MPL,* XXXIII, 268.

[20] *Opera Omnia Canonica* (12 vols., Venetiis, 1727), IX, 199.

bishop to whom the authority was given to ordain.[21] As Van Espen (1646-1728) pointed out, in its original sense the word was used in the Trullan Synod (692), wherein it was decreed: ". . . sine proprii episcopi scripta dimissoria in alienae ecclesiae catalogum referri." [22] Citing the Greek canonist Balsamon (ca. 1140-1195), he stated that a cleric who wished to go to another Church to become enrolled among the clergy of that Church had to bring with him two letters from the bishop who had previously ordained him, viz.: commendatory and dimissorial. The former served to prove that the cleric had received the orders which he claimed, and the latter served the purpose of permitting his incorporation among the clergy of the new Church as one who was free of all impediments.[23]

This character of dimissorial letters in the early Church came as a result of the legislation on the title of ordination, according to which no man was to receive ordination until he was enrolled in the service of a certain church from which he was to receive support.[24] Hallier asserted that there were instances when dimissorials were used with the meaning which is attached to them today. He furnished the example of an abbot who in the time of St. Gregory the Great (590-604) issued letters to a monk the while he intended at the same time to retain all his rights over the monk. The instances of this are rare, however, and in no way militate against the meaning of the term which has been set forth above.[25]

21 Devoti, *Institutionum Canonicarum Libri IV* (2 vols., Romae, 1830), tit. II, sect. V, n. 50, nota 2: P. Gasparri, *Tractatus Canonicus de Sacra Ordinatione* (2 vols., Parisiis-Lugduni, 1894), n. 863 (hereafter cited *De Sacra Ordinatione*); Van Espen, *Commentarius in Canones Juris Veteris ac Novi et in Jus Novissimum* (Lovanii, 1753), p. 370; McBride, *Incardination and Excardination,* pp. 155-156; Hallier, *De Sacris Elect. et Ordin.,* Pars II, sect. V, cap. III, art. 10, n. 6—*MTC,* XXIV, 1042.

22 *Jus Ecclesiasticum Universum* (10 vols., Lovanii et reperitur, Lugduni, 1778), Tom. I, pars II, sect. I, tit. IX, cap. 3, n. 2.

23 Van Espen, *Commentarius,* p. 370.

24 Moeder, *Proper Bishop for Ordination,* p. 40; Thomassinus, *Ecclesiae Disciplina,* Pars II, lib. I, cap. II, n. 7; Van Espen, *Jus Ecclesiasticum,* Tom. I, pars II, sect. I, tit. IX, cap. II, n. 6; Wernz, *Ius Decretalium,* II, n. 90.

25 *De Sacris Elect. et Ordin.,* Pars. II, sect. V, cap. III, art. X, n. 6—*MTC,* XXIV, 1042.

3. *The Form of Dimissorials*

An example of these dimissorials, which demonstrates the proper matter and form, was published by the I General Council of Nicaea (325) and was incorporated in the *Decree of Gratian* as a model for later centuries.[26] To forestall all possible contingency of fraud the bishops worked out a system by which the genuinness of these letters could be easily ascertained. It consisted of a series of Greek alphabetic characters incorporated in the document, each of which had a special significance. One of these characters stood for the name of the bishop to whom the letters were addressed, another represented the city of his diocese, another represented the name of the bishop issuing them. From this it can be seen that these letters were always sent to a definite bishop. They were not issued to a cleric whose destination had not been ascertained by the bishop who issued them. This also meant that a request had first to be received by that bishop before he would issue them. An indication of this is found, for example, in the letter of Pope Innocent I referred to above.[27] The protection afforded by this system lay either in the fact that the characters were kept secret among the bishops of the Council, or in the fact that they had to be written in the bishop's own hand.[28]

[26] "Sanctissimo in Christo fratri summa dulcedine karitatis amplectendo A., illius civitatis episcopo, Y., illius ecclesiae praesul, perpetuae beatitudinis optat in Christo salutem. Ω.Y.A.Ω. De cetero noverit sancta fraternitas vestra, quod iste clericus, Hermannus nomine, nostra in parochia instructus ac detonsus, parvitatem nostram rogavit, quatenus illi commendaticias litteras conscriberemus, quibus vestrae celsitudini commendatus sub tuitione vestri regiminis degere posset; cuius voluntati consentientes secundum canonicam auctoritatem litteras ei dimissorias dedimus, per quas et ipsi concedimus, ut sub vestro magisterio divini servituti insistens suae deserviat utilitati, et vobis licentiam tribuimus, ut, si dignum eum iudicaveritis, ad sacros ordines promoveatis. Commendatum ergo eum curae vestrae suscipite, et nostris ex partibus absolutum in vestrarum ovium numero custodite. Quas litteras, ut vigore veritatis firmatae indubitanter a vobis suscipiantur, litteris grecis, ut canonica docet auctoritas, confirmare sategimus. Sancta Trinitas vestram beatitudinem ad regimen sanctae suae ecclesiae perpetualiter bene valere concedat, 'Αμήν. —C. 2, D. LXXIII.

[27] Cf. *supra*, p. 2.

[28] McBride, *Incardination and Excardination*, pp. 155-158; Baronius (1538-

Article II. From the Sixth Century to the III Lateran Council (1179)

With the progress of time a fairly compact body of laws was being drawn up with regard to dimissorial letters. From the sixth to the twelfth centuries there was an absence of papal legislation.[29] As for the general councils, the I Council of Nicaea (325) remained the only one that had legislated on the matter. There was, however, no dearth of legislation emanating from provincial councils and diocesan synods.

1. *The Necessity for Dimissorials*

Whereas in the first five centuries most of the councils had confined themselves merely to legislating that permission was needed for the ordaining of strangers, in the following centuries the law with regard to the necessity of letters became much more explicit.

One of the first councils during this time to state expressly that letters were needed for this purpose was the III Council of Orange, held in the year 538. The seventeenth canon of this Council decreed that clerics who for any reason whatsoever were staying outside their diocese were not to be ordained to higher orders without the written consent of their bishop.[30] In the Province of Galicia similar

1607) believed that this part of the proceedings of the Council was kept secret—*Annales Ecclesiastici* (37 vols., Vols. I-XXVIII, Barri-Ducis, 1864-1875, Vols. XXIX-XXXVII, Parisiis, 1876-1883), Anno 325, T. IV, n. 167. The same author offered an explanation of the system, nn. 163-169; likewise Hallier, *De Sacris Elect. et Ordin.*, Pars II, sect. V, cap. III, art. X, n. 4—*MTC*, XXIV, 1038.

29 Pope Gregory the Great (590-604) several times in settling disputes mentioned the *cessio*, which was another word used for *dimissio*, but on the whole he made no contribution to the development of the law in this regard. Cf. Gregorius I (590-604), *Ianuario Archiepiscopo Caralis Sardiniae—Monumenta Germaniae Historica, Gregorii I Papae Registrum Epistolarum* (4 vols., ed. L. M. Hartmann post Pauli Ewaldi obitum, Berolini, 1887-1899), Tom. I, Liber I, n. 81; Gregorius I, *Iohanni Episcopi Arimensi, op. cit.*, Tom. II, pars 2, Liber XIV, n. 11; Gregorius I, *Cypriano Diacono, op. cit.*, Tom. I, Liber VI, n. 20.

30 *Monumenta Germaniae Historica, Legum Sectio III, Concilia Aevi Karolini* (Tom. I, II, pars I, II, ed. A. Werminghoff, Hannoverae et Lipsiae, 1906-

legislation was decreed by the I Council of Braga (561), of which the eighteenth canon stated that a cleric from another diocese was not to be ordained *"nisi forte signata ipsius scripta susceperit."* [31]

In 692 a council was convoked at Constantinople. This Council has come to be known in history as the *Quinisextum,* or the Trullan Synod. It drew up 102 disciplinary decrees, which were intended to be a supplement to the preceding ecumenical councils. It has been considered as an ecumenical council among the Eastern Orthodox Churches, but was never accepted as such in the West. Some of its canons, however, were incorporated into the legislation of the Western Church, as long as they did not contradict the true faith, good morals, and the decrees of Rome.[32] Among its decrees was one, the seventeenth, which stated the need of written dimissorials, and which, as was pointed out in the preceding chapter, showed clearly the meaning of the word as used at that time.[33]

In 743 Pope Zachary (741-752) convoked a synod at Rome. In canon 11 of this Synod it was ordered that clerics from other cities could not be ordained without dimissorials from their respective bishops.[34]

According to Thomassinus and those who shared his opinion, the third canon of the Council of Ravenna (997) marked a turning point in the history of dimissorial letters. This canon, which expressly forbade bishops to ordain any candidates from other dioceses

1908), Tom. I, p. 78 (hereafter cited *MGM, Conc.*). Cf. also Bruns, II, 196-199, who lists this as canon 15.

[31] Bruns, II, 34.

[32] Schroeder, *Disciplinary Decrees,* p. 128; Hefele and Leclercq, *Histoire des Conciles,* III, pars I, 560-581.

[33] *Supra,* p. 7: ". . . statuimus, ut a mense Januario praeteritae quartae indictionis, nullus omnino clericus, in quocumque sit gradu, potestatem habeat sine proprii episcopi scripta dimissoria, in alienae ecclesiae catalogum referri. . . ." —Mansi, XI, 951; c. 1, C. XXI, q. 2.

[34] "Sed et hoc interdicimus, ut nullus episcoporum audeat iuxta sanctorum canonum statuta . . . aut alterius civitatis clericum sine dimissoriis sui Episcopo suscipere vel ordinare neque eum usurpet nisi episcopus ejus precibus exoratus concedere voluerit, . . ."—*MGH, Conc.*, Tom. II, pars I, p. 17. Cf. also Mansi, XII, 384.

regardless of whether or not they already were clerics,[35] according to them marked a change in emphasis in the matter of competency for ordination, and consequently for the issuing of dimissorial letters. Whereas in the earlier centuries the factor of ordination was all important, thenceforward, according to them, the person's origin became the determining factor. They explained the change by noting that in the early Church not all the provinces and cities had their own bishops. Therefore men born in those cities which lacked bishops had more ready occasion not to attach themselves to any other bishop than to him who first had imposed hands upon them. As time went on and the Church became more widely diffused, the number of bishops in the cities and provinces increased. As a result of this it seemed most equitable that the bishop should choose those who were to be his ministers from among those whom he had baptized and whose lives and moral conduct he had been able to observe practically from their childhood.[36]

The Council of Benevento was convoked by Pope Urban I in 1091. From it there issued certain disciplinary decrees, one of which forbade any bishop to ordain a cleric from another diocese without dimissorial letters and the commendation of his bishop.[37]

For the most part regulars were still governed by the laws which regulated the ordination of seculars. The Council of Agde (506) prescribed that, at least with regard to the *monachi vagantes*, re-

[35] ". . . neque alterius dioecesanos vel parochianos recipere aut promovere seu retinere praesumat sine canonicis epistolis . . ."—Mansi, XIX, 220.

[36] Thomassinus, *Ecclesiae Disciplina*, Pars II, lib. I, c. I, n. 13; Petra, *Commentaria*, V, n. 66.

[37] C. 3—Mansi, XX, 739. Cf. also I Auvergne (535), c. 11—*MGH, Conc.*, Tom. I, p. 68; III Orleans (538), c. 6—Mansi, IX, 16; V Orleans (549), c. 5—*MGH, Conc.*, Tom. I, p. 102; V Arles (554), c. 7—*MGH, Conc.*, Tom. I, p. 119; Chalon-sur-Sâone (649), c. 13—Bruns, II, 267; VI Paris (829), lib. I, cap. 36—*MGH, Conc.*, Tom. II, pars II, pp. 635-636; Meaux (845), c. 51—Mansi, XIV, 831; Mainz (888), c. 15—Mansi, XVIII A, 68; Tribur (895), c. 27—Mansi, XVIII A, 130; Nantes (896), c. 7—Mansi, XVIII A, 168; Rouen (1050), c. 9—Mansi, XIX, 753; Gerona (1078), c. 12—Mansi, XX, 520; London (1138), c. 7—Mansi, XXI, 512.

ligious should not be ordained unless their abbot had given testimonials to them.[38]

Dating from the middle of the ninth century (847-852) came the pseudo-Isidorian forgeries, which consisted of four rather closely connected collections of canonical enactments. The authors of these forgeries sought to reform certain of the abuses current in the Church by producing forged legislation from the past. Their main preoccupation was to fortify the position of the ordinary against all encroachments. So cleverly did they mingle authentic pronouncements with the spurious that the forgery remained concealed for many centuries. Included in these collections were decretals, supposedly deriving from some of the early popes, and touching on the question of ordinations, which decretals were not to be found in any other earlier collections, so that any knowledge of them had to depend completely upon these forgeries.[39]

Among these was a letter of Pope Calixtus I (217-222) purportedly written in the year 218 and supposedly sent to the Bishops of France, in which letter the pope forbade the bishops to exercise judgment in court or to confer sacred orders outside their own territory.[40] In another decretal Sylvester I (314-335) forbade bishops to receive any strangers into their clergy unless they had been vouched for in writing by five bishops.[41] In still another decretal, designated as written to the Oriental Bishops, Julius I (337-352) forbade any bishop to retain or ordain a person from another diocese without the consent of his own bishop, the superior authority of the Holy See in such matters being, of course, always duly safeguarded. If anyone in violation of this precept nevertheless

[38] C. 27: "Monachi etiam vagantes ad officium clericatus, nisi iis testimonium abbas suas dederit, nec in civitatibus nec in parochiis ordinentur."—Bruns, II, 151.

[39] Van Hove, *Prologomena,* pp. 305-311.

[40] C. 1, C. IX, q. 2; Mansi, I, 737; Jaffé, n. 86. The last named lists this as spurious.

[41] C. 1, D. XCVIII; Hinschius, *Decretales Pseudo-Isidorianae et Capitula Angilramni* (Lipsiae, 1863), p. 451 (hereafter cited *Decretales*).

undertook to confer orders, his act was branded as invalid in its desired effect.[42]

While the traditionally accepted concept of dimissorials was contemplated in the legislation of all the councils throughout the period here considered, the terms used to give expression to this concept varied greatly. Some councils used the very term dimissorials. From this precise usage no difficulties emerged. But the use of different terms by other councils, and especially by the authors, furnished occasion for much confusion. Thus some authors spoke of the *litterae pacificae,* inasmuch as the use of the dimissorial letters made for peaceful relations between the bishops.[43] But there were also other terms used such as *litterae commendatitiae.* While this latter for the most part did not deal with ordinations at all, and its nature somewhat corresponded to the modern *celebret,* except that it was given to lay people as well as to clerics, still the term was used by some councils with the meaning of dimissorials.[44] By other councils the *litterae dimissoriae* were termed *litterae formatae,* for the reason that they were to be drawn up in certain definitely established forms.[45] But, again, the latter term was applied to many other kinds of letters in use in the early Church. Still other councils referred to the *litterae dimissoriae* as *litterae canonicae,* inasmuch as they fulfilled the requirements of the councils in this matter.[46] The greatest cau-

[42] Mansi, II, 1185; Hinschius, *Decretales,* p. 468. This letter is branded as spurious by Jaffé, n. 196.

[43] Cf. Hallier, *De Sacris Elect. et Ordin.,* Pars II, sect. V, cap. III, art. X, n. 5—*MTC,* XXIV, 1040. This author cited the examples of the Councils of Antioch and Chalcedon as well as the Greek canonists Balsamon and Zonaras of the twelfth century. He claimed that these canonists identified the *litterae dimissoriae* with the *litterae pacificae.*

[44] Council of Ravenna (997), c. 3: "ut nullus Episcoporum alterius clericum sine commendatitiis litteris recipiat . . . aut aliquem promoveat ad sacrum ordinem . . ."—Cf. *supra,* p. 11.

[45] Council of Benevento (1092), c. III: ". . . sine formata epistola et commendatitione sui episcopi eum recipere, aut in sua ecclesia eum ordinare, praesumat . . ."—Mansi, XX, 739. Cf. also Council of Ravenna, *supra,* p. 11.

[46] Council of Meaux (845), c. LI: "litteras canonicas ab episcopo . . ."—Mansi, XIV, 831. Cf. also Council of Ravenna, *supra,* p. 11.

tion must be exercised then when it remains to be determined just what a council meant in any particular place when it used one or more of these terms.[47]

2. *The Nature and Form of Dimissorials*

From the sixth to the twelfth century the nature of dimissorial letters underwent no change. They were still instruments by means of which one became incorporated with the clergy of the ordaining bishop. As has already been pointed out, Thomassinus believed that a change whereby these documents were required on the part of lay candidates as well as of clerics occurred during these centuries.[48]

It is known that the form letters as issued by the I General Council of Nicaea (325) were still in use in the early eleventh century, for the sample form letter which was reproduced in the *Decree of Gratian* dated from the time of Burchard, who was the Bishop of Worms between 1002 and 1025.[49] In some cases a bishop who had received a cleric who was properly equipped with the requisite letters later allowed the same cleric to transfer to a third bishop with the proper authorization for that bishop to ordain him. An example of this procedure is found in a dimissorial issued in the year 768 by Luitadus, Bishop of Vinchy, to Wenilo, Archbishop of Rouen, in which the latter was given permission to ordain the deacon Wifadus, who had formerly been consigned to Luitadus by Ebbo, Archbishop of Rheims.[50] In this letter the Greek characters as prescribed by the Council of Nicaea were still used. The same is true

[47] Hallier, *De Sacris Elect. et Ordin.*, Pars II, sect. V, cap. III, art. X, n. 5—*MTC*, XXIV, 1041; Lupus, *Opera Omnia*, IX, 199; Van Espen, *Commentarius*, pp. 228-229.

[48] *Supra*, pp. 10-11.

[49] *Supra*, p. 8.

[50] Hallier, *De Sacris Elect. et Ordin.*, Pars II, sect. V, cap. III, art. X, n. 8—*MTC*, XXIV, 1047. The names and dates given by Hallier in this letter do not accord with the facts of history since Ebbo became Archbishop of Rheims only in 816. Cf. Gams, *Series Episcoporum Ecclesiae Catholicae* (Ratisbonae, 1873), pp. 608 and 614.

also of a letter dating from the time of Pope Urban II (1088-1099), and sent by Durandus, Bishop of Clermont, to Rodulfus, Archbishop of Tours.[51]

This procedure was not followed in all letters, however, for Hallier pointed to a letter post-dating the time of Marculfus, who about the middle of the eighth century had compiled two books of formularies dealing with the practices of the bishops' chanceries and courts, in which letter the Greek characters do not appear, but instead there is to be found the signature of the bishop, as the letter itself indicated: ". . . et ut hae litterae firmiorem obtineant dignitatem, meliusque eis fides adhibeatur, manu nostra eas subter firmavimus." [52]

The I Council of Braga (561) expressly ordered that such letters be signed in the hand of the bishop himself.[53] According to Hallier, the II Council of Chalon-sur-Sâone (813) went so far as to demand that the names of the bishop and of the city be impressed upon the letters with lead. An examination of the text of the canon, however, seems to indicate that this regulation referred rather to letters given to priests who were being excardinated than to dimissorials as such, although by extension it could be argued that the same requirement existed for the issuance of dimissorial letters.[54]

It was still the practice to send the letters to some particularly designated bishop, as can be seen not only from the fact that the letters continued to be drawn up in the form first employed by the Council of Nicaea, but also from a canon of a synod held in Rome in the year 826.[55] From this canon it can also be seen that the

[51] Hallier, *op. cit.*, Pars II, sect. V, cap. III, art. X. n. 8—*MTC,* XXIV, 1048.

[52] *Loc. cit.*

[53] C. 8—*supra,* p. 10.

[54] C. 41: "Presbyter proprio loco dimisso ad aliud migrans nequaquam recipiatur. . . . Litteras etiam habebit, in quibus sint nomina episcopi et civitatis plumbo impressa."—*MGH, Conc.*, Tom. II, pars I, p. 282; Hallier, *De Sacris Elect. et Ordin.*, Pars. II, sect. V, cap. III, art. X, n. 3—*MTC,* XXIV, 1038.

[55] C. 18: "Episcopus subiecto sibi sacerdoti, vel alii clerico nisi ab alio postulatus dimissòrias non faciat, ne ovis quasi perdita aut errans inveniatur, sed per consensum unius in alterius inveniatur ovili."—*MGH, Conc.*, Tom. II,

letters were to be issued only when the bishop who wished to ordain the candidate had asked for them. While there indeed were cases wherein the bishops granted the letters at the request of the cleric, yet these cases were of such rare occurrence that one cannot rightly consider them as revealing any consistent usage or current practice.[56]

pars II, p. 575; c. 1, D. LXXII. The *Glossa Ordinaria* interpreted the words *ab alio postulatus* as pointing to the request of the receiving bishop. Cf. also the Synod of Rome (743)—*supra*, p. 10.

[56] Hallier, *De Sacris Elect. et Ordin.*, Pars II, sect. V, cap. III, art. X, n. 7—*MTC*, XXIV, 1044.

CHAPTER II

FROM THE III LATERAN COUNCIL (1179) TO THE COUNCIL OF TRENT (1545-1563)

DURING this period there is to be noted the same insistence upon the need of dimissorial letters which prevailed in the preceding centuries. As time went on, moreover, additional legislation, which made further demands in the way of documents required for ordination, made its appearance.

ARTICLE I. DIMISSORIAL LETTERS

The system whereby every cleric was to be assigned to a benefice as his title of ordination failed, with the passage of the centuries, to fulfill the purpose for which it was instituted. The number of benefices which could guarantee to the cleric an adequate support was necessarily limited, and so when bishops, in view of their desire to have a large number of clerics because of the honors accorded to the clerical state, ordained large numbers of men, the result was that the Church became overrun with clerical *vagi* or *acephali.*

To remedy such a situation, Pope Alexander III (1159-1181) in the III General Council of the Lateran (1179) issued a decree to the effect that any bishop who ordained a man to the diaconate or to the priesthood without a certain title would have to support that cleric out of his own personal resources, unless the subject in question had sufficient material wealth to provide for himself from his own resources or patrimony.[1]

Though issued to remedy the abuse of bishops who ordained men without a title, the decree was misconstrued as an official declaration of a new policy regarding the title of ordination. From it was

[1] C. 5: "Episcopus, si aliquem sine certo titulo, de quo necessaria vitae percipiat, in diaconum vel presbyterum ordinaverit, tamdiu necessaria ei subministret, donec in aliqua ei ecclesia convenientia stipendia militiae clericalis assignet; nisi forte talis qui ordinatur, extiterit, qui de sua vel paterna haereditate subsidium vitae possit habere."—c. 4, X, *de praebendis et dignitatibus,* III, 5; Mansi, XXII, 220.

deduced the legitimacy of the title of patrimony as a title of ordination, although in the tenor of the canon itself any foundation for this interpretation is sought in vain.[2] No longer, therefore, according to the law of the Church was every cleric through the very act of his ordination assigned to a particular church, and thus it became possible for a cleric to receive ordination from a bishop and yet not become permanently incorporated with the clergy of that bishop. As a consequence of this, dimissorial letters could be issued simply for the ordination of a candidate by a strange bishop, his own bishop still maintaining all rights over him, and the cleric remaining incorporated in his original diocese of incardination. The evolution of the term dimissorials was thus rendered complete.[3]

Many of the councils of this period merely reiterated the legislation of the preceding centuries.[4] There were some, however, which added new elements to the legislation. The Synod of Valencia (1255) forbade the archdeacon to present clerics of another bishop for ordination without letters from their proper bishop, which letters were to be handed over to the ordaining bishop.[5] The Provincial

[2] Stephen of Tournay, writing between 1192 and 1203, seems to have been the first to advance this interpretation of the canon—*Epistola CXIV—MPL,* CCXI, 477. This interpretation is also to be found in Ioannes Andreae, *In VI Libros Decretalium Novella Commentaria* (6 vols. in 5, Venetiis, 1581), tit. *de praebendis et dignitatibus,* c. *Episcopus* (III, 5, 1-3). Cf. also Fagnanus, *Commentaria in Libros Decretalium* (5 vols. in 3, Venetiis, 1697), ad c. 4, X, *de praebendis et dignitatibus,* III, nn. 24-26; Many, *Praelectiones de Sacra Ordinatione* (Parisiis, 1905), p. 333 (hereafter cited *De Sacra Ordinatione*); Claeys-Bouuaert, *De Canonica Cleri Saeculari Obedientia* (Lovanii, 1904), p. 205. Gasparri (*De Sacra Ordinatione,* n. 591) was of the opinion that this came about rather from a response of Innocent III to the Archbishop of Besançon, which is found in c. 23, X, *de praebendis et dignitatibus,* III, 5, than from this canon of the Lateran Council.

[3] Moeder, *Proper Bishop for Ordination,* pp. 40-41.

[4] Council of Rouen (1231), c. 10—Mansi, XXIII, 215; Synod of Gerona (1261), statutum 13—Mansi, XXIII, 931; Council of Aquileia (1282)—Mansi, XXIV, 434; Council of Milan (1287), c. 29—Mansi, XXIV, 882; Synod of Bayeux (1300), c. 3—Mansi, XXV, 80; Council of Lambeth (1330), c. 6—Mansi, XXV, 894-895; Council of Avignon (1455), c. 17—Mansi, XXXII, 188.

[5] "Item dicimus Archdiaconibus, ne praesentent clericos aliorum episcopatum sine litteris episcoporum propriorum, quas tradant episcopo, cum sigillo pendenti: . . ."—Mansi, XXIII, 892.

Council of Mainz (1261) forbade the ordination of *peregrini* or *clerici ignoti* without the commendatory and dimissorial letters of their bishop, or at least the testimony of the cathedral chapter.[6]

Pope Clement IV (1265-1268) issued a decree in which he established certain regulations regarding the ordination in Italy of men from other countries. The purpose of the decree was to prevent the reception of orders by men who were perhaps excommunicated, apostates, or otherwise unworthy for the reception of orders in their own country.[7] This legislation applied to Germans, French, Spaniards, and in general to all born in any country outside of Italy, but not to those from the islands adjacent to Italy.[8] No bishop in Italy was to ordain such men without the special permission of the Pope, or without letters from the bishop to whom they were subject by reason either of origin or of benefice. These letters were to make mention, besides the data concerning age and fitness, of the reason why that bishop was unable or unwilling to ordain the candidate in question. This was the initial occasion when it was prescribed that this last element was to receive mention in these letters. In later years it came to be a requirement for all such letters, not just for this particular case. As a later interpretation showed, this decree applied only to seculars, not to regulars.[9] While it seemed to speak only of clerics who wished to be ordained, it was believed that it applied equally to lay candidates.[10] Severe penalties were established for the violation of this law. The one ordained was to be suspended and the ordaining prelate was also to receive a fitting penance. While the law

[6] C. 33—Mansi, XXIII, 1091-1092. (Canon 17 of the same Council established very strict regulations to prevent fraud with regard to these letters.) A similar wording is found in the Council of Fritzlar (1287), c. 10—Mansi, XXIII, 728.

[7] C. 1, *de tempore ordinationis et qualitate ordinandorum,* I, 9, in VI°.

[8] Many, *De Sacra Ordinatione,* pp. 168-170; Honorante, *Praxis Secretariae Tribunalis Cardinalis Urbis Vicarii* (2. ed., Romae, 1762), c. X, nota 3 (hereafter cited *Praxis Secretariae*).

[9] S. C. Ep. et Reg., 30 dec. 1617—cited in Barbosa, *Juris Ecclesiastici Universi Libri Tres* (Lugduni, 1660), lib. I, c. XXXIII, n. 57.

[10] *Glossa Ordinaria,* ad c. 1, *de tempore ordinationis et qualitate ordinandorum,* I, 9, in VI°, v. *clerici.*

distinctly called for letters, yet Gasparri, even in this case, believed that an explanation in writing was not an absolute necessity.[11]

Further specification was given to that law in a decree of Pope Boniface VIII (1294-1303). It was the purpose of this decretal not so much to establish the necessity of dimissorial letters—that had been quite well established by that time—but rather to determine just who was authorized in law to issue these letters.[12] Whereas Clement IV had listed two possible sources of competency relative to the conferring of ordination and the issuing of dimissorial letters, Boniface added a third, viz., acquired domicile.[13] He then excluded *inferiores praelati* and *officiales* from granting such dimissorial letters. Innocent III (1198-1216) before him had forbidden the archdeacon to issue them.[14] The restrictive legislation as it affected the *officialis* was later restated in the I Provincial Council of Cologne (1536), canon 29.[15]

Hallier held that the decretal of Boniface revoked also the privilege by which abbots and certain religious superiors had been allowed to issue these letters.[16] The vicar general likewise needed a special mandate for the granting of dimissorial letters, but when the bishop was away for a long period of time the vicar general was authorized to issue them. Just what distance from his diocese was postulated on the part of the bishop, or what length of time in the duration of his absence, before the vicar general was authorized to act in this matter was left to the prudent judgment of the vicar general himself. While the see was vacant the cathedral chapter, or he to whom the administration of the spiritual affairs of the diocese pertained for that

[11] *De Sacra Ordinatione*, n. 862.

[12] C. 3, *de tempore ordinationis et qualitate ordinandorum*, I, 9, in VI°.

[13] Cf. McBride, *Excardination and Incardination*, pp. 45-54, for a fuller treatment of this phase.

[14] C. 8, X, *de officio archdiacono*, I, 23. Cf. also Potthast, *Regesta Pontificum Romanorum inde ab a. post Christum natum 1198 ad a. 1304* (2 vols., Berolini, 1874-1875), n. 835 (hereafter cited *Regesta*).

[15] Mansi, XXXII, 1221.

[16] *De Sacris Elect. et Ordin.*, Pars II, sect. V, cap. III, art. X, n. 4—*MTC*, XXIV, 1054.

time, could give the required permission. In this phase of the history there was no limitation with regard to the power of the chapter in this matter.

In 1314 the II Council of Ravenna was convoked. This Council prescribed that simple dimissorial letters were not sufficient for the conferring of orders unless they were at the same time testimonials concerning the life and training of the candidate and were presented to the bishop at least two days before the day on which the orders were to be conferred.[17]

In accordance with the decretal of Boniface these letters had to be issued by the bishop of the candidate, or by his vicar general, in the case as designated by the Pontiff. The conciliar statute was intended as binding on all except mendicants and certain other privileged exempt religious whose possession of the same privilege was acknowledged as certain. A further requirement was enacted in the Council of Béziers, held in the year 1300. This Council ordered that the candidate was not to be granted the letters until he had been examined and found worthy, and express mention of the executed compliance with this demand was to be made in the letter.[18]

With regard to the penalty in store for the violation of these laws, the II Council of Lyons (1274) established that a bishop who presumptuously ordained clerics from another diocese thereby lost for one year the right of conferring orders.[19] The subjects of a bishop thus suspended could receive ordination from a neighboring bishop during the period of the suspension. This penalty was confirmed in the Bull *Cum ex sacrorum,* issued by Pope Pius II (1458-1464) on November 17, 1461.[20]

[17] Rubrica II—Mansi, XXV, 537.

[18] C. 7—Mansi, XXV, 361. Canon 1 of the same Council, in speaking of those who were to receive tonsure, stated that the Constitution of Boniface VIII was strictly to be adhered to.—Mansi, XXV, 359.

[19] C. 15: "Eos qui clericos parochiae alienae absque superioris ordinandorum licentia, scienter, seu affectata ignorantia, vel quocumque alio figmento quaesito, praesumpserint ordinare, per annum a collatione ordinum decernimus esse suspensos; iis quae iura statuunt contra taliter ordinatos in suo robore duraturis."—c. 2, *de tempore ordinationis et qualitate ordinandorum,* I, 9, in VI°; Mansi, XXIV, 91.

[20] *Bullarum Diplomatum et Privilegiorum Sanctorum Pontificum Taurinensis*

The Provincial Council of Sens (1528) established a very definite procedure to be followed in the issuance of dimissorial letters lest unworthy candidates should be ordained. The candidate was to approach his bishop, who in turn was to inquire into his age, education, morals, and benefice or patrimony. The bishop, was to observe these formalities with the same diligence that he himself was required to observe if he personally ordained the candidate. If thereupon he deemed it fitting to grant the letters, he was to make express mention in the letters that he had observed the prescribed solemnities. If for a reasonable cause the candidate could not present himself to his bishop for this examination, then the clause *"Super quo conscientiam tuam oneramus"* was to be inserted in the letters with the result that the onus for the examination was thus placed upon the ordaining bishop. These letters, in any case, were not to be given to any cleric unless he had a benefice or possessed an adequate patrimony.[21]

Article II. Other Requisite Documents

In the Council of Exeter (1287) is to be found one of the first instances of a statute which required documents even for those who were being ordained in their own dioceses. This Council required letters from the archdeacon which testified regarding the parental origin and good morals of the candidate. Religious and also such as were endowed with a benefice were exempted from this requirement.[22]

As has been seen, a number of councils demanded that a candidate be equipped with testimonials as well as with dimissorials. This double demand is exemplified in the decrees of the Council of Mainz (1261).[23] The third canon of the Council of Sens (1528) ordered that, for the ordination of one of his subjects, a bishop was to have testimonial letters from the candidate's pastor. These letters

Editio (24 vols. et Appendix, Augustae Taurinorum, 1857-1872), V, 165-166 (hereafter cited *Bullarium*).

21 Mansi, XXXII, 1185-1186.

22 C. 8—Mansi, XXIV, 797.

23 *Supra*, p. 19.

were to contain sworn statements, furnished by two or three trustworthy witnesses, testifying to the required age and blamelessness of life of the candidate.[24]

In a letter to the Bishop of Modena, a special requirement was set forth by Pope Innocent III (1198-1216) for anyone who had been promoted to minor orders by the Roman Pontiff. Such a cleric required the special permission of the Holy See to receive higher orders from any other bishop.[25]

[24] Mansi, XXIII, 1185.

[25] C. 12, X, *de temporibus ordinationis et qualitate ordinandorum,* I, 11; Potthast, *Regesta,* n. 1173.

CHAPTER III

FROM THE COUNCIL OF TRENT (1545-1563) TO THE CONSTITUTION *SPECULATORES* (1694)

Article I. Tridentine Legislation

In 1538 the group of Cardinals and other prelates appointed for the sake of inquiring into the needs for reform within the Church reported to Pope Paul III (1534-1549) that the first and greatest abuse was the lack of care and diligence in connection with the ordination of clerics, and especially of priests. As a result of this neglect, so they reported, men who were absolutely unworthy were admitted to the lofty office of the priesthood.[1] Hence it was not strange that one of the tasks assigned to the Fathers of the Council of Trent was the restatement and, where necessary, the reformation of the laws of the Church regarding the sacrament of Orders. It is against the background of this report that the laws of the Council of Trent with regard to ordinations are to be viewed.

1. *Testimonial Letters*

For the first time in the history of the legislation of the Church a conciliar law which was of the character of a universal law made it necessary even for those who were being ordained by their own bishop to present testimonials. Previously only in the case wherein a candidate was being ordained by a bishop other than his own had such letters been required. But henceforth all those who were being promoted to minor orders had to present to the ordaining

[1] "Primus abusus in hac parte est ordinatio clericorum, et praesertim presbyterorum, in qua nulla adhibetur cura, nulla adhibetur diligentia; quod passim quicumque sint, imperitissimi sint, villissimo genere orti, sint malis moribus ornati, sint adolescentes, admittantur ad sacros ordines, et maxime ad presbyteratum, ad characterem, inquam, Christum maxime exprimentem."—Consilium Delectorum Cardinalium et Aliorum Praelatorum de Emendanda Ecclesia—Mansi, XXXV A, 349.

prelate testimonials from their pastor and also from the head of the school which they attended.[2] For those who were to be promoted to Sacred Orders even more stringent requirements were established. Such candidates were required to report to their bishop one month before the ordinations. The bishop then deputed their pastors, or other priests, according to his discretion, to announce publicly in their parish churches the names of those desiring to be ordained. At the same time the priest so deputed was diligently to seek information from trustworthy sources regarding the parentage, the age, the morals, and the life of the candidate. Upon complying with this demand he was to transmit to the bishop testimonial letters declaring the results of his inquiry, and testifying to the making of the required announcement in the parish church.[3]

In another decree the Council declared that candidates were not to be promoted to tonsure unless they had already been confirmed and instructed in the rudiments of the faith, and unless they knew how to read and write. There was to be, moreover, at least a probable conjecture that the candidate was embracing the clerical state, not that he might fraudulently escape from the toils of civil justice, but rather that he might render faithful service to Almighty God in that state.[4] While in this decree there was no explicit statement to the effect that these qualifications had to be set down in writing, still this decree served in many places as the basis for laws which required testimony in the form of letters of the presence of these qualifications.[5] The same was true of the decree of the Council which re-

[2] Conc. Trident., sess. XXIII, *de ref.*, c. 5. Use is made of the text and translation of the text of the Council by Schroeder (1875-1942), *Canons and Decrees of the Council of Trent* (St. Louis: B. Herder, 1941).

[3] Conc. Trident., *loc. cit.* It is interesting to note that the original draft of this canon required that these letters be signed by four of the older priests among the clergy of the diocese and also by four of the more outstanding parishioners, as well as by the pastor. In the course of the discussions on the canon, however, this requirement was omitted. Cf. *Concilium Tridentinum, Diariorum, Actorum, Epistularum, Tractatuum Nova Collectio* (ed. Societas Goerresiana, 13 vols., Friburgi Brisgoviae: Herder, 1901-1938), IX, 479 (hereafter cited *Coll. Goerresiana*).

[4] Conc. Trident., sess. XXIII, *de ref.*, c. 4.

[5] An interesting example of how far this decree could be stretched, as it were, is furnished by Honorante, who stated that if in Rome an only son wished

quired as a prerequisite for promotion to the diaconate and the priesthood that the candidate have assisted at the ecclesiastical functions celebrated in the church to which he was assigned.[6]

2. *Dimissorial Letters*

Through the centuries it had been one of the most fundamental laws with regard to ordination that every candidate receive his ordination at the hands of his own bishop. It was from the neglect of complying with that fundamental and often repeated law that so much evil had come. It is not surprising then to find this law stated once more among the decrees of the Tridentine Council. It was required, furthermore, that if anyone asked to be ordained by another bishop, under any pretext whatsoever, even in consequence of a special rescript, such a bishop could rightfully ordain him only if the probity of his life and morals was established by testimony from his own bishop. The penalty established for the violation of this law applied both to the ordaining prelate, who was suspended from the conferring of orders for one year, and to the one ordained, who was suspended, for as long a time as his ordinary saw fit, from the exercise of the orders he had received.[7]

Barbosa (1589-1649) stated that on the strength of this decree a bishop who ordained the subject of another, even in that bishop's own diocese and in possession of the needed dimissorials, incurred this penalty if the candidate lacked the testimony of his own bishop for the requisite approval of the candidate's life and morals.[8]

Apart from the fact that these letters were to contain permission to ordain, there had been nothing in the previous general legislation of the Church as to the requisite contents of the letters. By the

to be ordained it was necessary for him to seek a dispensation, on the assumed grounds that such a candidate was entering the clerical state simply with a view to freeing himself of all incumbent responsibilities.—*Praxis Secretariae*, c. I, nota 4.

[6] Conc. Trident., sess. XXIII, *de ref.*, c. 13.

[7] Conc. Trident., sess. XXIII, *de ref.*, c. 8. Cf. also sess. XXIII, *de ref.*, c. 3, and sess. XIV, *de ref.*, c. 1.

[8] *Collectanea Doctorum in Varia Concilii Tridentini Decreta et Canones* (Lugduni, 1657), ad Sess. XXIII, *de ref.*, c. 8, n. 31, p. 213.

Tridentine legislation, however, it was required that they also mention the cause why the candidate's own bishop could not ordain him. This was required, moreover, in writing, and for the validity of the letters.[9]

The power of titular bishops, of abbots, and of cathedral chapters in connection with the authorization of ordinations and the issuance of dimissorial letters became precisely defined and limited.[10] The wording of the decree dealing with titular bishops gave rise to a discussion whether, by the legislation of this Council, the permission to ordain the subject of another had of necessity to be conceded in writing. The decree had stated that such bishops could not rightfully ordain any candidate without the express consent or the dimissorial letter from the candidate's own bishop.[11]

Passerini (1595-1677) held that this consent could be given orally, except when it was given to an absent bishop, in which case it had to be given in writing.[12] Gasparri (1852-1934), by pointing to the disjunctive phrasing of the decree, denied that consent had to be granted in writing. He stated that it could be given orally as long only as the ordaining bishop could be absolutely certain that the permission had been given, for example, when the consent was given in the presence of that bishop.[13]

Pax Jordanus (early 17th century) was perhaps the only author who disagreed with this interpretation. He distinguished between the permission to ordain and the granting of the dimissorial letter. The former was tendered to the ordaining bishop and could be offered orally; the latter was given to the ordinand and had to be executed in

[9] Conc. Trident., sess. VII, *de ref.*, c. 11.

[10] Conc. Trident., sess. XIV, *de ref.*, c. 2; sess. XXIII, *de ref.*, c. 10; sess. VII, *de ref.*, c. 10.

[11] Conc. Trident., sess. XIV, *de ref.*, c. 2: ". . . absque sui proprii praelati expresso consensu aut litteris dimissoriis. . . ."

[12] *Commentaria in Primum Librum Sextum Decretalium* (2 vols., Venetiis, 1698), I, cap. *Cum nullus*, III, Quaest. II, Art. I, n. 134, p. 365 (hereafter cited *Commentaria*).

[13] *De Sacra Ordinatione*, n. 862. Cf. also Monacelli (+1715), *Formularium Legale Practicum Fori Ecclesiastici* (3. ed., 4 vols. in 3, Romae, 1844), Pars I, tit. IV, Form. V, nota 4, p. 107 (hereafter cited *Formularium*).

writing. [14] All authors agreed, however, that as a matter of fact the permission also was usually given in writing.

Even at the time of the Council of Trent the terminology with regard to these letters was not uniform. The Council indeed referred to them as dimissorial letters. But it is interesting to note that the original draft of one of the decrees of the Council equated dimissorial letters and commendatory letters.[15] They were also called *reverendae litterae* by the Council.[16] It is known that this name was also used in the designation of these letters in Spain. They were so called either because they were issued by the most reverend bishop, or because the letters began with that word. Hallier (1595-1659) offered the latter explanation, and thereupon added that such letters were both commendatory and dimissory.[17]

Lest the severity of these laws in their absolute requirement of dimissorials should become the occasion for another abuse, the Council established the amount of the fee which notaries might exact for the execution of these letters as one-tenth of a gold florin. This fee became chargeable, however, only when the notary received no salary for such work.[18]

Article II. Period Between the Council of Trent and the Constitution *Speculatores*

In time the decrees of the Council of Trent were duly promulgated. But if they were to achieve the reforms for which they were intended, it was necessary that the individual bishops should see to

[14] *Opera Omnia* (3 vols., Coloniae Allobrogum et Lugduniae, 1729), Tom. I, Lib. III, tit. VI, n. 143, pp. 199-200.

[15] *Coll. Goerresiana,* IX, 480.

[16] Conc. Trident., sess. VII, *de ref.,* c. 10: ". . . litteras dimissorias seu reverendas, ut aliqui vocant. . . ."

[17] *De Sacris Elect. et Ordin.,* Pars II, sect. V, cap. III, art. XI, n. 1—*MTC,* XXIV, 1049. Pirhing (1606-1679), *Jus Canonicum in V Libros Decretalium* (5 vols., Dilingae, 1674-1678), Lib. I, tit. XI, n. 52 and Schmalzgrueber (1663-1735), *Jus Ecclesiasticum Universum* (5 vols. in 12, Romae, 1843-1845), Lib. I, tit. XI, n. 43, both gave the former explanation for the use of the term.

[18] Conc. Trident., sess. XXI, *de ref.,* c. 1.

their enforcement in their respective sees. From the effort to achieve such an enforcement and from the doubts and difficulties which arose in connection with it there evolved a still further determination regarding the requisite documents preliminary to the conferring and the receiving of orders.

1. *Testimonial Letters*

The IV Provincial Council of Milan, one of a series of Councils which Saint Charles Borromeo (1538-1584) convoked in order to effect the reforms intended by the Council of Trent, was held in 1576. This Council drew up a very detailed list of the documents required by candidates for ordination. Though this enactment reflected a purely particular legislation, still it is of interest for the purposes of this study. Candidates for ordination were to bring testimony of their having been born of a legitimate marriage, or, if not born of such a marriage, of their having obtained a dispensation from the irregularity involved. They were also to bring testimony showing that they belonged to the diocese in which they sought to receive ordination, whether by reason of origin, of benefice, of acquired domicile, or of any other legitimate title. Signed letters from the pastor giving testimony regarding their life and morals, and from the head of the school, or from the rector of the seminary, if they attended a seminary, or from others whom the bishop might choose, as well as testimony of their attendance at schools of Christian doctrine were also required.

Those who were to receive tonsure also had to bring with them testimony of their reception of the sacrament of confirmation, of their frequent attendance at church and of their inclination toward a clerical life, of their reception of Holy Communion during the year, and testimony from their pastors, or from the priests to whom they were entrusted by the bishop, regarding a founded hope that they would be able to persevere in the clerical training. The Council admitted, however, that a bishop might promote a man to tonsure even though he lacked testimony regarding the candidate's reception of Holy Communion during the year and regarding his attendance at schools of Christian doctrine.

For those being ordained to minor orders there was required, in addition, testimony of the reception of tonsure, or of the last order conferred, testimony of the exercise of that office in the church to which they had been attached, testimony of their wearing the clerical garb, and testimony of their frequent use of confession and of the reception of Holy Communion.

For major orders the candidates were required to present testimonials regarding the requisite age, regarding their beneficial revenue as sufficient for their sustentation, regarding their attendance at the spiritual exercises in preparation for the reception of orders, and regarding the previous publication of their names in their parish churches.[19]

With regard to the requirement of attendance at specified spiritual exercises, it is interesting to note that Pope Alexander VII (1655-1667), when establishing regulations in 1662 to be followed in the ordinations to be conferred in Rome and the six adjoining suburbicarian sees, made the same requirement for that area as St. Charles had made for the Province of Milan almost one hundred years earlier[20] Many of the requirements listed by the Council of Milan are also to be found in other councils of the period here considered, but in none are they so detailed.[21]

According to Barbosa (1589-1649), those who had been granted by the Holy See the privilege of receiving orders from any bishop in communion with the Apostolic See did not require dimissorials from their own bishops, but did require testimonials from them con-

[19] Pars II, § VIII—Mansi, XXXIV A, 233-240.

[20] Const. *Apostolica solicitudo,* 7 aug. 1662—*Bullarium,* XVII, 52-53. Monacelli cited a decree of the Congregation of Bishops and Regulars of October 9, 1682, as his own basis for this requirement.—*Formularium* Pars I, tit. III, Form. I, p. 85.

[21] Council of Malines (1507), *De Ordinandis*—Mansi, XXXIV A, 582; V Provincial Council of Milan (1579), *De Initiandis Ordinis Sacramento*—Mansi, XXXIV A, 443-446; Council of Rouen (1581), *De Episcoporum Officiis,* 14—Mansi, XXXIV A, 632; Bordeaux (1583)—Mansi, XXXIV A, 759; Sorrento (1584), XXVI, *De Sacramento Ordinis*—Mansi, XXXVI bis, 296; Sienna (1599), c. XV, *De Sacramento Ordinis*—Mansi, XXXVI bis, 536; Cambrai (1631), Titulus XII, *De Sacramento Ordinis*—Mansi, XXXVI ter, 178.

cerning the probity of the candidates' lives.[22] The Sacred Congregation of the Council ruled that the same was true in the case of a bishop ordaining a candidate from another diocese when the latter had become his subject by reason of the conferral of a benefice.[23]

2. *Dimissorial Letters*

The III Provincial Council of Milan (1573) stated that if the dimissorial letters lacked the required testimony of the bishop as to the candidate's life, morals, etc., the cleric was to be considered as not having asked for the letters at all, and was therefore not to be ordained. For major orders, the Council continued, the letters had also to contain mention of the age of the candidate and of his title of ordination, and a statement giving an estimate of the income from his benefice, pension or patrimony.[24]

The IV Provincial Council of the same province (1576) also laid down regulations with regard to dimissorial letters by adding further specifications to the laws of the Council of Trent. Letters were not to be granted for the reception of many orders, and the time for the receiving of the orders for which they were granted was to be stated in them. This time, generally, could be extended for one or two months, after which time the letters would be of no value. If no determination was made regarding the time during which the order was to be received, the bishop was not to ordain on the authority of such letters unless they were recently written, renewed, or confirmed, i.e., not more than two or three months before the date of the proposed ordination. Those who were absent from their diocese, or away from their superior, for any length of time were to

22 *De Officio et Potestate Episcopi,* P. II, alleg. 7, n. 15, p. 220; Passerini, *Commentaria,* n. 141, p. 366.

23 S. C. C. *Tirasonen.,* 1596—Pallottini, *Collectio omnium conclusionum et resolutionum quae in causis propositis apud Sacram Congregationem Cardinalium S. Concilii Tridentini Interpretum prodierunt ab eius institutione anno MDLXIV ad annum MDCCCLX, distinctis titulis alphabetico ordine per materias digesta* (17 vols., Romae, 1868-1893), XVI, n. 46, p. 83 (hereafter cited Pallottini).

24 Mansi, XXXIV A, 152. Cf. also Council of Bordeaux (1583), XIV, *De Sacramento Ordinis*—Mansi, XXXIV A, 759; Council of Bitonto (1571), *De Examine Ordinandorum*—Mansi, XXXVI bis, 63.

present testimonial letters prepared not only by their bishop or superior, but also by the priest with whom they had been staying, or written by his authority and signed by him, in addition to the regular dimissorial letters.[25]

The II Council of Ravenna (1582) enacted similar legislation. It prescribed that there were not to be issued any letters in which permission was granted to receive more orders than one might licitly receive at one time, and that the time for which the letters were to be considered valid was always to be stated in the letters themselves.[26]

According to Passerini (1595-1677), a decree of the Congregation of the Council ruled that the testimony concerning the life and character of the candidate which was demanded by the Council of Trent when the candidate was being ordained by a bishop other than his own was not required on the part of lay persons, and therefore that the law did not apply in the promotion to tonsure.[27]

The authors of the post-Tridentine period in the sixteenth and seventeenth centuries helped to fix and determine the question of the form and contents of these letters. Hallier (1595-1659) pointed out that the letters were of two types, general and specific. They could be sent to a certain determinate bishop, or they could be sent to any bishop in communion with the Apostolic See. Furthermore they could be general or specific in the sense that they might be granted for all orders, or for certain orders only.[28] Letters which

[25] Pars II, § VIII—Mansi, XXXIV A, 231-233. The same rule as to the date is given by Honorante, *Praxis Secretariae,* Cap. VI, nota 2, where he cited two decrees, one from the Congregation of the Council in 1666, and the other from the Congregation of Immunity in 1624, as proof thereof. He believed that the dimissorial letters might be accepted even after three months when the ordinand had remained in Rome all during the time and had favorable testimony for his good character. This was the practice of the Roman Curia. Cf. also Lucidi, *De Visitatione Sacrorum Liminum* (3. ed., aucta per Josephum Schneider, 3 vols., Romae, 1883), I, 172; Ballerini-Palmieri, *Opus Theologicum Morale* (3. ed., 7 vols., Prati, 1898-1901), V 764.

[26] *De Sacramento Ordinis,* 6—Mansi, XXXVI bis, 841.

[27] *Commentaría,* I, Cap. *Eos qui,* II, n. 18, p. 350. This author gave no indication of the date of this decree or of the person in whose favor it was issued.

[28] *De Sacris Elect. et Ordin.,* Pars II, sect. V, cap. III, art. XI, n. 2—*MTC,* XXIV, 1049. For a sample of such a general letter, cf. the same author, *ibid.,*

were granted for minor orders, or even for orders absolutely, were not valid for major orders unless, when given for orders absolutely, the candidate in whose favor they were given was already an acolyte.[29]

Most of the authors included in their treatment of the subject a list of the essential elements as far as the contents were concerned. In general, all agreed to the following enumeration:

1. The recommendation of one's own ordinary.

2. The reason why one's own bishop was unable to ordain one. The cause did not have to be that of sickness.

3. The orders for which the letters were given.

4. The form of concession, i.e., to a certain bishop or to any bishop in communion with the Apostolic See.[30]

3. *The Ordination of Regulars*

From very early times it was believed necessary that religious should be ordained by the bishop of the place in which the monastery was located.[31] Likewise from early times it was considered necessary for the ordination of regulars that the consent of the abbot be obtained.[32] In the thirteenth century with the rise of the mendicant orders a change appeared. Since they were moved about from one monastery to another, Pope Clement IV (1265-1268) gave to these religious the privilege of being promoted to orders by any bishop

n. 26—*MTC,* XXIV, 1067. Cf. also Passerini, *Commentaria,* I, Cap. *Cum nullus,* III, Quaest. II, Art. I, n. 131, p. 365; Jordanus, *Opera Omnia,* Tom. I, lib. III, n. 141, p. 199.

[29] Pirhing, *Jus Canonicum,* Lib. I, tit. XI, n. 66; Honorante, *Praxis Secretariae,* Cap. VI, nota II, p. 77; Monacelli, *Formularium,* Pars I, tit. IV, Form. V, nota 5, p. 108; Gasparri, *De Sacra Ordinatione,* n. 883.

[30] Barbosa, *De Officia et Potestate Episcopi,* P. II, alleg. 7, n. 21, pp. 221-222; Passerini, *Commentaria, ibid.,* n. 140, p. 336; Pirhing, *Jus Canonicum, loc. cit.*

[31] Council of Africa, c. 80—Bruns, I, 175.

[32] Council of Agde (506), c. 27—Bruns, II, 152; Council of Lerida (523), c. 3—Bruns, II, 21.

in Communion with the Holy See.[33] The concession of this privilege was confirmed by Pope Sixtus IV (1471-1484) in his Constitution *Regimini universalis*.[34]

By the time of the Council of Trent almost all religious orders enjoyed this privilege either by way of direct grant or by way of an acknowledged mutual participation with the other orders. The Council stressed, more than once, the necessity of each candidate's being ordained by his own bishop.[35] As a result there arose the question whether or not this new law bound regulars despite the privileges which they had received from the earlier popes.

Pope Pius V (1566-1572) in his Constitution *Etsi mendicantium Ordines* of May 16, 1567 declared that the law of the Council of Trent in regard to dimissorials was not binding on regulars, and that therefore they could receive ordination from any bishop in communion with the Holy See, and thus did not need the permission of their local ordinary for the reception of orders at the hands of some other bishop.[36] Pope Gregory XIII (1572-1585), on March 1, 1573, changed this provision, and in answer to a *dubium* submitted by the Carthusians in the same year stated that in order to be ordained by another bishop it was necessary that they should secure the express permission of the ordinary of the place in which their house was located. Thus it became necessary for them to receive ordination from their local ordinary or to obtain from him written letters which gave permission for the ordination to be conferred by some other bishop.[37]

The Provincial Council of Malines which was held at Louvain in 1574 prescribed that religious who had received orders from one bishop and then approached another bishop for promotion to higher orders were not to be promoted until they had furnished testimony,

[33] Const. *Virtute conspicuos*, 21 iul. 1265, § 7—*Bullarium*, III, 737.

[34] 31 aug. 1474, § 3—*Bullarium*, V, 218.

[35] Conc. Trident., sess. VIII, *de ref.*, c. 11, and sess. XXIII, *de ref.*, c. 8.

[36] § 7—Pallottini, XVI, p. 73, n. 1.

[37] Pallottini, *loc. cit.*

regarding the orders received, from the bishop who had conferred the lower orders.[38] The IV Council of Ravenna (1592) required that regulars who sought to be promoted to orders needed the testimony of the superior of their religious orders that they had made profession in that order.[39]

Regulars were likewise exempted from the prescription of the Council of Trent which required the previous publication of the names of the candidates for the subdiaconate, as well as the testimonials which were required by the same Tridentine decree. For them the testimony of their superior sufficed, and therefore the testimonials from their pastor and school master were not necessary.[40]

Pope Clement VIII (1592-1605), in a decree emanating from the Congregation of the Council and confirming a previous decree issued by the same Congregation,[41] prescribed that, when a regular was being sent to another bishop for ordination, the cause why he was being sent to a bishop other than his own was to be stated in the letters. The cause for which he might be sent was also established by the same decree, viz., the absence of his own bishop from the diocese at that time, or, in the event of his presence, the fact that he was not conferring ordinations at the time proposed for the ordination of the regular.[42]

In answer to a *dubium* submitted to it, the same Congregation declared that regulars did not need dimissorial letters from the bishop of the place of origin, but that it sufficed that they observe the form prescribed by Pope Clement VIII, viz., the presentation of dimissorial letters from their superior.[43] A further exemption was granted to

[38] *Sub titulo de Ordinandis*—Mansi, XXXVI bis, 129.

[39] *De Sacramento Ordinis,* § 2—Mansi, XXXVI bis, 842.

[40] S. C. C., *Mediolanen.,* aug. 1587—*Codicis Iuris Canonici Fontes,* cura Emi Petri Card. Gasparri editi (9 vols., Romae [postea Civitate Vaticana]: Typis Polyglottis Vaticanis, 1923-1939; Vols. VII-IX ed. cura et studio Emi Iustiniani Card. Serédi), n. 2185 (hereafter cited *Fontes*).

[41] S. C. C., *Hispalen.,* 11 ian. 1596—Pallottini, XVI, p. 73, n. 1.

[42] S. C. C., 15 mart. 1596—*Fontes,* n. 2294. This regulation was renewed in another decree: S. C. Ep. et Reg., *Minorum Observantium,* 11 ian. 1683—*Fontes,* n. 1754.

[43] S. C. C., *Senonen.,* 28 febr. 1654—*Fontes,* n. 2734.

regulars when the Congregation of the Council declared that the stringent regulations enacted by Pope Urban VIII (1623-1644) with regard to the *ultramontani* in Rome [44] did not apply to them[45]

[44] Const. *Secretis,* 11 sept. 1624—*Fontes,* n. 205. In addition to the prescription that such candidates needed written dimissorials which stated the cause why their own bishop did not ordain them, this document demanded that these letters had to be shown to and approved by the Apostolic Nuncio of the province of the issuing bishop, and in turn the signature of the Nuncio had to be shown to and approved by the Cardinal Vicar of Rome, even though the latter did not plan or propose to conduct the ordination personally.

[45] S. C. C., *In Nucerina Paganorum,* 29 nov. 1670—Pallottini, XVI, p. 77, n. 13: *Bullarium,* XIII, 263-265.

CHAPTER IV

FROM THE CONSTITUTION *SPECULATORES* (1694) TO THE CODE OF CANON LAW (1918)

DESPITE the safeguards established by the Council of Trent and the subsequent decrees which emanated from the Holy See, abuses continued to appear in connection with ordinations. For this reason Pope Innocent XII (1691-1700) found it necessary to issue the Constitution *Speculatores* on November 4, 1694.[1] While it concerned primarily the question of the proper bishop for ordination, it necessarily treated also of dimissorial and testimonial letters. Through its provisions the Pope hoped to remove fraud, abuse and scandal in this matter. From it sprang many of the decrees and decisions which with reference to ordinations appeared at a later time. Thus Pope Innocent's Constitution helped to give to this consideration in the Church's law its final form. For the purpose of this study, then, some of its provisions must be considered here as the next major phase in the development of this law.

ARTICLE I. TESTIMONIAL LETTERS

According to the prescriptions of this Constitution, a man who had been promoted to tonsure by his own bishop could not permissibly be advanced to higher orders by another bishop on the title of a benefice obtained in the latter's diocese apart from testimonial letters furnished by the bishop of the candidate's place of origin and domicile, in which letters the bishop testified regarding the parentage, age, morals, and life of the candidate. These letters were to be shown to the ordaining bishop, and thereafter were to be preserved among the records of the curia. Mention of these letters was to be made by the ordaining prelate in the certificate of ordination issued by

[1] *Fontes*, n. 258.

him.[2] This was a more stringent demand than that made by the Council of Trent when in similar cases it required merely a letter from the ordinand's bishop.[3]

Furthermore, if perchance a candidate for orders happened to be born outside the diocese in which his father had his domicile, then the actual place of his birth was not to be considered as the place of his origin. If, however, a candidate had remained outside the place of his origin in the actual place of his birth for a period of time sufficient for the contracting of a canonical impediment, it was required of him to present a testimonial letter from the bishop of that place as well as from the bishop of his place of origin and domicile before he could rightfully be admitted to orders.[4]

Another precaution established by Pope Innocent XII concerned those who were being ordained in the diocese in which they had their domicile, but whole rightful place of origin was some other diocese. If the candidate resided in the diocese of origin for such a period as to be capable of contracting a canonical impediment to ordination, it was required of him to present testimonial letters from the bishop of the diocese of origin.[5] Even when a bishop had the right to ordain

[2] *Ibid.*, § 3—*Fontes,* n. 258. Cf. Council of Rome (1725), tit. VI, c. IV—*Acta et Decreta Sacrorum Conciliorum Recentorum, Collectio Lacensis* (7 vols., Friburgi Brisgoviae, 1870-1890), I, 355 (hereafter cited *Collectio Lacensis*); Gasparri, *De Sacra Ordinatione,* n. 726; Many, *De Sacra Ordinatione,* p. 309; Ferraris, *Prompta Bibliotheca Canonica, Iuridica, Moralis, Theologica, necnon Ascetica, Polemica, Rubricistica, Historica* (ed. novissima, 9 vols., Romae, 1885-1899), "Ordo," art. III, nn. 14-18 (hereafter cited *Bibliotheca*).

[3] Sess. XXIII, *de ref.*, c. 8.

[4] Innocentius XII, Const. *Speculatores,* 4 nov. 1694, § 4—*Fontes,* n. 258. Cf. Gasparri, *De Sacra Ordinatione,* n. 728. The amount of time for which it became necessary to obtain such letters was interpreted by most of the authors as six months after the completion of the candidate's seventh year. E.g., Ballerini-Palmieri (*Opus Theologicum Morale,* V, 763) and Genicot (*Theologiae Moralis Institutiones* [4. ed., 2 vols., Lovanii, 1902], II, 484) were of this opinion. Many (*De Sacra Ordinatione,* pp. 313-316) inclined to the belief that the length of the period of time in question was indeed the lapse of six months, but divergently from the more common view he held that this lapse of time occasioned the need of added testimonial letters only when it supervened the candidate's attainment of the age of puberty.

[5] *Ibid.*, § 5—*Fontes,* n. 258.

the candidate by reason of the latter's connection with the bishop as a member of the bishop's household,[6] testimonial letters were required both from the bishop of the place of origin and from the bishop of the place of domicile.[7]

The bishop who ordained in violation of the provisions of this Constitution was by that very fact suspended from the conferring of orders for one year, and the one so ordained was likewise suspended from the exercise of the orders he had received, for as long a period as his own ordinary saw fit to determine in his discretion. Further penalties could be imposed if the bishop deemed them necessary.[8]

Mention of this need for testimonial letters was frequently repeated in the legislation which followed upon this Constitution. There were also further legislative developments relative to the requisite content of these letters. Much of this legislation was of a particular character. It is interesting, however, because in time it frequently found its way into the general legislation. An example of this was the Constitution *Apostolici ministerii,* which was issued with a view to restoring ecclesiastical discipline in the kingdom of Spain. It ordered that, before issuing testimonial letters in compliance with the Constitution *Speculatores,* the bishop was to examine the candidate, and then was to include in his letter the testimony regarding the fitness of the candidate as determined through the examination.[9]

[6] Cf. Conc. Trident., sess. XXIII, *de ref.,* c. 9.

[7] Const. *Speculatores,* § 6—*Fontes,* n. 258. Cf. Wernz, *Ius Decretalium,* II, n. 29; Gasparri, *De Sacra Ordinatione,* n. 736; Santi, *Praelectiones Iuris Canonici* (5 vols. in 3, Ratisbonae, 1903-1905), Lib. I, tit. XI, n. 32 (hereafter cited *Praelectiones*); McBride, *Incardination and Excardination.* p. 60. The last named holds that testimonial letters in this case were to be obtained merely from the bishop of the place of origin, or merely from the bishop of the place of domicile rather than from both. The common opinion was that they were required from both, although the wording of the Constitution itself did not seem to favor this interpretation. The section in question reads: ". . . absque eius propriae originis scilicet seu domicilii praelati testimonialibus litteris." Many (*op. cit.,* p. 309) was of the same opinion as McBride.

[8] *Ibid.,* § 8—*Fontes,* n. 258. Cf. Many, *op. cit.,* p. 161.

[9] Innocentius XIII (1721-1724), 23 maii, 1723, § 6—*Fontes,* n. 280; *Bullarium,* XXI, 931-942.

Of special importance was a decision of the Sacred Congregation of the Council with regard to a certain type of testimonial letter. The letter in question read:

> Testamur Clericum Laurentium Meldicheschi nostrae Dioecesis in minoribus Ordinibus constitutum, nullo excommunicationis, irregularitatis, aut cuiusvis alterius canonici impedimenti vinculo, saltem quoad sciamus, innodatum existere, neque ullo crimine postulatum, sed esse bonis ac honestis moribus praeditum, ac talem, qualem in sortem Domini vocatos decet.[10]

The ordaining bishop accepted this letter as suitably authorizing him for the conferring of orders, even though it made no mention of having been issued for that purpose. His action was called into question on this point by the bishop who had issued the letter, and also on the ground that the letter lacked testimony regarding the candidate's parentage or age. The former argued that, as far as the question of testimony regarding the candidate's parentage was concerned, the mere omission of this testimony did not render the letter unsuited or insufficient as authorization for the ordination, since the letter expressly stated that the candidate had received minor orders, and therefore it could be legitimately presumed that he was not affected with any irregularity on that score. The latter bishop argued that the letter was merely the type of letter regularly issued to a cleric who was about to depart from his diocese, and consequently did not imply any authorization whatsoever for the conferring of higher orders upon the cleric.

The Congregation was asked whether the testimonial letter which the cleric had requested from his bishop sufficed for the conferring of higher orders upon him, that is, whether it satisfied the provisions of the Constitution *Speculatores*. On July 18, 1733, the Congregation answered in the affirmative.

[10] S. C. C., *Pientina seu Ilcinen. Ordinationis,* 18 iul. 1733—*Thesaurus Resolutionum Sacrae Congregationis Concilii* (167 vols., Romae, 1718-1908), VI, 131-136 (hereafter cited *Thesaurus*). Cf. Gasparri, *op. cit.*, n. 724. Ferraris, *Bibliotheca,* "Ordo," art. III, nn. 88-95; Bouix, *Tractatus de Episcopo* (2 vols., Parisiis, 1859), II, 154-156.

The case was soon taken up again for further consideration by the Congregation, and on August 8 of the same year the original decision was reversed.[11] In this decision the Congregation stated that it was the purpose of the legislator, Innocent XII, through this requirement of testimonial letters to prevent all fraud possible. For the accomplishment of this it was necessary, according to the Congregation, that it be clearly stated in the letters that they were being issued for the reception of orders, even though there was lacking in the Constitution *Speculatores* any express mention of this requirement. The Congregation adverted to the existing customary usage, as well as to the examples of testimonial letters issued in Rome as favoring this interpretation. These letters clearly expressed not only the general fact that they were issued for the sake of authorizing a promotion to orders, but also the specific fact that they were issued in authorization of the candidate's promotion to a particularly designated clerical order.

The letter was declared insufficient, moreover, because it lacked testimony regarding the candidate's legitimate birth. The fact that he had already been promoted to minor orders did not make testimony on this point less necessary. Again, the letter failed to mention that the candidate had attained the age required by the Council of Trent [12] for major orders. While the Congregation conceded that this information could be ascertained from other documents, it stated that it was preferable that it be obtained from the bishops of the place of origin and of domicile, since these knew the candidate, and thus the very possibility of any deception was more effectively obviated.

In deciding that the letter had to contain express mention of the fact that it was issued for the sake of authorizing a promotion to major orders, the Congregation added an important observation. It declared that it did not suffice if the letter merely stated that the candidate had fulfilled all the requirements of obligations relating

[11] S. C. C., *Pientina seu Ilcinen. Ordinationis,* 8 aug. 1733—*Thesaurus,* VI, 147-152. Gasparri, besides treating this case very thoroughly, also related another similar case.—*De Sacra Ordinatione,* n. 891.

[12] Sess. XXIII, *de ref.,* c. 12.

to his status in minor orders. The letter definitely had to state that the candidate, in the opinion of the bishop, was worthy to be promoted to major orders.

In conclusion, the Congregation pointed out that there was an immense difference between dimissorial letters and testimonial letters. The former bestow upon another bishop the right to promote a candidate to orders; the latter merely testify to the fitness of the candidate for promotion to orders.[13]

A further specification as to the contents of these letters came some years later when the same Congregation ruled that they were to be testimonials, not regarding the knowledge or studies of the candidate, but simply regarding his parentage, age, life, and character. It stated that fraud would be sufficiently precluded if the bishop of the place of origin, before allowing the exercise of orders, subjected to an examination any cleric who had been ordained in another diocese and then returned to this bishop's diocese.[14]

With regard to the necessity for testimonial letters in accordance with the Constitution *Speculatores,* an interesting case was presented to the Congregation of the Council in 1792. A certain bishop had ordained to minor orders and to the subdiaconate a candidate who was his subject by reason of origin in the diocese. The cleric, John Rossetti by name, obtained a permanent chaplaincy in another diocese, and then requested the bishop of that diocese to ordain him to the diaconate and the priesthood. The new bishop consented, but the first bishop refused to grant the requested testimonial letters. The Congregation, when asked whether it was permissible for the new bishop to ordain the subdeacon without having obtained the testimonial letter, answered in the affirmative.[15] This decision established a precedent for cases of this kind.

[13] S. C. C., *Pientina seu Ilcinen. Ordinationis,* 8 aug. 1733—*Thesaurus, loc. cit.* Cf. Gasparri, *op. cit.*, n. 706; Gallagher, *Examination of the Qualities of the Ordinand,* The Catholic University of America Canon Law Studies, n. 195 (Washington, D. C.: The Catholic University of America Press, 1944), pp. 28-30.

[14] S. C. C., *Bergomen., Ordinationis seu Literarum Testimonialium,* 18 iun. 1746—Pallottini, XVI, p. 109, n. 168.

[15] S. C. C., *In Fabrianen., Ordinationis,* 21 aug. 1792—Pallottini, XVI, p. 120, n. 193.

An example of a particular law which in time had an influence on the general law of the Church came from the Provincial Council of Tuam (1817), in Ireland. This Council ordered that no candidate should be promoted to major orders without an authentic document that attested to the completion of at least two years of his theology course.[16] It is one of the first examples of a statute which required candidates to fulfill a definite part of their theology course as expressed in terms of specified years. The Council of Trent had established a requirement in this regard, which was, however, very general. It required that the candidate should be instructed in letters and in those things which pertained to the exercise of the order to be received.[17] According to Honorante (18th century) it was the practice in Rome to require testimony of attendance at a seminary, or at a mission house as he called it, for a specified period of time. For tonsure this specified time was two months,[18] for minor orders it was six months,[19] for the subdiaconate one year,[20] and one additional year for the diaconate and the priesthood respectively.[21]

The question of time spent in a seminary came up for consideration in another regard in a problem submitted to the Congregation of the Council. It concerned the ordination of a man who had spent some years in a seminary in another diocese, and who thereupon was ordained without having obtained testimonials from the bishop of that diocese. The Congregation decided that in the case as presented neither the ordaining prelate nor the ordinand was to be disquieted. For the future, however, in similar circumstances testimonial letters were to be requested for the time spent in a seminary in another diocese.[22]

16 C. XXII—*Collectio Lacensis,* III, 766.

17 Sess. XXIII, *de ref.,* c. 13.

18 *Praxis Secretariae,* cap. I, V, p. 2.

19 *Ibid.,* cap. II, IV, p. 29.

20 *Ibid.,* cap. III, VII, p. 36.

21 *Ibid.,* cap. IV, VI, p. 56, and cap. V, V, p. 60.

22 S. C. C., *Spoletana et Reatina, Ordinationis,* 23 nov. 1839; 11 iul. 1840—Pallottini, XVI, p. 117, n. 187.

Inasmuch as many candidates moved about from one seminary to another in the course of their studies, the II Plenary Council of Baltimore (1866), in legislating for the Church in the United States, ordered that in addition to the other requirements, bishops should demand from such men testimonial letters, signed by the rectors of the different seminaries, and stating what studies the candidate in question had completed. They should require, moreover, letters from the pastor of any place in which such men had stayed for a notable time.[23]

The Constitution *Speculatores* contemplated the situation in which a man who was being ordained outside the diocese of his origin had remained in that diocese after having attained the age at which he became capable of incurring a canonical impediment. Accordingly, this Constitution provided that such a candidate should not be promoted to orders as long as he had not received testimonial letters from that bishop.[24]

However, it did not contemplate the situation in which a candidate remained in a diocese long enough to contract an impediment when that diocese was not simultaneously the diocese of his origin. Some denied that in such cases letters offering testimony concerning the candidate's life and character, and especially regarding his freedom from any impediment, needed to be obtained from that bishop according to the provisions of the Constitution of Pope Innocent XII. The reason they gave was that the document was subject to a strict interpretation. They also objected on the grounds that the requiring of letters in such a case involved too much inconvenience to justify such a demand.[25] According to the common opinion, however, testimonial letters were deemed necessary, for although Pope Innocent had not expressly considered this situation, yet the generic

[23] *Concilii Plenarii Baltimorensis II, in Ecclesia Metropolitana Baltimorensi, a die VII ad diem XXI Octobris, A. D. MDCCCLXVI, Habiti, et a sede Apostolica Recogniti, Acta et Decreta* (Baltimorae: John Murphy, 1894), n. 332, p. 169 (hereafter cited *Acta et Decreta*).

[24] Cf. *supra*, p. 38. The II Plenary Council of Baltimore required such letters regardless of the age of the candidate who had departed from the diocese of his origin.—*Acta et Decreta*, n. 321, p. 169.

[25] Many, *De Sacra Ordinatione*, p. 316.

scope and the whole force of the provisions of his Constitution seemed definitely to point to a like requirement in such a case as well.[26]

The question was definitely settled in the Constitution *Apostolicae Sedis* of Pope Pius IX, issued on the 12th day of October, 1869.[27] By the provisions of this document it clearly became necessary to request testimonial letters from all ordinaries, without limitation, in whose dioceses the candidate had stayed for that period of time which was considered sufficient for the contracting of a canonical impediment, even though he had not been born there.[28]

For the application of this law in the case of men who had attended seminaries in other dioceses [29] there arose a problem for which a solution was sought from the Holy Office by the bishops of Austria. They contended that the ordinary of the diocese in which the seminary was situated usually knew nothing of the candidates. As a result he was forced to obtain the information necessary for the issuance of these letters from the rector of the seminary. This information was already contained in the testimonial letter issued by the rector. In view of all this the bishops asked if they might ordain these candidates without letters from the other bishop. The Holy Office answered in the negative. It granted, however, that in any particular case in which there would be grave difficulty in obtaining such letters the bishops might confer orders without having

[26] Gasparri, *De Sacra Ordinatione,* n. 729. Decisions from the Congregation of the Council are alleged for both sides of this question, the most recent seeming to favor the common opinion. Honorante (*Praxis Secretariae,* Cap. XV, n. 6, pp. 162-163) in his day admitted that the matter was by no means clear.

[27] *Fontes,* n. 552.

[28] *Ibid.,* V, art. 3. Cf. Gasparri, *loc. cit.;* Pennacchi, *Commentaria in Constitutionem* APOSTOLICAE SEDIS (2 vols., Romae, 1883), II, append. XLIV, pp. 365-385; Santi, *Praelectiones,* Lib. I, tit. XI, nn. 39-44; Many, *De Sacra Ordinatione,* p. 316; Téphany, *Constitution* APOSTOLICAE SEDIS: *Commentaire* (Tours, 1883), pp. 476-484; Huguenin, *Constitutionis* APOSTOLICAE SEDIS *Brevis Explanatio* (Parisiis, 1887), p. 60.

[29] As has been seen above, it was considered necessary, even before the issuance of this Constitution, to obtain letters for these from the bishop of the place in which the seminary was located. Cf. *supra,* p. 43.

obtained them, provided that from other sources they could be morally certain of the fitness of the candidates. This faculty was granted for a period of ten years.[80]

According to Many (+1922), though candidates for the reception of orders were by law required to obtain testimonials from the local bishop for the time spent in his diocese whenever in consequence of dimissorials from their own bishop they were being ordained at the seminary located in that diocese, yet in Paris and, so it was said, in Rome also, candidates were sometimes ordained without having obtained such testimonial letters. The reason which was advanced as warranting this mode of action was the following. It was felt that the law was sufficiently fulfilled through the attestations made by the rector of the seminary in proposing the candidate for ordination, together with the dimissorial letters from his own bishop.[81]

When the testimonial letters were purely negative in content, i.e., when they stated that the candidate was unknown, and accordingly offered no testimony for or against his fitness, it was the practice of the Holy See to grant permission to supply for this defect through a suppletory oath on the part of the candidate himself. It was necessary that this faculty be requested from the Holy See.[82]

Towards the close of the nineteenth century, an Instruction was directed to the bishops of America by the Congregation for the Propagation of the Faith with regard to priests and candidates for the priesthood who had emigrated to America. It concerned particularly the natives of Poland who had received all orders, or only some, in Italy, and then emigrated to America with commendatory

[80] S. C. S. Off., 28 oct. 1887—*Analecta Ecclesiastica* (Romae, 1893-1911), IV (1896), 206-207. Cf. Santi, *Praelectiones,* Lib. I, tit. XI, Appendix, n. 5. This decision was confirmed on July 14, 1894, by the Congregation of the Council in *Parentina et Polen.,* which outlined the history of the question and enumerated the decisions, both for and against the present stand, which had been handed down in the course of time.—*Acta Sanctae Sedis* (41 vols., Romae, 1865-1908), XXVII (1894), 159-162 (hereafter cited *ASS*).

[81] *De Sacra Ordinatione,* p. 322.

[82] S. C. C., *Urgellen.,* 26 ian. 1895—*Fontes,* n. 4293. Cf. also Many, *op. cit.,* p. 325. According to the response this applied only to soldiers, but the authors extended it to other cases also.

letters from some Italian bishop. The American bishops were warned that such were not to be admitted to their clergy, either as priests or as candidates for the priesthood, if they did not possess testimonial letters also from the Congregation itself.[33] These letters attested to their permission to leave their diocese, to their freedom from censures, and to the good morals of the candidate. In a later decree, however, which treated in more detail the whole question regarding the ordination of those who had arrived from other countries, no mention was made of this special requirement.[34]

Another group to receive special consideration in this regard were those who had been in military service and thereupon became candidates for ordination. Such men were required to present testimonial letters from the ordinary of the place in which they had spent three months or more.[35] This requirement applied only to those who had been in military service. It did not concern those who had left their diocese for any other reason. For the latter it was necessary to present such letters only when they had been absent for six months or more.[36] If the candidate was unable to establish his freedom through testimonial letters from the respective ordinaries, or through other documents, then the Holy See gave permission for the supplying of this defect through a suppletory oath.[37]

[33] 25 febr. 1896—*Collectanea S. Congregationis de Propaganda Fide* (2 vols., Romae, 1907), n. 1918. Cf. also S. C. de Prop. Fide, 2 maii, 1898—*Analecta Ecclesiastica*, VI (1898), 355.

[34] S. C. C., decr. *A primis*, 20 iul. 1898—*Fontes*, n. 4307.

[35] S. C. C., *Firmana*, 9 sept. 1893—*Fontes*, n. 4288. This document confirmed a decree previously issued with regard to religious. Cf. S. C. super Statu Regulari, 27 nov. 1892—*ASS*, XXV (1893), 635.

[36] S. C. C., *Urgellen*, 26 ian. 1895—*Fontes*, n. 4293. According to Many (*De Sacra Ordinatione*, p. 313), this and the preceding two decrees noted in the preceding footnote referred only to clerics who had been in the armed forces, and not to lay persons, formerly soldiers, who later sought admission to the clerical state. Moreover, these decrees were not authentic interpretations of the universal law, since neither the decision of 1893 nor that of 1895 mentioned that it had been issued *"R. Pontifice consulto,"* or *"relatione facta ad R. Pontificem,"* which kind of mention had been required by Pope Sixtus V in his Bull *Immensa* (Jan. 22, 1588) if the decrees or interpretations of the Congregations were to have universal application and force.

[37] S. C. S. Off., 12 mart. 1896—*Analecta Ecclesiastica*, IV (1896), 290.

The three months' period referred to in these decisions was to be understood as a temporal duration of three continuous months. Hence a soldier could have spent more time than a total of three months in some diocese and still not have been required to present testimonials from that ordinary, inasmuch as the stay was so interrupted that he did not in any one stretch spend three continuous months there.[38] The bishop had the right, however, to inquire into the fitness of the candidate and to require testimonials in the event of a shorter stay if none of the periods of sojourn extended to three continuous months, or he could even demand a suppletory oath under the same circumstances if he deemed it necessary. The decision applied also to those who had been absent from their dioceses for other reasons. In such cases, however, the space of time which necessitated the obtaining of testimonial letters was six months rather than three.

In Spain, according to a decree of 1894, the bishops of that country were not to confer orders upon those who had been in military service, unless these had previously obtained testimony concerning their lives and characters from the Pro-vicar for the armed forces. It was sufficient for such candidates to obtain this testimony but once, that is, before the first order was conferred, unless after receiving some orders they had returned to military service. These letters were to be signed by the Military Vicar.[39]

According to Honorante, if the candidates for orders in the Oriental Rites were being ordained in Rome, it was necessary that they obtain the permission of the Cardinal Vicar of Rome, called the *Exercenda,* in order to be promoted to orders by the bishops of their own rites.[40] The Synod of Lebanon (1736) in legislating for

[38] S. C. C., *Pragen,* 25 iun. 1904—*Fontes,* n. 4318.

[39] S. C. C., 5 apr. 1897—*Analecta Ecclesiastica,* IX (1901), 253. This decision, in answer to a question submitted by the Bishop of the Island of Goa, referred to the decree of 1894 and summarized its prescriptions. The original decree is not to be found in the 1894 volume of the *Thesaurus,* nor in the *ASS,* nor in the *Analecta Ecclesiastica.* There was a similar practice in Italy—S. C. Consist., 2 ian. 1917—*Acta Apostolica Sedis, Commentarium Officiale* (Romae, 1909—), IX (1917), 16 (hereafter cited *AAS*).

[40] *Praxis Secretariae,* Cap. XIII, V, p. 139.

the Maronites listed the documents which were required by candidates of that rite for ordination. For the most part the requirements were the same as those in the Western Church. Included as requisites in the list were the testimonials regarding the probity of life, the age, the knowledge, the service of the Church, the title of ordination, and the exercise of the orders already received.[41]

On December 22, 1903, the Vicariate of the City of Rome issued an Instruction with regard to the conferring of orders in that city. In this Instruction were enumerated the documents required of candidates for orders. Inasmuch as it seems to sum up quite well the documents which through the centuries had come to be regarded as necessary for a candidate in his promotion to orders, and also in view of its influence in later legislation, the contents of the Instruction are inserted here. The documents which the candidate had to present were the following:

I. For Tonsure and Minor Orders:

1. Petition for admission to First Tonsure, or to Minor Orders, addressed to the Cardinal Vicar of Rome;
2. Testimony
   (a) regarding baptism;
   (b) regarding the lawful wedlock of the parents;
   (c) regarding the free state of the candidate with reference to the time that had elapsed since he became fourteen years of age;
   (d) regarding the first clerical tonsure or the last Minor Order received;
   (e) regarding the candidate's life and morals (furnished by the pastor);
   (f) regarding the frequent reception of the sacraments;
   (g) regarding the studies of the candidate (furnished by the prefect of the school);
   (h) regarding the life of the candidate (furnished by the prefect of clerics).
3. Certification that proper provision was made before the reception of Tonsure for the care of the parents or other relatives.

[41] Pars II, Cap. XIV, *De Sacramento ordinis,* nn. 20-31—*Collectio Lacensis,* II, 237-240.

II. For Major Orders:
1. Petition for admission to Sacred Orders.
2. Petition for a dispensation from the observance of the interstices, if such was needed.
3. Testimony
(a) regarding baptism when the order of subdeaconship or priesthood was to be conferred;
(b) regarding the last Order received;
(c) regarding the exercise of the ministry in the subdiaconate and the diaconate;
(d) regarding the completion of one full year of theological studies for the subdiaconate, of two full years for the diaconate, and of three full years for the priesthood;
(e) regarding the free state of the candidate for the subdiaconate;
(f) regarding the candidate's life and morals (furnished by the pastor);
(g) regarding the frequent reception of the sacraments;
(h) regarding the life of the candidate (furnished by the prefect of clerics);
(i) regarding the title of ordination for the subdiaconate;
(j) regarding the candidate's exemption from military service;
(k) regarding the required publications in the candidate's own parish church and also in the Lateran Basilica (the latter peculiar to Rome);
(l) regarding the fulfillment of the spiritual exercises during the ten continuous days preceding the ordination.[42]

According to a declaration of the Congregation for Religious, testimonial letters issued in favor of religious were to contain a very detailed account of the progress made by the candidates in their studies. With regard to the theology curriculum, the letters were to state the name of the school in which they had pursued their

[42] *Ex Vicariatu Urbis—ASS*, XXXVI (1903-1904), 510-512. Similar enumerations may also be found in the *Instructio pro ordinandis in civitate et dioecesi Neapolitana*, issued by the Provincial Council of Naples, June 7-9, 1699 —Mansi, XXXVI ter, 830; in Monacelli, *Formularium*, Pars I, tit. III. form. I; and in Honorante, *Praxis Secretariae*, Cap. I-V. Monacelli (*op. cit.*, Pars I, tit. III) listed specimen formularies of all these different testimonials.

course, the date of their entrance into that school, the date of the completion of their course, and finally the fact that they had successfully undergone an examination in the theological subjects taught in the school. With regard to the lower studies, i.e., the humanities and philosophy, the letters were to state what studies had been pursued, the name of the school, the number of academic years spent in these studies and the measure of success that attended the examination.[43] This declaration extended to religious all over the world, and not merely to those in Italy. It included, moreover, those institutes and communities whose members were bound merely by a promise of perseverance.[44]

Article II. Dimissorial Letters

On the whole but little advance was made in the law on dimissorial letters. With the Council of Trent and the subsequent decrees the law in this regard seemed almost to have reached the point of complete development. The Provincial Council of Naples (1699) prescribed that dimissorial letters were to be directed to a particular bishop rather than to any bishop. This was required for the validity of these letters.[45] However, this conciliar provision remained purely a particular law. As Many pointed out, no universal law prescribed that the dimissorials had to be directed to some designated particular bishop.[46]

These letters had to be issued, however, to a certain determined candidate. They could not be issued to a class of candidates, e.g., to all who would seek them in the next year. Such was the decision of the Congregation of the Council in answer to a question from some bishops of the New World. This question concerned a bishop who had granted such letters, as he was about to die, to some subjects designated by name, and at the same time to all others who should ask for them in the next year.[47]

[43] 7 sept. 1909—*AAS,* I (1909), 701-704.

[44] S. C. de Rel., 31 maii 1910—*Fontes,* n. 4402; *AAS,* II (1910), 449-450.

[45] Caput VII, n. 13—Mansi, XXXVI, ter. 750.

[46] *De Sacra Ordinatione,* p. 163.

[47] S. C. C., *Mexicana,* 24 apr. 1700—*Fontes,* n. 2978.

According to Petra (1662-1747), a candidate who had obtained letters for his promotion to Sacred Orders, although no simultaneous mention was made of minor orders, was allowed by the Sacred Congregation of the Council to receive minor orders also on the strength of such letters. He added, however, that in such a case it was a safer practice to have recourse to the Congregation.[48] Gasparri noted that the happening of such a case was scarcely within the realm of the possible, since the bishop was supposed to testify in the letters concerning the last order received by the candidate.[49]

The Congregation of Bishops and Regulars ordered that when abbots *nullius* granted such letters they were to include in them a phrase stating that they were not to be accepted as sufficing for an authorized promotion to orders until after the candidate had presented proper dimissorial letters from the bishop whose see bordered on the territory of the abbacy.[50]

Pope Benedict XIV (1740-1758) ordered that candidates in the Italo-Greek rites were not to be promoted to orders or even to first tonsure until they had obtained dimissorials from their Latin diocesan bishops.[51] Those being ordained in Rome required also dimissorial

[48] *Commentaria,* III, n. 51, p. 84. This author cited the decision of the Congregation as *In Andegaven.*, 22 iun. 1707. Likewise a bishop who received dimissorials for one who had not received the sacrament of confirmation could confirm such a candidate, even though the latter was not that bishop's subject, for in such a case the ordaining prelate could legitimately presume the consent of the candidate's proper bishop. Cf. also Barbosa, *De Officio et Potestate Episcopi,* alleg. 30, n. 14.

[49] *De Sacra Ordinatione,* n. 883.

[50] S. C. Ep. et Reg., *Regien.*, 11 apr. 1766—*Analecta Iuris Pontificii* (Romae, 1855-1869; Parisiis, 1872-1891), XII (1873), 103.

[51] Const. *Etsi pastoralis,* 26 maii, 1742, § VII, n. VIII—*Continuatio Bullarii Romani Benedicti XIV* (3 vols. in 4, Prati, 1845-1847), I, 205; *Fontes,* n. 328. This document renewed the prescriptions of Pope Clement VIII (1592-1605), established in his Instruction *Sanctissimus* of August 31, 1595, § 4, which declared a suspension for the Greeks who were promoted to Sacred Orders when they had not previously obtained dimissorials from the Latin diocesan bishop, and an irregularity when despite the suspension they exercised the orders which they had wrongfully received—*Bullarium,* X, 211-213; *Fontes,* n. 179. Cf. Honorante, *Praxis Secretariae,* Cap. XIII, n. 4, pp. 142-144; Ferraris, *Bibliotheca,* "Ordo," Art. III, n. 78.

letters from the Congregation for the Propagation of the Faith, signed by the Prefect and by the Secretary, and directed to the Cardinal Vicar of the City. These letters were also to indicate the title on which the candidate was being ordained.[52]

With regard to the length of time for which these letters were valid after their issuance, there was no express ruling of the Holy See. The authors were of the opinion, however, that they continued to be valid for two, four, or at most six months. Monacelli (+1715) argued for the fitness of this in consideration of the purpose inherent in the law. These letters called for testimony concerning the life and character of the candidate, which in the space of six months could have changed considerably.[53] Gasparri noted that in Rome the Cardinal Vicar of the City conceded letters which were valid for two months with reference to tonsure, for four months with reference to minor orders, and for six months with reference to any of the Sacred Orders.[54]

For the candidate who had been absent from his diocese over a long period of time for reasons other than studies, the letters were to contain testimony simply regarding his parentage, his age, his baptism and confirmation, the orders already received by him, and the death of his wife in the event that he had earlier contracted a marriage. No attestation was to be made regarding his freedom from impediments. In such cases it was the practice to give the testimony exclusively for the time spent in the diocese of the bishop who granted the letters, the period of absence being duly noted. It was then necessary for the candidate to obtain another letter in which the testimony was to be given for the time of his absence.[55]

A letter by means of which a bishop granted to another bishop the permission to exercise all acts of spiritual jurisdiction over one of his clerics who now resided in the diocese of the second bishop, so that the latter might consider the cleric as his own, did not satisfy

[52] Honorante, *op. cit.*, Cap. XIII, I, p. 138.

[53] *Formularium,* Pars I, tit. IV, form. II, n. 2, p. 104.

[54] *De Sacra Ordinatione,* n. 884.

[55] Gasparri, *op. cit.*, nn. 677 and 886; Monacelli, *op. cit.*, Pars I, tit. IV, form II, n. 3, p. 104.

the requirements for either dimissorial or testimonial letters.[56] However, the letters which were granted to a lay person who was about to depart from his diocese, and who thereupon might well become the subject of some other bishop, proved sufficient under restrictive conditions for the candidate's promotion to tonsure and even to Sacred Orders. They sufficed if they were granted for a just cause and at the same time were directed to a certain bishop, if, in addition, all the rules for incardination and excardination were followed, and if, finally, the oath as required by the Constitution *Speculatores*[57] had been duly taken before the reception of tonsure. It was understood that these various conditions had to be verified cumulatively. The candidate was not to be allowed to take this oath before he had reached his majority.[58]

Without a just cause a bishop could not rightfully deny such letters to his clerics when these requested them from him. If a denial was made without a just cause, the candidate could have recourse to the Holy See.[59] In some such cases of recourse the cleric was granted permission to be promoted to higher orders by any Catholic bishop.[60]

Gasparri summed up very well what should be contained in these letters. First they should contain a recommendation concerning the life and character of the ordained, and then an expression of the reason why the proper bishop was unable to confer the orders himself. The latter could be omitted when the letters were given to a candidate who happened to be residing in the diocese of the bishop who became authorized through these letters to ordain him, for in that case the reason was quite obvious, viz., the absence of the candidate from his own diocese. There was also to be an express de-

[56] S. C. C., *S. Miniatis et Collen., Ordinationis* 24 apr. 1830—quoted in Gasparri, *op. cit.*, n. 891.

[57] *Fontes,* n. 258.

[58] S. C. C., decr. 24 nov. 1906—*Fontes,* n. 4330.

[59] S. C. Ep. et Reg., *Verulana Aquinaten et Neapolitana,* 16 iul. 1841—*Collectanea in Usum Secretariae Sacrae Congregationis Episcoporum et Regularium,* cura Bizzarri (2. ed., Romae, 1885), pp. 474-476. This decision cited the decision *In Rhenen.*, 21 apr. 1668, of the Congregation of the Council.

[60] S. C. C., *Anicen., Ordinationis,* 23 mart. 1878—Quoted by Gasparri, *op. cit.*, n. 890. Cf. also Lucidi, *De Visitatione Sacrorum Liminum,* I, 181.

termination of the orders for which the letters were issued, of the length of time for which they were to be considered valid, and name of the bishop who was to confer the orders. Finally, the letters were to be signed by the bishop who granted them, as well as by the chancellor, although the omission of the signature of the latter did not affect the validity of the letters.[61]

With regard to the dimissorials issued by religious superiors for their subjects, Pope Benedict XIV (1740-1758), in his Constitution *Impositi Nobis,* ruled that such were of no value if they lacked an authentic attestation, made by the vicar general, the chancellor, or the secretary of the bishop, which stated the absence of the bishop from the diocese at the time or confirmed the assumption that the bishop would not preside at ordinations in his diocese at the next regularly occurring time established by law for the conferring of orders. A bishop who ordained a man when the dimissorials lacked this attestation incurred the same penalty that befell any bishop who undertook to confer orders without having obtained any dimissorials at all.[62]

[61] *De Sacra Ordinatione,* n. 885; Wernz, *Ius Decretalium,* II, n. 29; Many, *De Sacra Ordinatione,* p. 164. Specimens of the letters may be found in Monacelli, *Formularium,* Pars I, tit. IV, form. I-III, and also Gasparri, *op. cit.,* allegatum II.

[62] 27 febr. 1747—*Fontes,* n. 376. Pope Clement VIII, by means of a mandated decree which the Sacred Congregation of the Council issued on March 15, 1596, had ordered the regular superiors, when they issued their dimissorials to some outside bishop, to make mention in their letters of the absence of the local diocesan bishop, or of the circumstance that he would not preside at ordinations on the next regular occasion for the conferring of orders. But he had not at the same time required that the statement of the superiors be attested by someone of the diocesan officials.—*Fontes,* n. 2294.

Part Two

Canonical Commentary

CHAPTER V

DOCUMENTS REQUIRED FOR THE RECEPTION OF TONSURE AND MINOR ORDERS

Article I. Preliminary Notions

Canon 993 of the Code of Canon Law, which treats of the documents which must be presented by the candidate for orders, contains an introductory paragraph which defines and delimits those who are governed by the prescripts contained therein. In the first place, the subjects are described as *promovendi,* and therefore comprise all those who are to be promoted to orders, those who have the intention of receiving any orders whatsoever. These in turn are further limited by what is stated in the succeeding phrases. Of all these, the canon legislates only for seculars and candidates who are members of a religious institute which, in so far as ordinations are concerned, is ruled by the law as established for seculars.[1]

Saeculares is the word used by the Code in this connection. As used in the Code this word is applicable both to laymen and to clerics.[2] It is clear therefore that this canon applies not only to those who are about to enter the clerical state through first tonsure, but also to those who have already entered that state and now desire to ascend to some higher order.[3] While certain religious are included under this canon, the present chapter will deal solely with seculars.

[1] In general it may be said that these include all non-exempt religious. The ordination of religious will be treated in a subsequent chapter.

[2] McBride, *Incardination and Excardination,* p. 308.

[3] Gallagher, *Examination of the Qualities of the Ordinand,* p. 49.

As to the orders for which this canon legislates, there is no limitation whatsoever in the law. Thus it applies not only to orders, major or minor, strictly so called [4] but also to the first clerical tonsure, since, as canon 950 points out, the words *ordo, ordinatio,* when used in the law, comprehend not only the orders listed in canon 949, but also tonsure, unless the nature of the case demands otherwise. In this chapter only tonsure and minor orders will be considered. Major orders will be treated in the following chapter.

In speaking of the presentation of the prerequisite documents, the Code uses the word *afferant*. From the use of this word it is not to be inferred that the candidate himself will actually carry these documents to the bishop. As Wernz-Vidal well point out, under the present arrangement with regard to seminary training for the candidates for the priesthood, the task of obtaining these documents, and especially the testimonial letters which may be required, devolves upon the rector of the seminary.[5] It would be wise for him to obtain these reasonably well in advance of the date of ordination, in order that he may provide for any unforeseen difficulties which may arise. This, however, is merely a matter of practice. The obligation in law still rests upon the individual candidate, because it is he who is bound to prove his fitness for ordination.[6] A further indication that such is the case is found in the Constitution *Speculatores* of Innocent XII, in which that Pontiff enjoined this obligation upon the candidate himself.[7]

The examination or inspection of the documents here listed pertains to the proper bishop of the ordinand inasmuch as the right and duty of judging the fitness of the candidate is placed upon him by the Code.[8] This will be the case even when the student is to be

[4] Can. 949—*Codex Iuris Canonici Pii X Pontificis Maximi iussu digestus Benedicti XV auctoritate promulgata* (Romae: Typis Polyglottis Vaticanis, 1917. Reimpressio, 1934).

[5] *Ius Canonicum* (7 tomes in 8 vols., Romae: apud aedes Universitatis Gregorianae, 1923-1938. Tom. IV, Pars I, 1934; Tom. IV, Pars II, 1935), Tom. IV, Pars I, n. 270, footnote 534. Cf. also Many, *De Sacra Ordinatione,* p. 323.

[6] Many, *De Sacra Ordinatione, loc. cit.*

[7] 4 nov. 1694, § 3—*Fontes,* n. 258.

[8] Can. 968, § 1.

ordained by another bishop, since in such an event his own bishop will be required to issue dimissorial letters, and he is expressly enjoined from doing so before he has obtained all the testimonials required by law.[9] He may delegate this examination to others and, as a matter of fact, he usually delegates the rector of the seminary, who does this as part of the entire examination of the candidate.[10]

Throughout this title the word *testimonium* is frequently employed.[11] In this connection it refers to an attestation of a particular fact issued by one who is competent to certify the existence of the said fact.[12] While the canons do not explicitly state that these attestations must be made in writing ,it may be legitimately inferred from a later canon, which speaks of preserving all documents concerning ordination,[13] that such was intended. Certainly it is the almost universal practice to demand these attestations in written form, and the very nature of the situation demands some sort of enduring record.

Article II. Documents Required in Every Case

1. *The Petition*

Canon 992 of the Code states that all, whether secular or religious, who are to be promoted to orders are, at an opportune time, to manifest to their bishop or to any other person who takes the place of the bishop in these matters their intention to be ordained. They may do this personally or through another. This canon is not restricted, as is canon 993, to religious governed by the law of seculars. The Council of Trent made it necessary for all candidates for major orders to make such a manifestation one month before ordination.[14] According to Gasparri, who wrote at the close of the last century, before the Code all who desired to be ordained were bound to make this manifestation to the bishop or his delegate.[15]

[9] Can. 960, § 1.

[10] Many, *De Sacra Ordinatione*, pp. 323-324.

[11] Cans. 993, 1°, 2°, 3°; 1001, § 3. Cf. also can. 960.

[12] Gallagher, *op. cit.*, p. 51.

[13] Can. 1010, § 1: ". . . et omnia singularum ordinationum documenta accurate serventur."

[14] Conc. Trident., sess. XXIII, *de ref.*, c. 5.

[15] *De Sacra Ordinatione*, n. 668.

In the present canon it seems clear that the Code has canonized what was a pre-Code practice based ultimately on Tridentine legislation, and has made this manifestation or petition, for it is both, an altogether necessary condition for any ordination.[16] The Church has learned through bitter experience the harm that can be wrought through the ordination of one who receives orders under constraint from without. To safeguard herself as well as the candidate, she now demands that he make a specific request for ordination indicating not only his freedom in so doing, but also his willingness to assume the weighty obligation of the state which he desires to enter, or of the higher orders which he desires to receive.[17] According to Cappello, this prescription of itself binds *sub gravi,* since the law here treats of a matter of great importance.[18]

As to the form or contents of this petition, the canon makes no specification apart from the fact that it is to be a manifestation of one's intention to receive tonsure or orders. An Instruction from the Sacred Congregation of the Sacraments, however, as issued in 1930, is much more definite and specific.[19] According to the Instruction, at least two months before the date set for the ordination each candidate must present to the rector of the seminary a petition, in this case, for tonsure and minor orders. This petition, which must be written in the candidate's own handwriting and signed by him, will state that he requests these orders absolutely of his own free will.[20] The rector in turn will present the petition to the bishop.

Thus one petition suffices for tonsure and the four minor orders. It is not necessary to present a new petition each time the candidate

[16] Coronata, *Institutiones Iuris Canonici, De Sacramentis* (3 vols., Taurini-Romae: Marietti, 1943-1946), II, n. 170 (hereafter cited *De Sacramentis*).

[17] Coronata, *loc. cit.*

[18] *Tractatus Canonico-Moralis de Sacramentis* (3 vols. in 6, Taurinorum Augustae: Marietti, 1935-1945). Vol. I, 4. ed. 1945; Vol. II, Pars III, 1935; Vol. III, Pars I et II, 4. ed., 1939), Vol. II, Pars III, n. 530 (hereafter cited *De Sacramentis*).

[19] Instr. *Quam ingens,* 27 dec. 1930—*AAS,* XXIII (1931), 120-127. A translation of this important Instruction may be found in Bouscaren, *The Canon Law Digest* (2 vols., Milwaukee: Bruce, Vol. I, 1934; Vol. II, 1943), II, 463-473.

[20] Instr. *Quam ingens,* § 2, 1—*AAS,* XXIII (1931), 122.

is to be advanced in the clerical state through the reception of minor orders.[21] It must be written by the candidate; while it is sufficient for him merely to sign a printed form drawn up by the rector yet it is preferable for the candidate to write the entire petition in his own hand in order that his complete freedom be assured. It is difficult to see how Cappello[22] and Regatillo[23] can justify their stand that for tonsure and minor orders the petition may be made orally, particularly when these authors make explicit reference to the Instruction. Larraona, writing at the time of the issuance of the Instruction, pointed out that advisedly no form was proposed for the petition, in order that the candidate might be free to phrase his petition in his own words and thus further insure his freedom in so doing.[24] The ordinary, nevertheless, may well demand that some special element be included in the petition, for example, that the candidate while petitioning for tonsure and minor orders declare also his intention of proceeding ultimately to the priesthood.[25]

According to the Code all candidates are bound to present this petition, both secular and religious, including the quasi-religious, i.e., those who live in common but without public vows.[26] The Instruction *Quam ingens,* however, legislates only for secular candidates. Therefore the specifications concerning the petition as found therein do not apply to the petition of candidates in religious or quasi-religious institutes. The petition to be presented by these will be treated separately in a subsequent chapter. According to the Code it is to be presented to the bishop or to those who take his place in this matter. Blat teaches that it should be presented to the proper bishop for ordination as prescribed in canon 956.[27] Accordingly, it could

[21] Coronata, *De Sacramentis,* II, n. 170; Aertnys-Damen, *Theologia Moralis* (14. ed., 2 vols., Taurini: Marietti, 1944), II, n. 573.

[22] *De Sacramentis,* Vol. II, Pars III, n. 530.

[23] *Ius Sacramentarium* (2 vols., Santander: Sal Terrae, 1945-1946), II, n. 142.

[24] "Animadversiones"—*Apollinaris* (Romae, 1928—), IV (1931), 207-210.

[25] Can. 973, § 1.

[26] Blat, *Commentarium Textus Codicis Iuris Canonici* (5 vols. in 6, Romae: Collegio Angelico, 1919-1927), Lib. III, Pars I (De Sacramentis), n. 370 (hereafter cited *De Sacramentis*).

[27] *De Sacramentis, loc. cit.*

also be directed to the Prelate or Abbot *Nullius*,[28] to the prefect or vicar apostolic,[29] or to any other who acts for the bishops in this matter, such as a priest delegated for this purpose, or whoever is empowered to issue dimissorial letters, viz., with certain restrictions, the vicar general,[30] the vicar capitular or administrator.[31]

2. *Proof of the Reception of the Sacraments*

A. Baptism

The sacrament of orders can be validly conferred only upon those who have been baptized.[32] A baptism of water is absolutely necessary for the reception of baptism as a sacrament, and hence all who have not yet received the sacrament of baptism are excluded from the possible reception of the sacrament of orders, even though they may be catechumens.[33] The theological reason for this is quite clear. Baptism of water and it alone is the door to all the other sacraments.[34] Therefore before its reception the subject is, by divine law, completely incapable of receiving any of the other sacraments.[35] It is because the reception of the sacrament of baptism is so absolutely necessary that the Church demands proof of its reception before admitting a candidate to the clerical state.[36] For those clerics who are candidates for advancement in orders the furnishing of proof for the reception of the sacrament of baptism is not required, since its reception is lawfully presumed from the fact that for the reception of the first tonsure such proof has already been presented.

The principal agency provided by the Code as a means of proving the fact of baptism is the parochial record of baptism or the baptismal

[28] Can. 215, § 2 and can. 957, § 1.

[29] Can. 294, § 1 and can. 957, § 1.

[30] Can. 958, § 1, 2°.

[31] Can. 958, § 1, 3°. Cf. also can. 198, § 1.

[32] Can. 968.

[33] Cappello, *De Sacramentis,* Vol. II, Pars III, n. 353; Wernz-Vidal, *Ius Canonicum,* Tom. IV, Vol. I, n. 205.

[34] Can. 737.

[35] S. Thomas Aquinas, *Summa Theologica* (22. ed., 6 vols., Taurini-Romae; Marietti, 1939), Suppl., q. XXXV, a. 3.

[36] Can. 993, 1°.

register.[37] It may also be substantiated by either of two documents, namely, an official baptismal certificate, or an authentic copy of the baptismal record.[38] The Code clearly distinguishes between these written instruments derived from the baptismal register. A certificate relates the sense or the essential facts contained in the record, while a copy, on the other hand, is a literal, word for word, reproduction of the record itself.[39] Both are public documents and as such presuppose a proper authentication. For this it is necessary that they be signed by a public official such as the ordinary, the pastor, or an ecclesiastical notary.[40] Assistant pastors or curates do not inherently possess the power to authenticate parish documents. The Code nowhere gives them such power.[41] Coronata apparently allows the assistant to sign these documents.[42] In doing so, however, he seems to be speaking more of an assistant who is taking the place of, or substituting for, the pastor, and thus is acting with parochial power.[43] It is generally admitted today that a word for word copy of the

[37] Sullivan, *Proof of the Reception of the Sacraments.* The Catholic University of America Canon Law Studies, n. 209 (Washington, D. C.: The Catholic University of America Press, 1944), p. 51.

[38] Can. 1813, § 1, 4°.

[39] Coronata, *Institutiones Iuris Canonici* (5 vols., Taurini-Romae: Marietti, 1936-1946. Vols. I and II, 2. ed., 1939; Vol. III, 2. ed., 1941; Vol. IV, 2. ed., 1946; Vol. V, 1936), III, n. 1342 (hereafter cited *Institutiones*).

[40] Can. 1813, § 1, 4°.

[41] Augustine, *A Commentary on the New Code of Canon Law* (8 vols., Vol. IV, 1921; Vol. VII, 1921, Vol. VIII, 1922; St. Louis, B. Herder Book Co.), VII, 217 (hereafter cited *Commentary*); Wanenmacher, *Canonical Evidence in Marriage Cases* (Philadelphia: Dolphin Press, 1935), p. 208; Willett, *The Probative Value of Documents in Ecclesiastical Trials,* The Catholic University of America Canon Law Studies, n. 171 (Washington, D. C.: The Catholic University of America Press, 1942), p. 56; Sullivan, *Proof of the Reception of the Sacraments,* p. 59.

[42] *Institutiones Iuris Canonici,* III, n. 1342.

[43] Sullivan, *loc. cit.* This author points out that the discussion is quite theoretical since assistants can certainly be delegated for the purpose by the ordinary or the pastor, which delegation may be presumed if no other provision is made.

baptismal register is not required in proof of the fact of baptism. A certificate which contains the essential facts recorded therein would certainly suffice.[44]

Unless the contrary is specified in diocesan statutes, it is not necessary for the certificate to be presented to the ordinary for his approval. Cappello says that when the certificate is being sent to another diocese it would be advisable to obtain for it an approval from the curia of the diocese of baptism.[45] He admits, however, that this is by no means necessary. Failure to present it to the curia, even where there is a diocesan statute which calls for such a presentation, would not affect the value of the certificate in any way.

The Code does not treat the question of a photostatic copy of the baptism register as a method of proof. Sullivan is of the opinion, and it seems quite safe to follow, that if such is made under the supervision of the pastor it would certainly constitute full proof of baptism.[46]

The certificate should mention the name of the baptized, the date and the place of baptism, the name of the minister and the names of the sponsors and parents.[47] Any other information which may be found in the register, such as that regarding domicile, etc., need not be included. Regarding the subsequent annotations O'Rourke contends, despite the divergent wording of canon 470, § 2, that if the certificate is to be used merely in proof of the fact of baptism apart from all reference to the prospective contracting of marriage it would not be necessary to include them.[48] The certificate, even when these annotations are included, will prove fully only the essential elements recorded in the original baptismal register.[49]

44 Cappello, *De Sacramentis,* I, n. 185; Coronata, *De Sacramentis,* I, n. 159.

45 *Loc. cit.* Cf. also Coronata, *loc. cit.*

46 *Proof of the Reception of the Sacraments,* p. 57. It is proper, as this author suggests, that some statement of the pastor accompany the photostat. The statement should be attached to the document in such a way that the two are inseparable.

47 Can. 777, § 1. Cf. O'Rourke, *Parish Registers,* The Catholic University of America Canon Law Studies, n. 88 (Washington, D. C.: The Catholic University of America, 1934), pp. 45-56.

48 *Ibidem,* p. 12.

49 Willett, *The Probative Value of Documents,* p. 76.

In the great majority of cases the requirement of the Code regarding the production of proof for the fact of baptism will be satisfied through such documents. There can be times, however, when such documents are not available. May the bishop then fall back upon private documents, such as a letter written by some witness, a personal letter of the pastor in which he mentions the baptism of some child known to the recipient of the letter, or some document which was originally intended to be issued as a public document, but which was not drawn up by the proper official, or which remained destitute of some legal formality? Private documents may also be introduced as proof of the reception of baptism in the event that a public document cannot be obtained.[50] Such documents, however, are not to be immediately received at face value. The authorship of the document as well as the credibility of its contents must be established, since they lack the legal presumption of genuineness which the law grants to public documents.[51] Ultimately the value of any private document is to be estimated by the bishop according to the knowledge and credibility of its author. As long as the bishop can so satisfy himself on these points as to exclude all prudent doubt concerning the fact of baptism, no further proof will be required.[52]

What is to be done in those cases—and there will be many during times of war—when there cannot be procured any document whatsoever with which to prove the fact of baptism? The Code itself provides for such an eventuality. For proving the fact of baptism the testimony of one witness who is above all exception, or the oath of the candidate himself when he has received baptism in adult life,[53] will suffice as long as the rights of a third party are in no way jeopardized.[54]

If the accepted proof of baptism in any way entails injury to the rights of another, the attestation of one witness does not furnish full proof unless the witness can be included among those who are termed

[50] Cappello, *De Sacramentis,* Vol. III, n. 420.

[51] Willett, *op. cit.,* p. 90. Cf. can. 1814.

[52] Sullivan, *Proof of the Reception of the Sacraments,* p. 64.

[53] This is to be understood in the sense of canons 88, § 3, and 745, § 2, 2°, i.e., after the completion of his seventh year.

[54] Can. 779.

qualificati by the Code, i.e., public officials who testify under oath concerning acts performed in virtue of their office, e.g., pastors, notaries, ordinaries, etc.[55] Instances in which the rights of a third party would be jeopardized could occur, for example, when the acquiring of an inheritance would be blocked for such a person or a definitive declaration regarding the juridical status of a marriage would be adversely affected in view of the acceptance of proof furnished by a single witness in substantiation of the fact of baptism.[56]

Most of the authors teach no such jeopardy of rights is at stake when the conferral of tonsure or of orders follows upon the acceptance of proof furnished by a single but reliable witness relative to the fact of baptism, and therefore this method of proof may legitimately be substituted for the more common form of proof by means of a certificate when the latter is not available.[57] Gasparri expressed the opinion that in the absence of a baptismal certificate the fact of baptism may be proved in other ways, and he gives as an example the testimony of even one witness worthy of credence.[58] This is in agreement with a decree of the Holy Office of March 18, 1896, which declared that the testimony of one trustworthy witness suffices to establish the fact of baptism, and therefore the sacrament may not be repeated conditionally as long as there is one such witness to testify to the fact that the baptism was properly conferred.[59]

Gallagher points out that while strictly according to the wording of canon 779 its rule may be invoked in this matter, it is not altogether clear whether the Holy See will by means of an oath, either of one witness or of the candidate himself admit proof of the fact

[55] Can. 1791, § 1. Cf. Wernz-Vidal, *Ius Canonicum,* Tom. IV, Vol. I, n. 48.

[56] Coronata, *De Sacramentis,* I, n. 159; Sullivan, *Proof of the Reception of the Sacraments,* pp. 72-77.

[57] Coronata, *De Sacramentis,* II, n. 177; Regatillo, *Ius Sacramentarium,* II, n. 49; Davis, *Moral and Pastoral Theology* (4. ed., 4 vols., New York: Sheed and Ward, 1943), IV, p. 43; Woywod, *A Practical Commentary on the Code of Canon Law* (2 vols., 8. printing, revised by C. Smith, New York: Wagner, 1944), I, n. 679.

[58] *De Sacra Ordinatione,* n. 685.

[59] *Collectanea,* n. 1923; *Fontes,* n. 1177.

of baptism in relation to extremely important consequences.[60] He therefore advises that in cases wherein presumptions arising from Catholic parentage and education cannot be invoked, it would be preferable to seek the guidance of the Holy See. However preferable this may be in certain cases, it certainly cannot be made a general rule. As long as the rector of the seminary, or the ordinary, can arrive at moral certitude of the fact of the conferral of the sacrament, whether this is arrived at by means of a certificate, by means of the testimony of one witness, even though not qualified, who is worthy of credence, by means of an oath on the part of a candidate who has been baptized in adult life, or even by means of the presumption of baptism arising from the candidate's Catholic parentage and upbringing,[61] he may proceed to admit the candidate to tonsure. If despite whatever proof is presented there still remains a prudent doubt, then the candidate is to be baptized conditionally.[62]

In the ordinary case this process of proving the reception of baptism will not be necessary at the time the candidate is to be promoted to tonsure, since he will already have presented satisfactory proof of this fact at the time of his admission into the seminary.[63] Thus if the presented proof of the fact of baptism became no longer traceable at some time after the student's admission to the seminary, it would not be necessary, when the time arrives for the student to be promoted to tonsure, to demand this proof again, as long as the rector could attest to the fact that this proof had been presented. This attestation should be made in writing and preserved with the

60 *Examination of the Qualities of the Ordinand,* pp. 54-55.

61 The Holy See has ruled that where these presumptions exist the candidate is not to be baptized conditionally even though no other proof is available. Cf. c. 3, X, *de presbytero non baptizato,* III, 43; Innocentius III (1198-1216), *Veniens ad apostolicam,* 13 apr. 1206—Potthast, n. 2749; S. C. de Prop. Fide, instr., 30 sept. 1848—*Fontes,* n. 4825. Cf. also Noldin-Schmitt, *Summa Theologiae Moralis* (3 vols., Oeniponte-Lipsiae: Rauch, 1939-1940. Vol. I, 27, ed., 1940; Vol. II, 26. ed., 1939; Vol. III, 26. ed., 1940), III, n. 76; Merkelbach, *Summa Theologiae Moralis* (3. ed., 3 vols., Parisiis: Desclée, de Brouwer et Soc., 1938-1939), III, n. 167.

62 Can. 732, § 2.

63 Can. 1363, § 2.

other documents pertaining to the ordination.[64] If the rector were unable to make such an attestation, then proof of the reception of baptism would have to be demanded again in accordance with canon 993, 1°.[65]

According to the Instruction of the Congregation of the Sacraments,[66] the baptismal certificate, or other proof of baptism, should be appended to the candidate's petition for tonsure and minor orders. In practice, however, it seems sufficient for the rector merely to state that this document has been presented and is now on file at the seminary.[67]

B. Confirmation

The second attestation required by canon 993 for those who are about to make the transition from the lay state to the clerical state is that of the reception of the sacrament of confirmation. Unlike baptism, this sacrament in no way affects the validity of orders. Its reception is a requirement which is concerned solely with the consideration of licitness.[68] St. Thomas illustrated the intimate congruity inherent in the reception of this sacrament prior to the reception of tonsure or any of the orders, but he insisted that in the light of the divine law one cannot maintain that such a previous reception of the sacrament of confirmation is absolutely necessary.[69] As an ecclesiastical requirement it was first established as law for the universal Church in the Council of Trent.[70] The reason for the law is quite clear. Without this sacrament a person would not be considered sufficiently strong in the faith to be admitted to the clerical state and, moreover, it would not be fitting for those who have not yet been

[64] Can. 1010, § 1.

[65] Cf. Gasparri, *De Sacra Ordinatione,* n. 686.

[66] Instr. *Quam ingens,* 27 dec. 1930, § 2—*AAS,* XXIII (1931), 122.

[67] Gallagher, *Examination of the Qualities of the Ordinand,* p. 55. Cf. also Claeys Bouuaert-Simenon, *Manuale Juris Canonici* (3 vols., Gandae et Leodii: Apud Auctores in Seminariis Gandavensi et Leodiensi, 1930-1931, Vols. I and III, 3. ed., 1930; Vol. II, 1931), II, 209.

[68] Can. 974, § 1, 1°.

[69] *Summa Theologica,* Suppl., q. XXXV, a. 4.

[70] Conc. Trident., sess. XXIII, *de ref.,* c. 5.

made soldiers of Christ to be constituted the leaders of others through orders.[71] To make sure that the candidate has been confirmed, therefore, the Code demands that he present proof of this fact before he is allowed to enter the clerical state.

To prove this fact, as in the case of baptism, the ordinary means will be a certificate of confirmation, that is, a public attestation of a qualified official in authentic form certifying that according to the parochial record the person named has been confirmed. All that has been said heretofore concerning the baptismal certificate may be applied to the confirmation certificate. The parochial register of confirmation and authentic copies or certificates derived from this register are public documents, and as such are presumed genuine and therefore constitute the most secure method of proving the fact of the reception of this sacrament.[72]

With regard to the sacrament of confirmation there is a further source of proof regarding its reception, viz., the annotation of the fact in the baptismal register.[73] What of its probative value? The baptismal register testifies directly only to the reception of baptism. Accordingly it does not furnish full proof of any other facts noted therein.[74] Wanenmacher in treating the question of the annotation of marriage in this register, contends that such an annotation does not give full proof of the marriage of the person baptized.[75] His reason is that this annotation is not to be considered a direct and primary content of the baptismal register. It would certainly seem that the same argument would be applicable in the case of the annotation of confirmation in the baptismal register. Of itself, therefore, such a method of proof of the reception of confirmation would be insufficient. It would provide, however, a strong presumption for this fact in the absence of the original confirmation record.[76]

[71] Gasparri, *De Sacra Ordinatione*, n. 479.

[72] Sullivan, *Proof of the Reception of the Sacraments*, p. 108. Augustine (*Commentary*, IV, 517) contended that such certificates are to be issued by the bishop who confirmed or by one of his officials. But he did not specifically indicate who are to be considered his officials.

[73] Can. 470, § 2.

[74] Can. 1816. Cf. Willett, *Probative Value of Documents*, p. 76.

[75] *Canonical Evidence in Marriage Cases*, p. 229.

[76] Gallagher, *Examination of the Qualities of the Ordinand*, p. 56.

As in the case of baptism, so here, when the rights of a third party are in no way endangered, the testimony of one trustworthy witness, or the oath of the person himself if he received confirmation in adult life, suffices for proving the fact of confirmation.[77] Since the validity of orders does not in any way depend upon the reception of confirmation on the part of the candidate, it is safe to say that the rights of a third party would not be endangered through the lack of meeting the requirement of the law, and therefore this method of proof may be used for the candidate for tonsure.[78]

The minister of the sacrament, the pastor, the sponsor, or anyone else who witnessed the conferral, and who is worthy of credence, could supply the requisite information. Since in the Latin Church the administration of this sacrament is usually deferred until the child's seventh year,[79] the sworn affirmation of the candidate will serve as full proof of the reception of confirmation, provided, of course, that he can remember the event. There may be many instances in which the rector will be constrained to resort to one of these subsidiary methods of proof. When not even these are sufficiently strong enough to give him moral certitude that the candidate has been confirmed, then the sacrament should be administered conditionally.[80]

This attestation is required only for the conferral of first tonsure. It is not necessary to present proof again before the reception of minor orders, since the fact of confirmation was once and for all sufficiently established in connection with the conferral of tonsure.[81] Since this is also one of the documents which must be presented prior to a student's admission to the seminary, it will usually not be necessary to go through the process of proving this fact when the candidate is about to be tonsured, as long as the record of the proof is present in the seminary files, or the rector can attest to the fact that

[77] Can. 800.

[78] Coronata, *De Sacramentis,* I, n. 182; Gasparri, *De Sacra Ordinatione,* n. 685; S. C. C., *Interamnen,* 6 maii, 1617—*Fontes,* n. 2401.

[79] Can. 788.

[80] Can. 732, § 2.

[81] Can. 993, 1°.

a previous presentation of the proof was duly effected.[82] According to the Instruction this attestation is to be appended to the candidate's petition and forwarded to the bishop.[83] As with the proof of baptism, however, so here it seems sufficient merely for the rector to attest to the presence of this document in the seminary files.

C. Orders

For those clerics who are candidates for minor orders, it will not be necessary to present baptismal or confirmation certificates since proof of the reception of these sacraments was once and for all established prior to the conferral of tonsure.[84] In place of these the cleric is required to furnish proof of the conferral of tonsure or, if he has already received some minor orders, proof of the last order received.[85] He need not supply proof of all the orders previously received. It suffices that he supply proof simply of the last order received, for that in turn points by way of presupposition to the reception of all the previous orders.[86] The purpose of this requirement is to insure compliance with the law of the Code which prescribes that the orders are to be conferred in their proper succession, so that the omission of any is absolutely forbidden.[87]

The Code orders that the name of each candidate ordained, the name of the minister of ordination, and mention of the place and date of ordination be noted in a special book to be kept in the curia of the diocese of ordination.[88] It further orders that an authentic certificate of ordination be given to each ordinand. When a candidate is ordained not by his own bishop but by some other bishop who had dimissorials from the candidate's own bishop, the one thus ordained shall present this certificate to his own bishop for the purpose of the latter's recording of this ordination in a special book

[82] Can. 1363, § 2.

[83] Instr. *Quam ingens,* 27 dec. 1930, § 2, n. 2—*AAS,* XXIII (1931), 122.

[84] Gasparri, *De Sacra Ordinatione,* n. 687. Cf. *supra,* p. 61.

[85] Can. 993, 1°.

[86] Cappello, *De Sacramentis,* Vol. II, Pars III, n. 543.

[87] Can. 977 and can. 974, 5°. Cf. Wernz-Vidal, *Ius Canonicum,* Tomus IV, Vol. I, n. 221.

[88] Can. 1010, § 1.

to be kept in the archives of the curia.[89] These prescripts have binding force in relation to tonsure as well as with reference to orders strictly so called.[90] Thus when a candidate is ordained outside his own diocese a record of this ordination will be kept both in the diocese where the ordination was conferred and also in his own proper diocese.

The ordination record is a public document, and hence authentic copies drawn from it furnish full proof of the facts to which it directly testifies, viz., the reception of some particular order by a certain person, the date and the place of the ordination, and the identity of the ordaining prelate.[91] Documents emanating from the curia should, to be authentic, bear the seal of the curia together with the signature of a competent official such as the ordinary, or a qualified notary.[92] The chancellor is by his very office a notary in the diocese,[93] and so his signature together with the seal of the curia would certainly fulfill all the requirements for a public document.[94] The same value must be accorded to the certificate of ordination whether it bears the signature of the ordaining bishop, that of the chancellor, or that of some other notary along with the official seal of the bishop.[95] Gasparri noted that the presentation of this testimony is not absolutely necessary if the ordaining bishop himself

89 Can. 1010, § 2. Whether this prescript means that there should be two separate books in the curia for this purpose, or whether the notation of each is to be made in the same book is somewhat disputed. Vermeersch-Creusen (*Epitome Iuris Canonici* [6 ed., 3 vols., Mechliniae-Romae: H. Dessain, 1937-1946], II, n. 272 [hereafter cited *Epitome*]), indicate that one book suffices. Sipos (*Enchiridion Iuris Canonici* [Pecs: Ex Typographia "Haladas H. T.", 1926], p. 465) requires two books. For a fuller treatment of this problem, consult Sullivan, *Proof of the Reception of the Sacraments*, p. 117.

90 Can. 950.

91 Can. 1813, § 1, 4°, and can. 1816.

92 Coronata, *Institutiones*, III, n. 1341. Cf. can. 1813, § 1, 4°.

93 Can. 372, § 3.

94 Can. 373, § 1.

95 Can. 1813, § 1, 1°.

conferred the last order on the candidate, for in that event he is able either himself or through his chancellor to consult the ordination record should his memory fail him.[96]

But what is to be done when, as may very well occur, the ordination record is inaccessible, and when the candidate is unable to present at the particular time the certificate which he received at the time of the conferral of the last order? May the bishop then have recourse to other proofs as he may do in relation to the facts of baptism and of confirmation? The matter is not generally treated by the authors. Cappello draws an analogy with baptism and confirmation and then declares that proof of the reception of orders may be established through the testimony of even one trustworthy witness, or even through the oath of the candidate himself, provided that the rights of any third party are in no way endangered.[97] Among the witnesses he lists by way of example are the ordaining bishop, the ordinary of the place, the chancellor or the master of ceremonies. Wernz (1842-1914)-Vidal (1867-1938) also were of the opinion that one's ordination could juridically be established as a fact through proof offered by but a single witness.[98] It seems safe enough on the authority of these authors to supply for the defect of the ordinary means of proof through the testimony of one trustworthy witness. In the matter of the reception of the lower orders the rights of any third party seem not in any way to become involved in jeopardy.[99]

What is to be said of the oath of the candidate in this regard? Certainly he received the orders in adult life, and therefore certainly

[96] *De Sacra Ordinatione,* n. 704. Cf. Cappello, *De Sacramentis,* Vol. II, Pars III, n. 534.

[97] *Summa Iuris Canonici* (3 vols., Romae: apud aedes Universitatis Gregorianae, 1938-1940. Vol. I, 3. ed., 1938; Vol. II, 3. ed., 1939; Vol. III, 2. ed., 1940), II, n. 871.

[98] *Ius Canonicum,* Tom. IV, Vol. I, n. 299. Cf. also Vermeersch-Creusen, *Epitome,* III, n. 189 where the testimony of even one witness is admitted as valid proof.

[99] Regatillo in speaking of this method of proof rules it out in the matter of the *concursus* for a benefice, but indicates no similar exclusion of its use in the investigations prior to the reception of further orders.—*Ius Sacramentarium,* II, n. 165.

would be able to recall the event. Can a parallel be drawn with baptism and confirmation? Wernz-Vidal were of the opinion that the oath of the candidate would not furnish satisfactory proof.[100] As the basis for their opinion they cite the answer of Pope Innocent III (1198-1216) to the Patriarch of Constantinople, as recorded in the Decretals of Gregory IX (1227-1241).[101] In this reply the Pope rejected the admissibility of such a mode of proof whether with reference to the reception of orders or with reference to allowing clerics to minister in a new diocese. Such clerics, he answered, could be admitted only on the strength of arguments which gave the bishop sufficient certitude concerning the cleric's ordination. The same authors cited also a declaration of the Holy Office as an indication of the mind of the Church in this matter.[102] This declaration, however, seems not to have much bearing on the matter at hand.

Cappello is the only other author who treats the question. In one work he draws a complete analogy with baptism and confirmation, and admits proof through the oath of the one ordained.[103] In another work he speaks of an analogy with baptism and confirmation, but makes no specific mention of proof through the oath of the recipient of the order in question.[104] In neither work does he make reference to the subject as presented in the other. Gallagher, noting the discrepancy, inferred that the author may have changed his opinion on the matter, since the work in which he admits proof by oath is of an earlier date than the work in which he omits mention of it.[105] This can hardly be the explanation, however, since the later editions of the earlier of the two works still admit proof through the

[100] *Ius Canonicum,* Tom. IV, Vol. I, n. 299.

[101] C. 2, X, *de clericis peregrinis,* I, 22; bulla *Inter quattuor,* aug. 1206—Potthast, *Regesta,* n. 2860.

[102] 9 apr. 1704—*Collectanea S. Congregationis de Propaganda Fide seu Decreta, Instructiones, Rescripta pro Apostolicis Missionibus ex Tabulario eiusdem Sacrae Congregationis Deprompta* (Romae, 1893), n. 1170.

[103] *Summa Iuris Canonici,* II, n. 871. This volume appeared in 1930, and then again in 1934, in a first and a second edition.

[104] *De Sacramentis,* Vol. II, Pars III, n. 577. This volume in Part III appeared in 1935.

[105] *Examination of the Qualities of the Ordinand,* p. 57.

oath of the recipient.[106] Since in both works he speaks of an analogy of law, and then cites canons 779 and 800, which refer to the proof of the facts of baptism and confirmation respectively by means of trustworthy witness or the oath of the person involved, he seems to hold that one may follow the same form of procedure in proving the fact of the reception of orders when the rights of another are not jeopardized.

Can this opinion be followed in practice? It would be strangely inconsistent that the Church should allow a person, in certain cases by means of an oath to prove his own baptism, a fact upon which the validity of all the other sacraments depends, but would not allow a candidate for orders to prove the fact of the reception of lower orders by the same means. In the latter case the validity of the later orders would not depend upon the fact of the reception of the earlier orders, except perhaps in the case of the episcopacy.[107]

While it is true that Cappello cites no authority for his stand whereas Wernz-Vidal cited the authority of the Church for theirs, it must be noted that this authority is the nature of a pre-Code disciplinary law. Now according to canon 6, 6° any disciplinary law which is left unmentioned by the Code is for that reason no longer binding. Hence there is no question here of harmonizing pre-Code and post-Code law since there is no law in the Code to cover this situation. In such circumstances canon 20 prescribes that the norm of action is to be taken from laws established for similar cases. This Cappello seems to have done by drawing an analogy between the proof of the reception of orders and the proof of the reception of baptism and confirmation as established by the Code.[108] It is the opinion of the writer then that the opinion of Cappello may be followed and hence the candidate may be allowed, in the absence of other proof, to prove the fact of the reception of orders by taking an oath to that effect.

106 These later editions, the third and the fourth, appeared in 1939 and 1945 respectively.

107 Cf. Wernz-Vidal, *Ius Canonicum,* Tomus IV, Vol. I, n. 221 for a fuller discussion of this point.

108 Cans. 779 and 800.

What is to be done by the bishop in the following case: Due to the upheavals caused by war a cleric who has already received two of the minor orders finds himself in a new country. Having gone through the process of incardination, he is now a candidate for the two higher minor orders. It is discovered, however, that he lacks proof of the reception of the earlier orders, and no proof seems forthcoming. The bishop, acting on the opinion of Cappello, admits him to the two remaining minor orders merely on the strength of his declaration under oath that he has received the first two minor orders. By the time he is ready to receive subdeaconship, however, the bishop has died, and another bishop, who does not similarly accept the doctrine proposed by Cappello, has been appointed to the see. Must the new bishop hold up the ordination of the candidate to the subdiaconate pending directions from Rome or may he proceed to admit the man to major orders in consequence of his possession of proof that the candidate has received the order of acolyte? The case is admittedly a highly theoretical one. But for expediting the case it seems to the writer that the bishop may proceed to the ordination, unless there is some positive reason for doubting the reception of the lower orders beyond the mere lack of direct proof. If doubts did arise, then the bishop should have recourse to the Holy See.

Granted for the sake of argument that a parallel cannot be drawn with baptism and confirmation as regards the oath of the candidate, what of the suppletory oath? The Code allows the use of a suppletory oath as a means of proving a person's civil or religious status when that status cannot be otherwise determined.[109] Some authors allow the use of this method with reference to proving one's ordination.[110] It must be remembered, however, that in such instances the oath is merely suppletory. The Code, in allowing the use of it for establishing the status of a person, specifies that it is to be used only when partial proof has already been produced and there exists no further means of proof. Taken alone, then, the oath would not

[109] Can. 1830, § 1.

[110] Vermeersch-Creusen, *Epitome*, III, n. 208; Beste, *Introductio in Codicem* (ed. altera, Collegeville, Minn.; St. John's Abbey Press, 1944), p. 809.

furnish full proof, if the opinion of Wernz-Vidal is to be followed; some other proof would of necessity be required along with it.[111]

With regard to the candidates who have received some orders as Orientals and now with the permission of the Holy See [112] desire to receive higher orders in the Latin Church, proof is required with reference not only to the last order received, but with reference also to whatever orders have already been conferred in the other rite. The reason for this procedure is the need of presently supplying in the Latin rite whatever orders were not conferred in the Oriental rite.[113] Once the candidate has received orders in the Latin rite it will not be necessary again to require such proof.

3. *Testimonial Concerning Studies*

After the attestation regarding the reception of the prerequisite sacraments, the Code demands that the candidate present an attestation regarding the studies which he has completed.[114] It is clear from the divine law that knowledge proportionate to his state is necessary in the candidate. Hence the Church even from the earliest times excluded from ordination those who were illiterate and ignorant.[115] The Council of Trent further defined this requirement by prescribing as necessary for tonsure a knowledge of the rudiments of the faith as well as a knowledge of how to read and write.[116] These were, of course, minimum requirements.[117]

According to the Code, tonsure is not to be conferred before the start of the theology course.[118] As to minor orders no express provision is made. It seems quite certain, however, that these may be

[111] Cf. Sullivan, *Proof of the Reception of the Sacraments,* p. 122.

[112] Can. 955, § 2.

[113] Can. 1004; Benedictus XIV, const. *Etsi pastoralis,* 26 maii 1742, § VII, n. VII—*Fontes,* n. 328; Coronata, *De Sacramentis,* II, n. 199.

[114] Can. 993, 2°.

[115] Coronata, *De Sacramentis,* II, n. 74; Wernz-Vidal, *Ius Canonicum,* Tom. IV, Vol. I, n. 220; Gasparri, *De Sacra Ordinatione,* n. 556.

[116] Conc. Trident., sess. XXIII, *de ref.,* c. 11.

[117] Cappello, *De Sacramentis,* Vol. II, Pars III, n. 416.

[118] Can. 976, § 1.

conferred during the first year of theology if the bishop so desires.[119] This may be gathered from the provisions of canon 978, § 2, in which the duration of the interstices between tonsure and minor orders or between any one minor order and another is left to the discretion of the bishop. There is, therefore, no reason why the minor orders could not be conferred any time after the reception of tonsure. For the minor orders no attestation regarding the candidate's studies is required, since with regard to studies the Code establishes no minimum requirements for the reception of these orders. From the fact that tonsure has been conferred it is necessarily to be presumed that the candidate has begun his course in theology.[120]

The law states that tonsure may be conferred only after the commencement of the theology course. The interpretation as to the exact moment at which it can be said that this course has started is somewhat disputed. It is certain that it does not begin with the study of theodicy, for while it is true that this subject may be considered as theological, it is nevertheless considered, and rightly so, as part of the candidate's philosophical training.[121] According to one view, as expounded in *Periodica,* the theology course does not begin until the lectures have actually started.[122] What the writer of the article seems to be opposing, however, is any practice of conferring tonsure immediately after the conclusion of the course in philosophy, that is, in the present arrangement, at the start of the vacation period intervening between the last year of philosophy and the first year of theology. According to the liberal opinion, held by Cappello [123] and shared by Coronata,[124] the course is considered to have begun when the student is registered in the first year of theology and the school is officially opened, even though the lectures have not yet started.

119 Cappello, *ibid.,* n. 414.

120 Gallagher, *Examination of the Qualities of the Ordinand,* p. 60.

121 Anonymous, "De studiis requisitis ante ordinationem"—*Periodica de Re Canonica et Morali Utili praesertim Religiosis et Missionariis* (Brugis, 1905—; ab anno 1927; *Periodica de Re Canonica, Morali, Liturgica*), XII (1923), (9)-(10) (hereafter cited *Periodica*).

122 *Loc. cit.*

123 *De Sacramentis,* Vol. II, Pars III, n. 414.

124 *De Sacramentis,* II, n. 74.

Hence the rector may issue the required testimonial of the inception of the candidate's theological studies as soon as the candidate has enrolled in the theology course. Initiation of the course in theology presumes the completion of the required two year course in philosophy and allied sciences.[125]

In the majority of cases tonsure will be conferred after the close of the vacation period which intervenes between the second year of philosophy and the first year of theology. Since the attestation would be required some time prior to the conferral of tonsure, when may the rector issue it? It seems that he may issue it any time after the candidate has completed his philosophy course, provided that the tonsure is not to be conferred until the start of the theology course. But when the candidate is to be ordained by his own bishop, the testimony of required studies will be sufficiently manifest from the records of the seminary in which he has studied, so that it seems unnecessary that a formal attestation distinct from these should be required of the candidate. If he is to be ordained by another bishop, then the testimonial letter or dimissorial letter may contain testimony of the completion of the required studies, or a special attestation concerning this matter should be presented.[126] It seems to be in keeping with the provisions of the Instruction [127] that some mention of the candidate's standing with regard to his studies should be included in the personal information concerning his general fitness for the clerical state, which information the rector is directed to send to the bishop together with the candidate's petition for the reception of tonsure.

It is the mind of the Church that the student's years in theology should be spent in a seminary. In special cases, however, the bishop may for a grave reason dispense from this requirement,[128] in which case the student is to be entrusted to the care of a properly qualified and pious priest.[129] It would still be necessary, nevertheless, to pursue the actual course of study not privately but in a school estab-

[125] Can. 1365, § 1. Beste, *Introductio,* p. 526.

[126] Coronata, *De Sacramentis,* II, n. 177.

[127] Instr. *Quam ingens,* 27 dec. 1930, § 2, n. 2.—*AAS,* XXIII (1931), 122.

[128] Can. 972, § 1.

[129] Can. 972, § 2.

lished for this purpose.[130] Hence in any case it will be the rector of the seminary or, if there is no rector, the one who is taking his place, who will issue the required attestation.

With regard to the studies there is also required an attestation of the fact that the candidate has successfully passed an examination regarding the order or orders he is to receive. The content of the examination comprises such considerations as relate to the qualifications demanded of the candidate, the obligations assumed by him in the reception of the order, the nature of the order and its effects, the minister for its conferral, and the matter and form required in the act of its conferral.[131] This examination must be taken before the reception of the corresponding order or orders. It is obligatory upon all candidates, seculars and religious alike.

4. *Testimonial of the Rector*

In the case of our large seminaries the bishop very often cannot come to know his candidates well enough to pass judgment personally on their fitness for orders. He must rely, therefore, on the information concerning the candidate which is supplied to him by those who are better acquainted with the candidate. Chief among these is the rector of the seminary. Accordingly, the Code requires that before the admission of a candidate to tonsure or orders a testimonial of high moral character in his behalf is to be obtained from the rector of the seminary.[132] If, in accordance with canon 972, § 2, the bishop has permitted a candidate to live outside the seminary, this testimonial is to be obtained from the priest to whose care the candidate was entrusted. So important is this testimony that on the strength of it the bishop may reject the petition of the candidate without any further investigation.[133]

The Council of Trent prescribed that candidates for minor orders should present testimonials from the head of the school in which they

[130] Can. 976, § 3.

[131] Can. 996, § 1.

[132] Can. 993, 3°.

[133] Instr. *Quam ingens,* § 2, n. 2—*AAS,* XXIII (1931), 121.

were educated.[134] If the school happened to be a seminary or some other like college, it was the rector who was to issue this testimonial.[135] In canon 993, 3°, the Code seems to have adopted this legislation, and to have extended it to all orders alike, and not merely to the minor orders. In accordance with the defined terminology of canon 950 it extends also to tonsure.

The Code gives no instructions as to how the rector is to proceed in this matter. The Instruction, however, more than compensates for this silence by describing in great detail the process that is to be followed. It was not the mind of the Congregation that each and every step of the investigation should be carried out in every case, since at times one or another of them may be not only superfluous but even impossible. Observance of the Instruction whenever possible and feasible, however, will permit the bishop to proceed safely to the ordination of the candidate.[136]

After the bishop has received from the rector the petition of the candidate together with the required documents and the rector's personal information concerning the candidate, he shall, unless he judges from the information thus supplied that the candidate is not to be admitted to the clerical state, return the petition to the rector with a mandate to investigate, with his authority, the suitableness of the student as evidenced during his years in the seminary.[137]

Such is the process as described in the Instruction. What, however, of the usual practice in many seminaries whereby the rector makes these investigations before sending the petition to the bishop? Such a practice does not seem to contravene the purpose of this Instruction. Accordingly the bishop may ratify this act of the rector and thereupon judge the candidate on the basis of the investigation already made. Needless to say, the process outlined in the Instruction is to be preferred.

If for some reason the seminary happens to be without a rector, the one who is taking his place is to be delegated for this task. Furthermore, if the ordinary judges that the rector is not the person

134 Conc. Trident., sess. XXIII, *de ref.*, c. 5.

135 Gasparri, *De Sacra Ordinatione*, n. 692.

136 Instr. *Quam ingens*, 27 dec. 1930, § 1, n. 4—*AAS*, XXIII (1931), 122.

137 *Ibid.*, § 2, n. 4—*AAS*, XXIII (1931), 122.

to make a really helpful investigation in this or that particular case, then he shall give to some other ecclesiastic the power to make it in his place.[138] The rector or priest delegated for this task shall gather his information from the prefects of the seminary, if they are priests, from the professors, and from the members of the board of discipline,[139] heard singly and then together. The candidate's confessor, however, is not to be questioned.[140] The rector shall question these men upon the signs of a vocation in the candidate, such as his piety, modesty, chastity, inclination to take part in sacred functions, progress in studies, and moral character. Finally, he shall give his own judgment or opinion as to the character and dispositions of the candidate, a judgment that shall be entitled to great influence in the final decision of the ordinary.[141]

The Instruction then adds a further requirement, not prescribed by the Code, with respect to the investigation antecedent to the reception of tonsure or of minor orders. In order to study the matter more thoroughly, the bishop is likewise to secure from the student's pastor testimony as to his character, piety, signs of vocation, and especially as to his family background. The conduct of the candidate during his vacation periods shall be considered by the pastor in this regard. The pastor shall also testify to the free choice of the candidate in seeking the clerical state.[142] If the pastor is related to the young man by consanguinity or affinity, the bishop shall make use of one of the neighboring priests or pastors for this purpose.[143] After receiving all this information the ordinary shall ask the judg-

[138] *Loc. cit.* Cf. Larraona, "Animadversiones": "Ut patet, mens S. Congregationis est ut Ordinarius non per sese sed per alios et generatim per Seminarii Moderatores colligat notitias . . ."—*Apollinaris,* IV (1931), 208.

[139] Can. 1359, § 1.

[140] Can. 1361, § 3.

[141] Instr. *Quam ingens,* § 2, n. 5—*AAS,* XXIII (1931), 123.

[142] Instr. *Quam ingens,* § 2, n. 6—*AAS,* XXIII (1931), 123.

[143] *Ibid.,* § 2, n. 7.

ment of the rector or of those who take his place, as to the sincerity of the candidate.[144]

What is the relationship between the testimonial letter required by the Code and the testimonial required by the Instruction?[145] It seems that with regard to tonsure the testimonial required by the Instruction completely supplants the testimonial required by the Code. No other testimonial from the rector in addition to the testimonial required by the Instruction is needed. With regard to minor orders the same is not true. The Instruction makes this testimony a requirement only for tonsure, while the Code, without distinction, makes it a requirement for all orders. Hence it seems that some statement from the rector would be necessary before the candidate's reception of the minor orders, namely, a statement attesting to the candidate's fitness to be advanced to orders.

What if the seminarian had started his training in one seminary but later transferred to another, where he is now a candidate for tonsure or minor orders? Various possibilities can attend such a case. If the seminarian had been dismissed from the first seminary, it would have been necessary, with reference to his re-admission to a seminary, for the rector to have obtained from the authorities of the first seminary a statement indicating the cause of his dismissal as well as a testimonial concerning the character and morals of the candidate.[146] This refers only to those who have been dismissed from a seminary; not to those who have left voluntarily.[147] Moreover, it applies only to schools and colleges which are actually prepar-

144 *Ibid.*, § 2, n. 8. The Instruction here uses the words: ". . . de candidatis sincera fide . . ." It seems that this is to be understood as referring rather to the sincerity of the candidate's intentions in seeking orders than to the candidate's sincerity in religious belief.

145 Whether the testimonial required by the Code corresponds to the testimonial sent to the bishop together with the petition, or to the testimonial sent upon the completion of the investigations, seems purely theoretical and of little, if any, consequence.

146 Can. 1363, § 3.

147 Coronata, *Institutiones*, II, n. 940. Wernz-Vidal, *Ius Canonicum*, Tomus, IV, Vol. I, n. 698, footnote 64.

atory for the priesthood.[148] While the law does not make the same demand with regard to those who have left the seminary of their own free will, still some recommendation of the student's life and morals should be obtained from the first seminary.[149] When the time arrives for the candidate to receive tonsure or to be advanced to minor orders in the event that he had received tonsure in the first seminary, the rector, in issuing his testimonial, should make reference to the testimony obtained from the rector of the first seminary at the time of the candidate's admission.[150]

Should the transfer involve not only a change in seminaries but also a change in dioceses after the candidate has been incardinated through tonsure, then, whether he was dismissed from the seminary or whether he left it voluntarily, testimony regarding his life, morals, character, studies and so forth would have to be obtained as required by the Code for the process of incardination.[151] This testimony should also be consulted before the rector issues the testimonial for advancement in orders and mention of it should be made in the testimonial issued for the first reception of orders in the new diocese.

In the United States it is necessary for a student who has transferred from one seminary to another for any reason whatsoever to have letters from the superior of the seminary which he left. This was decreed by both the II (1866) [152] and the III (1884) [153] Plenary

148 Vermeersch-Creusen, *Epitome,* II, n. 697; Beste, *Introductio in Codicem,* p. 664.

149 Coronata, *loc. cit.*

150 Gallagher, *Examination of the Qualities of the Ordinand,* p. 68.

151 Can. 117, 2°. "Ex-seminarians, whether such by dismissal or by voluntary departure, if they be clerics are still incardinated in the diocese for which they were promoted. To be accepted elsewhere they must be incardinated."—McBride, *Incardination and Excardination,* p. 537.

152 Tit. III, *De Personis Ecclesiasticis,* cap. VII, *De Seminariis ecclesiasticis constituendis et ordinandis,* n. 180—*Acta et Decreta,* p. 110.

153 Tit. V, *De Clericorum Educatione et Instructione,* cap. II, *De Seminariis Majoribus,* n. 176—*Decreta Concilii Plenarii Baltimorensis Tertii, A. D. MDCCCLXXXIV* (Baltimorae: Typis Joannis Murphy et Sociorum, 1894), p. 90.

Councils of Baltimore. According to Hannan, this prescription is *praeter Codicem* and therefore still remains in force.[154]

It is quite clear that all these testimonials are to be made in writing, for according to the Instruction they are to be preserved secretly in the archives of the curia.[155] Moreover they are to be consulted by the bishop when the student asks to be advanced to the subdiaconate,[156] which demand in the law postulates some permanent record of the testimonials.

5. *Testimonial Concerning Spiritual Exercises*

As a final requirement in every case the candidate must present an attestation of the fact that he has performed the spiritual exercises which are required before advancement to tonsure or orders.[157] For tonsure and minor orders the required exercises consist of a retreat of three full days.[158] When minor orders are to be conferred a few days after tonsure, or when different minor orders are being conferred a few days apart, the ordinary may reduce the time of the retreat before the second ordination to one day.[159] When two minor orders are being conferred on the same day, then one retreat suffices for the reception of both orders.

The attestation to the making of this retreat in the case of seculars should be issued by the superior of the house, e.g., of the seminary in which the retreat was made.[160] It should state the name of the house and the number of days spent on retreat, and should also indicate whether the duration of the retreat was extended for the

[154] "Ex Seminarian and Novice"—*The Jurist* (Washington, D. C., 1941—), II (1942), 382.

[155] Instr. *Quam ingens,* § 1, n. 5—*AAS,* XXIII (1931), 122.

[156] *Ibid.,* § 3, n. 1—*AAS,* XXIII (1931), 125.

[157] Can. 1001, § 4.

[158] Can. 1001, § 1.

[159] This is derived by way of analogy from a declaration concerning the spiritual exercises prior to the reception of major orders. This declaration was issued by the Sacred Congregation of the Sacraments on May 2, 1928—*AAS,* XX (1928), 359. Cf. Cappello, *De Sacramentis,* Vol. II, Pars III, n. 552, and Coronata, *De Sacramentis,* II, n. 194.

[160] Can. 1001, § 4. Cf. Gasparri, *De Sacra Ordinatione,* n. 768.

number of days indicated in the Code, or was reduced in harmony with the declaration of the Congregation of the Sacraments.[161] Finally, it should be written, or at least signed, by the superior of the religious house as acting in his official capacity.

Article III. Documents Required in Special Cases

I. *Dispensations*

Canon 993 lists the documents which must be presented by all candidates. It does not rule out, however, the possibility that in certain cases other documents may be required. Among such cases would be those in which the candidate has received some dispensation whether from an irregularity, or from a simple impediment, or from the required interstices, or from the required age, studies, spiritual exercises, or from the publication of the banns. In the case in which a candidate who had married seeks to be ordained, he would, before his admission to the clerical state, be required to present proof of the death of his wife, or of the dispensation granted from a ratified but unconsumated marriage, or of the declaration of nullity,[162] or of the permission granted to him by the Holy See to receive orders.[163]

It is nowhere required that dispensations which affect the external forum must be granted in writing. Hence they may be granted in writing or orally, but in the latter case the granting of them should be noted in some manner in the book of ordinations.[164] For the internal non-sacramental forum the dispensations from irregularities are to be granted in writing and the fact that they were granted should thereupon be recorded in a secret book in the curia,[165] or, as Cappello suggests, in a secret book in the Sacred Penitentiary, when-

[161] Coronata, *ibid.*, n. 195.

[162] Cappello, *De Sacramentis*, Vol. II, Pars III, n. 499.

[163] *Ibid.*, n. 488.

[164] Gasparri, *De Sacra Ordinatione*, n. 234; Coronata, *De Sacramentis*, II, n. 168. Cappello, however, is of the opinion that these must be granted in writing. For his stand he offers no other authority than his own statement.—*De Sacramentis*, Vol. II, Pars III, n. 517.

[165] Can. 991, § 4.

ever there is danger of infamy if the record is preserved in the curia.[166] When the application for a dispensation has been made in the external forum, the execution of the rescript which granted the dispensation must be done in writing.[167]

Coronata [168] maintains that a dispensation from the simple impediments, even though granted only for tonsure and the minor orders, may be understood as a general dispensation, and hence may be utilized also with reference to the major orders. Whatever value is to be accorded to this opinion, it seems quite certain that a granted dispensation from the impediment which arises from the fact that the candidate has a non-Catholic parent will avail also for the major orders when the dispensation was granted with a view to the reception of tonsure or of the minor orders.[169]

These documents should be presented by the candidate and then be preserved together with all the other documents relating to his ordination.[170] Ordinarily, however, the petition for the dispensation will be forwarded through the bishop and the rescript will be sent to him for execution, so that he will have these documents at hand. In the case of a student who transfers from one seminary to another after he has received some dispensation, the rector of the second seminary must obtain some form of proof of the grant of the dispensation.

What if such proof in consequence, for example, of a disruption in the means of communication caused by a war, cannot be obtained? The authors do not discuss this possibility. If the candidate has already been admitted to tonsure or to some minor orders, and if the irregularity or the impediment was not contracted after the reception of the last order, then it is suggested that he be asked to take a

166 *Loc. cit.*

167 Can. 56. Cf. Hickey, *Irregularities and Simple Impediments in the New Code of Canon Law,* The Catholic University of America Canon Law Studies, n. 7 (Washington, D. C.: The Catholic University of America, 1920), p. 89; Vogelpohl, *The Simple Impediments to Holy Orders,* The Catholic University of America Canon Law Studies, n. 224 (Washington, D. C.: The Catholic University of America Press, 1945), p. 17.

168 *De Sacramentis,* II, n. 167.

169 S. C. S. Off., 6 dec. 1905—*Periodica,* II-III (1907), (66).

170 Can. 1010, § 1.

suppletory oath,[171] which together with the favorable presumption arising from the candidate's previous reception of orders seems to give the bishop sufficient assurance to proceed safely to his ordination. If there is any reasonable doubt concerning the grant of the dispensation, or concerning the orders for which it was granted, then a dispensation should be obtained *ad cautelam*.

2. *The Oath Demanded by Canon 956*

Canon 955 of the Code states that each candidate is to be ordained by his own bishop or by some other bishop who has received letters from the proper bishop. Ordinarily one claims his proper bishop and pastor through the establishment of a domicile or a quasi-domicile, as illustrated in the Code.[172] With regard to ordinations, however, this is not true. For the reception of orders special requirements are established by the Code for the claiming of one's proper bishop. According to canon 956, with regard to the ordination of seculars only the bishop of the diocese in which the candidate has a domicile and to which he can also point for his origin is the proper bishop for ordination. The bishop of the place in which the candidate has a simple domicile, that is, an acquired domicile which cannot be identified with the place of his origin, may also be the proper bishop for ordination, but in such a case the candidate is required to fortify with an oath his intention of remaining perpetually in that diocese. The canon makes three exceptions to this latter requirement, viz., when there is a question of promoting a cleric who has already been incardinated through tonsure, when there is question of promoting a candidate who is destined for the service of another diocese according to the norms of canon 969, § 2, and, finally, when there is question of promoting a professed religious who belongs to an institute which in the matter of the reception of orders by its members is governed by the law as established for seculars.

The purpose of the oath is to place such a candidate in the same position as the candidate who presents himself for ordination to a bishop who by reason of domicile together with the place of origin

171 Can. 1829.

172 Cans. 94, § 1, and 92.

is his proper bishop, and to remove all doubt as to the competence of the bishop in this regard.[173] The oath is assertory in character rather than promissory. It simply attests to one's intention of remaining in a given diocese. The candidate, therefore, is not bound to promise that he will remain perpetually, as he is bound to do when he is to be ordained to the subdiaconate on the title of service of the diocese.[174]

Furthermore, the intention of remaining perpetually in that diocese is to be understood with the restriction: *si nihil inde avocet*, and therefore the candidate for tonsure may very well place this or some similar restriction in his oath.[175] A qualified intention, however, such as the candidate's intention to remain provided that he is ultimately ordained to the priesthood in that diocese, would not suffice.[176] If through negligence the oath were omitted prior to the reception of tonsure, there would be no necessity for having the cleric take it later, for through the reception of tonsure he has become incardinated in the diocese for which he was promoted.[177]

In the vast majority of cases the candidate for tonsure will have already attained his majority.[178] What, however, of the exceptional case in which the candidate who must take the oath is still in his minority when the time arrives for his entrance into the clerical state? May he be allowed to take the oath despite the fact that a minor has the necessary domicile of his father or his guardian, and therefore cannot establish a domicile of his own?[179]

[173] Moeder, *The Proper Bishop for Ordination*, p. 52.

[174] Regatillo, *Ius Sacramentarium*, II, n. 51.

[175] Gasparri, *De Sacra Ordinatione*, n. 834; Costello, *Domicile and Quasi-Domicile*, The Catholic University of America Canon Law Studies, n. 60 (Washington, D. C.: The Catholic University of America, 1930), pp. 119-123.

[176] Cf. Costello, *op. cit.*, p. 123.

[177] Mahoney, "The Tonsure and Incardination"—*The American Ecclesiastical Review* (1905-1943 *The Ecclesiastical Review*, Philadelphia, 1889-1943; Baltimore, 1944—), LXXXII (1930), 398 (hereafter cited *AER* and *ER* respectively).

[178] Majority here is understood in the sense of canon 88, § 1, i.e., as implying the completion of the twenty-first year of one's life.

[179] Can. 93, § 1.

Up to and including the time of Saint Alphonsus (1696-1787) it was the accepted teaching that children after the age of puberty could acquire a domicile of their own.[180] In the course of time, however, there was a gradual reversal of practice and teaching, until it became the established opinion that until children attained their majority they retained the domicile of their parents and therefore could not acquire a domicile of their own.[181] Such being the case they could not take the oath, since they were completely dependent upon their parents for their domicile.

Among the post-Code authors who treat the problem, Cappello,[182] D'Angelo (1885-1930) [183] and McBride [184] deny this right to minors. They argue on the basis of canon 93, viz., that the minor has the necessary domicile of his parents and does not have the right to establish one of his own.[185] Consequently he cannot take an oath to maintain a domicile in a given diocese for the simple reason that he does not have any control over the matter of a domicile. The last named author bases his opinion also on a decree of the Congregation of the Council,[186] in which bishops were warned not to admit minors to tonsure, since these could undertake the obligation of remaining permanently in a diocese only with great dangers and difficulties.

On the other hand, Coronata [187] and Wernz-Vidal [188] grant them this right. They base their argument on the fact that in spiritual

[180] *Theologia Moralis* (ed. nova, 4 vols., cura Gaudé, Romae: Typis Polyglottis Vaticanis, 1905-1912), Lib. VI, n. 778.

[181] For a further explanation of this change, cf. Costello, *Domicile and Quasi-Domicile*, p. 58.

[182] *De Sacramentis,* Vol. II, Pars III, n. 329.

[183] "De Prima Tonsura—Consultatio"—*Apollinaris,* I (1928), 181-182.

[184] *Incardination and Excardination,* pp. 332-333.

[185] Chelodi (+1922), *Ius Canonicum de Personis* (3. ed., cura Ciprotti, Vicenza: Società Anonima Tipografica e Trento: Libreria Moderna Editrice, 1942), n. 929, and Vermeersch-Creusen, *Epitome,* I, n. 214. These do not treat the question of the oath, but do treat the question of a minor's incapacity to establish a domicile of his own.

[186] S. C. C., 21 nov. 1906—*Fontes,* n. 4330.

[187] *De Sacramentis,* II, n. 33.

[188] *Ius Canonicum,* Tomus IV, Vol. I, n. 196.

matters minors are not subject to their parents,[189] and therefore there is no reason why they cannot establish a domicile for the purposes of ordination independently of their parents. Consequently they may take the oath which canon 956 requires with a view to their reception of orders. If this were not admitted, so they argue, then the freedom granted by the law [190] for embracing the religious or the clerical state would be frustrated. Moeder [191] is of the same opinion. He contends that since the Code does not distinguish in this matter between those who are minors and those who have attained their majority there is no reason to deny this right to minors.

To the writer it seems that not much importance as really pertinent to the case in hand can be attached to the decree which the Congregation of the Council issued in 1906, and which McBride cites as proof of his position.[192] The Congregation was treating the question of the excardination and incardination of laymen, a practice then in existence. Consequently it was considering the case of a candidate who sought ordination in a diocese which not only was not the diocese of his origin, but moreover, was not the diocese of even his domicile.[193] It is clear, then, why the Congregation should warn of the dangers involved in admitting such candidates to tonsure while they were still minors. It was not considering the specific problem involved here.

There is, however, a decision which the same Congregation issued a few years earlier,[194] and which seems far more pertinent to the question at hand. In this decision the Congregation stated that, when the candidate is a minor, his father is to take the oath for him. Thus the Congregation clearly indicated that minors were not to be allowed to take this oath.[195] Moeder [196] attempts to explain away

[189] Cf. cans. 89; 555; 573; 971; 1648, § 3.

[190] Can. 971.

[191] *The Proper Bishop for Ordination*, p. 53.

[192] *Supra*, p. 89.

[193] 3°. "Verum cum obligato permanendi in dioecesi non propria . . ."—*Fontes*, n. 4330.

[194] *Romana et aliarum*, 21 aug. 1897—*Thesaurus*, CLVI, 916.

[195] In Lucidi's *De Visitatione Sacrorum Liminum*, I, 92, the same doctrine had been presented.

[196] *Op. cit.*, p. 52.

this decision by saying that it simply echoed the severe prescriptions of the Constitution *Speculatores,*[197] which was then the guiding norm with regard to ordinations. Inasmuch as this Constitution has been supplanted by the Code, so he argues, it no longer needs to be followed.

While it is true that the Constitution *Speculatores* was more exacting in some of its requirements than the Code,[198] still with regard to the oath in question there seems to be no difference. The Constitution and the Code alike require an oath on the part of the candidate to fortify his expressed intention of maintaining an acquired domicile in a given diocese. Hence Moeder's attempt to explain away the pertinent import of this decision of the Congregation of the Council seems altogether unwarranted. Furthermore, whenever there is doubt whether a prescription of the Code disagrees with the earlier law, then the present law is to be presumed to be in accord with the earlier law.[199] That seems to be the situation in the case here considered. Therefore either the father of the candidate must take the oath, or the reception of tonsure must be deferred until the candidate has attained his majority and thus is enabled to take the oath.

The oath may be rendered to the bishop himself, or to a delegate of his who may be either the rector of the seminary or some other priest.[200] A declaration of the rendering of the oath should be signed by the ecclesiastic before whom the oath is taken.[201]

The Code makes no provision for a written form of the oath. As with all other attestations in this regard, however, the very nature of the case demands some enduring record. Thus the practice of having the candidate write out the oath in his own hand, of having him then read it and swear to it in the presence of the person who

197 4 nov. 1694, § 5—*Fontes,* n. 258.

198 Thus a cleric could not be promoted to higher orders in another diocese in which he had acquired a benefice unless he presented testimonial letters both from the bishop of the diocese of domicile and also from the bishop of the diocese of origin as stated in § 3 of that Constitution.—*Fontes,* n. 258.

199 Can. 6, 4°.

200 Augustine, *Commentary,* IV, 423.

201 Mahoney, "The Tonsure and Incardination"—*ER,* LXXXII (1930), 398.

is receiving the oath, and of finally having the oath signed by the candidate and the bishop or his delegate, must be deemed satisfactory. A printed form of the oath which would be signed by the candidate and the person receiving the oath would seem equally satisfactory. In either case the document should be preserved with all the other documents relating to the candidate's ordination.[202]

3. *Testimonial Letters*

For those candidates who have spent in any other diocese a sufficient period of time for the contracting of a canonical impediment, it will be necessary to secure testimonial letters from the ordinaries of those dioceses, before the candidates may be admitted to the reception of tonsure or of minor orders.[203] These letters, which testify regarding the fitness of the candidate and particularly regarding his freedom from irregularities in so far as the bishop of that diocese is able to know, are required whenever the candidate has spent six months after attaining the age of puberty, or three months if he happened to be in military service, in a diocese other than that for the service of which he now seeks to receive orders.[204]

Since the law relating to these letters demands a somewhat lengthy treatment, it has been thought better by the writer merely to point out the fact that these letters are comprised among the required documents, and to reserve a more complete discussion to a subsequent chapter.

4. *Dimissorial Letters*

Each candidate is to be ordained by his proper bishop or by some bishop who has received legitimate dimissorials from the proper bishop.[205] These letters, by means of which the candidate's proper bishop gives to another bishop permission to ordain one of his subjects and at the same time bear witness to the candidate's fitness, will be treated in a subsequent chapter.

[202] Can. 1010, § 1.

[203] Can. 993, 4°.

[204] Can. 994, § 1. Cf. Coronata, *De Sacramentis,* II, n. 178; Cappello, *De Sacramentis,* Vol. II, Pars III, n. 536.

[205] Can. 955, § 1.

CHAPTER VI

DOCUMENTS REQUIRED FOR THE RECEPTION OF MAJOR ORDERS

Article I. Documents Common to the Reception of Major and of Minor Orders

1. *The Petition*

As has been pointed out in the preceding chapter,[1] the Code in treating the question of the petition for the reception of orders merely states that at an opportune time the candidate shall manifest his desire to be promoted to orders.[2] For tonsure and minor orders the Instruction of 1930 gives further determination to this requirement. For major orders, however, such is not the case. As a matter of fact, the Instruction does not treat of the petition at all in outlining the procedure to be followed in the testing of the candidate for major orders. It does mention the petition twice, but only incidentally. In speaking of the inquiries to be made before the reception of tonsure and of minor orders it states that the record of these is to be considered when the candidate requests advancement to the subdiaconate.[3] The other mention occurs in the Appendix of the Instruction with relation to the declaration which the candidate is to make before each of the major orders, in which these words are found: ". . . in presenting to the bishop my petition for the subdeaconship (or the deaconship, or the priesthood). . . ."[4]

As far as the authors are concerned, Coronata[5] and Regatillo[6] both teach that a separate petition is to be presented before the

[1] *Supra*, pp. 58-59.

[2] Can. 992.

[3] Instr. *Quam ingens*, § 3, n. 1—*AAS*, XXIII (1931), 125.

[4] Instr. *Quam ingens*, Appendix, Form I—*AAS*, XXIII (1931), 127.

[5] *De Sacramentis*, II, n. 127.

[6] *Ius Sacramentarium*, II, n. 142.

reception of each major order. There seems to be sufficient authority for this stand in the manner in which the Instruction listed the three orders separately in the phrase quoted above.

No exact form for the petition has been provided by the Congregation. But as with the petition for the reception of tonsure and of the minor orders, the ordinary may insist upon the inclusion of certain elements in it. All that has been said previously concerning that petition may be applied also to the petition for the reception of major orders.[7]

2. *Testimonial Concerning Orders*

Before admitting a man to the reception of one of the major orders the bishop must demand proof of the reception of the order immediately preceding the order in question. The method of proof as outlined in the treatment of this matter in the preceding chapter is equally applicable here.[8] In addition to assuring, as it does in the case of minor orders, the conferral of orders in their proper succession,[9] this testimony also serves to insure the observance of the proper interstices with regard to sacred orders.[10]

3. *Testimonial Concerning Studies*

Again, before the reception of any one of the major orders the candidate must present proof of the fact that he has pursued the required course of studies. For the subdiaconate, therefore, he must present testimony from the rector which attests to his completion of the third year of theology.[11] Coronata [12] is of the opinion that the phrase *"exeunte tertio cursus theologici anno,"* which is used by the Code in this connection, may be interpreted as pointing to any time within thirty or forty days before the end of the school

[7] Cf. *supra*, pp. 59-61.

[8] Cf. *supra*, pp. 70-76.

[9] Cans. 974, 5°, and 977.

[10] Can. 978, § 2.

[11] Can. 976, § 2.

[12] *De Sacramentis*, II, n. 75.

year. The same view is held by Cappello.[13] Blat interprets it as any time after Easter or Pentecost,[14] while for Regatillo two-thirds of the year suffices to fulfill this requirement.[15] He bases his opinion upon an Instruction of the Congregation of Seminaries and Studies according to which a student in a university who misses one-third of the school year cannot be given credit for the year.[16] Therefore, he argues, as long as the student completes two-thirds of the year he is to be given credit for a full scholastic year.

The diaconate is not to be conferred before the start of the fourth year of theology.[17] According to Cappello the fourth year may be considered as begun with the time of one's enrollment in it, which time may be a month or two before the actual start of classes.[18] Regatillo contends that the fourth year has started only after the curriculum has actually begun, but admits at the same time that Cappello's opinion may be held.[19]

The priesthood may be conferred only after the middle of the fourth year,[20] which provision may be interpreted as pointing to any time after the lapse of four and one-half months of the scholastic year, since the school year generally consists of nine months.[21] The difference of a few days more or less could be waived.[22] So long as the testimonial regarding the studies attests to the completion of these studies and is issued by competent authority, the necessary requirements in this regard are fulfilled.

13 *De Sacramentis,* Vol. II, Pars III, n. 414; *Summa Iuris Canonici,* II, n. 840.

14 *De Sacramentis,* n. 327.

15 *Ius Sacramentarium,* II, n. 88.

16 *Ordinationes,* 12 iun. 1931, Art. 29, § 1—*AAS,* XXIII (1931), 275.

17 Can. 976, § 2.

18 *De Sacramentis,* Vol. II, Pars III, n. 414.

19 *Ius Sacramentarium,* II, n. 88.

20 Can. 976, § 2.

21 S. C. Consist., 24 mart. 1911—*AAS,* II (1911), 181.

22 Coronata, *De Sacramentis,* II, n. 75; Cappello, *loc. cit.;* Regatillo, *loc. cit.;* Vermeersch-Creusen, *Epitome,* II, n. 246; Hannan, "Ordinations at Christmas"—*The Jurist,* I (1941), 153-154.

4. *Testimonial of the Rector*

After the candidate has made his petition for advancement to the subdiaconate, the rector is instructed to consult the record of the inquiries conducted prior to the reception of tonsure and the minor orders, preparatory to issuing a testimonial regarding the fitness of the candidate in so far as his life and character are concerned.[23] This of itself, however, will not suffice for the issuing of the testimonial; another inquiry, conducted after the manner prescribed for the investigation prior to the reception of tonsure, will be necessary. In such an inquiry it will not be necessary, however, to inquire into such things as the candidate's origin, family, past life and so forth, unless there is some ground to suspect that the information previously supplied was false. The candidate's character and moral qualities as manifested by his life in the seminary will be the important factor in the present inquiry.

For the diaconate it will usually be sufficient to consider the inquiry made prior to the reception of the subdiaconate. If, in consequence of circumstances which have arisen since the reception of that order, there should exist any doubt concerning the candidate's fitness, the doubt should be resolved by such inquiries as shall be deemed helpful or necessary.[24] The results of these inquiries, made in writing, should be forwarded by the rector to the bishop to be preserved with all the other documents relating to the candidate's ordination.

5. *Testimonial Concerning Spiritual Exercises*

This testimony should contain all that was prescribed for the testimony furnished prior to the reception of tonsure and the minor orders.[25] The only difference will occur in the length of the retreat. For sacred orders a retreat of six full days is required. If, however, the candidate is receiving two of these orders within six months, the ordinary may reduce the retreat before the diaconate,

[23] Instr. *Quam ingens,* § 3, n. 1—*AAS,* XXIII (1931), 125.

[24] *Ibid.,* n. 2—*AAS,* XXIII (1931), 125-126.

[25] Cf. *supra,* pp. 84-85.

but to not less than three full days.[26] When even this amount of time cannot be given to the spiritual exercises because of the great proximity of the reception of the orders, the Sacred Congregation of the Sacraments has allowed bishops to reduce the time to one full day, provided that six full days were devoted to these exercises before the first of the sacred orders to be received.[27] This reduction may be made not only in favor of the diaconate but also in favor of the priesthood, unlike the reduction which the Code allows to be made only in favor of the diaconate. Cappello [28] and Coronata [29] both teach that when the subdiaconate is to be conferred a few days after the order of acolyte has been conferred, the three days of spiritual exercises made prior to the reception of that order may be computed as part of the time required for the spiritual exercises which precede the reception of the subdiaconate.

Article II. Documents Peculiar to the Reception of Major Orders

1. *Publication of the Banns*

Among the laws emanating from the Council of Trent with regard to ordinations was one which required that before the reception of major orders the name of the candidate and his intention of receiving major orders should be announced publicly in the parish church.[30] The Code in continuing this legislation gave to it a more exact determination. The publication is to be made in the parish church of the candidate before his reception of each of the major orders.[31] It need be made only once, on a Sunday or on some other holy day of obligation during Mass, or on some other day at divine services which are attended by a large part of the faithful.[32] For a just cause the ordinary may dispense from

[26] Can. 1001, § 1.
[27] S. C. de Sacr., 2 maii, 1928—*AAS*, XX (1928), 359-360.
[28] *De Sacramentis*, Vol. II, Pars III, n. 525.
[29] *De Sacramentis*, II, n. 194.
[30] Conc. Trident., sess. XXIII, *de ref.*, c. 5.
[31] Can. 998, § 1.
[32] Can. 998, § 2.

this law, or he may demand that it be carried out in other churches as well as in the candidate's present parish church, or he may substitute for this public announcement the affixing of the name of the candidate to the door of the church. If this latter method is employed, the period of time during which the name remains posted is to include at least one day of precept.[33]

The pastor who makes this publication shall at the same time conduct an inquiry into the candidate's life and fitness for this sacred order. If the ordinary sees fit he may request others to make a similar investigation. The pastor shall then forward a testimonial letter containing the results of his inquiries and of the publication of the banns in accordance with the requirements of the Code.[34]

Coronata points out that this investigation by the pastor is of added importance when the candidate has been dispensed from the requirement of living in a seminary during his theology course.[35] When the candidate has been living in a seminary, however, he thinks that there is no need for a similar complete inquiry by and report from the pastor, since the requirements of the law appear sufficiently fulfilled through the inquiries carried out in accordance with the Instruction issued by the Sacred Congregation of the Sacraments in 1930.[36] In such cases, therefore, the author deems it sufficient for the pastor's testimonial letter to attest to the fulfillment of the law with regard to the publication of the banns and to indicate its results as to the discovery of any irregularity, impediment, or other reason that could legitimately bar the candidate from the reception of the orders.

While it is true that this legislation came originally from the Council of Trent, it is equally true that in some countries, including many places in the United States, this law was not closely observed.[37]

[33] Can. 998, § 1. Coronata points out that this cause, while it must be just, need not be grave.—*De Sacramentis,* II, n. 187.

[34] Can. 1000, § 1.

[35] *De Sacramentis,* II, n. 191. Cf. can. 972, § 1.

[36] *Loc. cit.*

[37] Gasparri, *De Sacra Ordinatione,* n. 701; Augustine, *Commentary,* IV, 524; Many, *De Sacra Ordinatione,* p. 306. The last named, writing in the year 1905, expressly mentioned the United States among these countries.

What is to be said of such neglect of the law? Cappello[38] and Gasparri[39] declared that it was an unreasonable custom, and therefore regardless of its age could not entail the abrogation of the law, since it is essential if a contrary custom is to abrogate law that it be reasonable.[40] Augustine, on the other hand, maintained that this custom could not be called unreasonable.[41] While it is true that there is no express reprobation of such a contrary custom in the Code, and that therefore it cannot be branded as unreasonable on that ground,[42] still it seems that the opinion of Cappello and Gasparri must be held, since such a custom is contrary to a law enacted for the safeguard and promotion of the common good and, as Cicognani points out, such a custom must be termed unreasonable unless it redounds to the advantage of the people.[43] In this case the law is certainly one which is intended expressly for the protection of the common good, as with all laws in this regard, and the contrary custom does not in any way contribute to the profit or advantage of the people. Hence it seems that the custom in question is unreasonable, and therefore regardless of its age cannot have or obtain the force of law.

2. *Declaration of Freedom*

After it has been judged that there is no canonical reason for withholding the candidate from promotion to the subdiaconate or other major orders, the Instruction directs that he make a declaration to the effect that he is receiving these orders altogether freely, and that he fully understands all the obligations annexed to these orders. This declaration, which is to be written in his own hand and confirmed with an oath,[44] is to be made before each of the major

[38] *De Sacramentis,* Vol. II, Pars III, n. 547.

[39] *Loc. cit.*

[40] Can. 27, § 1.

[41] *Commentary,* IV, p. 524, note 23.

[42] Can. 27, § 2.

[43] *Commentarium ad Librum Primum Codicis Iuris Canonici,* recognitum et auctum a Dino Staffa (2 vols., Romae: Ex Officina Typographica Romana "Buona Stampa," 1939-1942), II, 131 (hereafter cited *Commentarium*).

[44] Instr. *Quam ingens,* § 3, n. 1—*AAS,* XXIII (1931), 125.

orders. The form that it is to take is indicated in the Appendix to the Instruction.[45] But the language to be used in that declaration was not specifically prescribed. The very purpose of the statement, that is, to insure the freedom of the candidate and his willingness to assume the obligations of sacred orders which he declares he fully understands, seems to dictate that the statement be executed in the language that is best known to him, viz., his own tongue. If it is to be executed in Latin the student should be provided with a copy of the statement sometime before he is asked to swear to it, in order that he may become fully aware of its contents. This document is to be preserved together with all the other documents pertaining to the candidate's ordination, and if ever there should be instituted a process for a declaration of nullity of the ordination on the ground that the candidate did not act freely in presenting himself for the reception of the order, he is to be confronted with the document in which he professed his full freedom of action.[46]

3. *Title of Ordination*

One of the requisites for the licit advancement of a candidate to major orders is the possession by the candidate of a canónical title of ordination,[47] that is, a legitimate guarantee of adequate means for his future livelihood.[48] For seculars, according to the Code, the ordinary title is the title of a benefice.[49] When this title is lacking, the title of patrimony or pension may be substituted for it. If, finally, the candidate does not possess even one of these, he may be advanced on the title of service of the diocese, or, in places subject to the Congregation for the Propagation of the Faith, on the title of the mission.[50] For regulars the title is the title of solemn religious profession, or, as it is called, the title of poverty.[51] For religious of

[45] *Ibid., Appendix,* Form 1—*AAS,* XXIII (1931), 127.

[46] S. C. de Sacr., 9 iun. 1931—*AAS,* XXIII (1931), 485.

[47] Can. 974, § 1, 7°.

[48] Coronata, *De Sacramentis,* II, n. 81. Cf. Conc. Trident., sess. XXI, *de ref.,* c. 2; Cappello, *De Sacramentis,* Vol. II, Pars III, n. 423.

[49] Can. 979, § 1.

[50] Can. 981.

[51] Can. 982, § 1.

simple prepetual vows it is the title of the common table, or of the congregation, or some other similar title according to the constitutions.[52] All other religious as far as this matter is concerned are ruled by the norms established for seculars.[53] Hence, before admitting a man to the subdiaconate, the bishop should have some proof of the availability of such a title for the candidate, and also of the security and sufficiency of that title.

The Code prescribes that ecclesiastical offices are to be conferred in writing,[54] and since a benefice [55] includes the notion of an ecclesiastical office [56] it follows that it, too, should be conferred in writing. This is usually the case, and consequently there should be no difficulty in establishing proof of the possession of a benefice as the title of ordination. It seems desirable that the bishop have an authenticated copy of this document, or an attestation of its existence and location, drawn up for inclusion with the other documents relating to the ordination. If that document were lost or otherwise became not available at the time the candidate seeks advancement to the subdiaconate, the bishop would have to rely upon the methods of proof as outlined in the Fourth Book of the Code to supply for this defect. This is a theoretical rather than a practical problem, however, since in practice this title is seldom used today in consequence of the fact that for the conferral of almost all benefices the priesthood is required, while a title is required before the reception of the subdiaconate.[57]

With regard to the title of patrimony, if the candidate intends to establish this title from his own goods, then it will be necessary for him to determine and designate individually, in writing, the goods or titles which he intends to set aside as his patrimony. If

[52] Can. 982, §2.

[53] Can. 982, § 3.

[54] Can. 159. This is required for licitness, not for validity.—Coronata, *Institutiones,* I, n. 214.

[55] Can. 1409: "Beneficium ecclesiasticum est ens iuridicum a competente ecclesiastica auctoritate in perpetuum constitutum seu erectum, constans officio sacro et iure percipiendi reditus ex dote officio adnexos."

[56] Coronata, *ibid.,* n. 205.

[57] Regatillo, *Ius Sacramentarium,* II, n. 94.

others wish to provide this title for him, it will be necessary for them to do likewise. In addition, in this latter case, the bishop should see to it that this donation is made in accordance with the provisions of the civil law as well as of the ecclesiastical law.[58] When a pension is to serve as the title of ordination some written proof of the grant of the pension as well as of its adequacy should be demanded.

For the candidate who is being ordained on the title of service of the diocese or of the mission, it will be necessary for him to take an oath promising to devote himself perpetually to the service of the diocese or of the mission, under the authority of the local ordinary.[59] This oath should be taken before the ordinary or before someone delegated by the ordinary, such as the rector of the seminary or college, and a copy of it in the handwriting of the candidate should be transmitted to the bishop.[60]

4. *Profession of Faith and Oath Against Modernism*

One of the final requirements for the reception of sacred orders is a profession of faith to be made before the subdiaconate.[61] Under the common law prior to the Code all those who were to receive any

[58] Cf. Coronata, *De Sacramentis,* II, n. 85.

[59] Can. 981.

[60] These prescripts were contained in an Instruction of the Congregation for the Propagation of the Faith as issued on April 27, 1871. They extended to all what had previously been the practice of the Pontifical Colleges.—*Fontes,* n. 4878; *Collectanea,* n. 1369. Cf. also Many, *De Sacra Ordinatione,* n. 145, pp. 351-354; McBride, *Incardination and Excardination,* pp. 142-143; Coronata, *De Sacramentis,* II, n. 91. The formula for this oath was provided in the Instruction. It may also be found in McBride, *loc. cit.* This formula made it necessary for priests ordained on these titles to obtain permission from the Holy See before entering a religious institute if they so desired. This is no longer true with regard to those who have been ordained on the title of service of the church or of the diocese; it is still true with regard to those who have been ordained on the title of the mission. Cf. Vermeersch-Creusen, *Epitome,* II, n. 250; McBride, *op. cit.,* p. 528. A form which may be used for the former will be found in Appendix II of this work.

[61] Can. 1406, § 1, 7°.

of the major orders were bound by this requirement.[62] Later this obligation was restricted to those who were to receive the subdiaconate, but the ordinary had the right to require it also before the reception of the diaconate and the priesthood if he saw fit to make such a demand.[63] In the Code no such right is given to the ordinary, but he has the right by virtue of the previous legislation which remains in force until expressly abrogated.[64]

An accompaniment of the profession of faith is the oath against Modernism. The requirement of this oath was established by Pope Pius X in his Motu proprio *Sacrorum Antistitum*.[65] Like the profession of faith it needs to be made only before the reception of the subdiaconate. Though this *Motu proprio* was issued before the Code, and though no mention of the required oath is made in the Code, still, according to a decree of the Holy Office it remains in force[66] until it is expressly abrogated by the Holy See. The ordinary has the right to demand that the candidate take this oath also before the reception of the other major orders.[67] The formula for this oath was provided in the *Motu proprio*. The document attesting to the fulfillment of the law with regard to the profession of faith and the oath against Modernism is to be preserved in the archives of the curia.

The oath is to be taken before the local ordinary or his delegate in which capacity the seminary rector may be appointed.[68] When there is a group of candidates, it suffices for one of the group to read the oath, provided that each of the candidates swears to it and signs the formula.[69] They should be given copies both of the pro-

[62] C. 6, D. XXIII; Cf. Canavan, *Profession of Faith*, The Catholic University of America Canon Law Studies, n. 151 (Washington, D. C.: The Catholic University of America Press, 1942), p. 87.

[63] S. C. Consist., 24 mart. 1911—*AAS*, III (1911), 181-182. This refers directly to the oath against Modernism, but by extension may be applied to the profession of faith also.

[64] S. C. S. Off., 22 mart. 1918—*AAS*, X (1918), 136.

[65] 1 sept. 1910—*Fontes*, n. 689; *AAS*, II (1910), 655-680.

[66] 22 mart. 1918—*AAS*, X (1918), 136.

[67] S. C. Consist., 24 mart. 1911—*AAS*, III (1911), 181-182.

[68] Can. 1406, § 1, 7°. Cf. Coronata, *Institutiones*, II, n. 970.

[69] S. C. Consist., 25 oct. 1910—*AAS*, II (1910), 856-857.

fession of faith and of the oath against Modernism sometime before the actual rendering of the oath, in order that they may fully understand the contents of these documents.[70] Usually this oath, the profession of faith, and the oath required by the Instruction *Quam ingens*[71] are all taken at the same time.

[70] Motu propr. *Sacrorum Antistitum,* 1 sept. 1910—*Fontes,* n. 689.
[71] *Supra,* pp. 90-91.

CHAPTER VII

TESTIMONIAL LETTERS

ARTICLE I. GENERAL CONSIDERATIONS

1. *Nature and Contents*

THE Council of Trent in legislating concerning minor orders decreed that it was necessary for the candidate to present a testimonial letter from his pastor as well as one from the head of the school which he attended.[1] As they are to be considered in this chapter, however, testimonial letters as prerequisites for ordination date from the Constitution *Speculatores* of Innocent XII (1691-1700),[2] and more exactly from the Constitution *Apostolicae Sedis* of Pope Pius IX (1846-1878),[3] which have already been treated at some length in the historical section of this study.[4]

In the treatment which follows, only those testimonial letters which are required by canon 993, 4°, viz., those which are to be issued by the bishop of a diocese as covering that period of time which the ordinand has spent in that diocese, will be considered. It is true that the Code demands other testimonials, e.g., from the pastor [5] and from the rector of the seminary,[6] but it is felt that these have already received sufficient treatment in the preceding chapters. With regard to the testimonial letters to be furnished by the major superiors of religious orders in such cases wherein these letters are required,[7] treatment has been reserved to a subsequent chapter.

1 Conc. Trident., sess. XXIII, *de ref.*, c. 5. There had been similar legislation previous to this, but it was of a particular nature, e.g., Council of Exeter (1287) and Council of Sens (1528). Cf. *supra*, pp. 22-23.

2 4 nov. 1694—*Fontes*, n. 258.

3 12 oct. 1869—*Fontes*, n. 552.

4 Cf. *supra*, pp. 44-45.

5 Can. 1000, § 1.

6 Can. 993, 3°.

7 Can. 993, 5°.

In so far as the determination of the form, the nature, and the contents of these letters is concerned, the Code is of but little help. While it explicitly refers to them as letters, still the authors hold that this testimony need not be given in writing.[8] It is, however, the universal practice today to use writing for this purpose. That this should be so can be seen from the fact that this testimony is to be preserved in the archives of the curia, a requirement which demands some sort of permanent form for it.[9] Moreover the failure to commit this testimony to writing in some way could very well lead to abuses and dangers.

When the proper bishop can obtain nothing but oral testimony concerning the candidate, he may proceed to the conferring of orders so long as he can be certain of the accuracy and authenticity of the testimony. It is certain that in so doing he would not become liable to the penalty listed in canon 2373, 2°, for bishops who ordain without the proper testimonial letters.[10] In such eventuality, which seems quite theoretical today, the bishop should make some attestation to the reception of this testimony in order that there may be a record of it for the future.

Under the law prior to the Code these letters were to contain testimony concerning the parentage, the age, the morals, and the life in general of the candidate.[11] However, since this legislation has now been supplanted by the Code, what is to be said with reference to the contents of these letters under the present law? In canon 994, § 2, the Code, in referring to these letters, speaks of the case in which the bishop is unable to testify that the candidate has not incurred a canonical impediment during the time spent in that bishop's diocese.[12] The letters then are to testify to the presence

[8] Cf. Coronata, *De Sacramentis,* II, n. 178.

[9] Can. 1010, § 1. The Constitution *Speculatores* expressly ordered that this testimony was to be shown to the bishop and to be preserved by him in the acts of the curia.—*Fontes,* n. 258. Cf. also, Cappello, *De Sacramentis,* Vol. II, Pars III, n. 538; Gasparri, *De Sacra Ordinatione,* n. 708; Regatillo, *Ius Sacramentium,* II, n. 146.

[10] Coronata, *De Sacramentis,* II, n. 178.

[11] Const. *Speculatores,* § 3—*Fontes,* n. 258.

[12] ". . . tempore quo in suo territori moratus est, nullum canonicum impedimentum contraxisse, . . ."

or absence of canonical impediments in the candidate. But what is to be understood by the term "canonical impediment?" According to the Code, an impediment to sacred orders may take the form of an irregularity, which is a permanent impediment,[13] or of a simple impediment.[14] Most of the authors agree, therefore, that these letters should be concerned chiefly with these.[15]

There is no reason, however, why a consideration of the candidate's moral qualities should not also be included.[16] This should certainly be done when the bishop is aware of something in the candidate's life or morals, as evidenced during the time spent in the bishop's diocese, which, while not constituting a canonical impediment strictly so-called, nevertheless renders the candidate untfit for the priesthood.[17] This may be done either in the testimonial letter itself or in a separate private letter.[18] On the other hand, it would not satisfy the requirements of the Code were the bishop to testify exclusively concerning the candidate's moral qualities, and nowhere

[13] Cans. 983-985.

[14] Can. 987.

[15] Cf. Cappello, *De Sacramentis,* Vol. II, Pars III, n. 540; Regatillo, *Ius Sacramentarium,* II, n. 146; Aertnys-Damen, *Theologia Moralis,* II, n. 573.

[16] Wernz-Vidal, *Ius Canonicum,* Tomus IV, Vol. I, n. 271; Gallagher, *Examination of the Qualities of the Ordinand,* p. 75.

[17] Cappello, *De Sacramentis, loc. cit.* Coronata (*De Sacramentis,* II, n. 178) is of the opinion that in some cases, e.g., when the candidate is being ordained by the bishop of a diocese in which the candidate has obtained a benefice, or when he is being ordained by another bishop for the service of that diocese, these letters should also testify concerning the parentage, age, etc. In view of all the requirements of the Code which have already been considered, this seems hardly necessary.

[18] Cappello, *De Sacramentis,* Vol. II, Pars III, nn. 536, and 540. This author seems to waver in his teaching in this regard. In the first mentioned reference he states that this should form a separate letter, while in the latter reference he states that it may be included in the testimonial letter or in a private letter. In practice it will usually be found necessary to use a separate letter for this, since the testimonial letter ordinarily is a form letter, leaving no room for such matters.

to state whether the candidate has incurred any canonical impediment during the stated period of time, since these impediments may coexist with the best of morals in any particular candidate.[19]

It is clear, then, that the testimony to be furnished in these letters is not to be confused with the testimony regarding the reception of baptism, of confirmation, or also of previously conferred orders, or with the testimony of the seminary rector. Nor are the letters themselves to be confused with the dimissorial letters, for they do not confer the right to ordain another's subject, the conferring of this right being constituted as the proper function of the dimissorial letters. With all this in view, one may hope to formulate a definition of testimonial letters, the essential elements of which one may see stated in the definitions given by any of the authors on the subject. Testimonial letters may be defined as declarations made by a competent authority, acting in his official capacity, attesting to the fitness of the candidate for the reception of orders, and particularly to his freedom from impediments during the time covered by the letters.[20]

This attestation must be given expressly for the purpose of the conferral of orders. Thus a testimonial letter issued for the acquisition of a benefice, or for entrance into a religious institute, would not satisfy the requirements of the law with regard to ordinations.[21] The reason for this is quite evident, viz., a special fitness and holiness is required for the reception of orders, and the testimonial letters are intended as an aid to the bishop in arriving at a decision whether that fitness is present in the candidate.

These letters may be issued for the reception of all orders or of only certain orders, e.g., of tonsure and the minor orders. If given

[19] Toso, "Consultationes"—*Jus Pontificium* (Romae, 1920-1940), V (1925), 40-42.

[20] Cf. Coronata, *De Sacramentis,* II, n. 178; Many, *De Sacra Ordinatione,* p. 308; Blat, *De Sacramentis,* n. 37; Gasparri, *De Sacra Ordinatione,* n. 536; Regatillo, *Ius Sacramentarium, loc. cit.;* Vermeersch-Creusen, *Epitome,* II, n. 262; Wernz-Vidal, *Ius Canonicum, loc. cit.;* Gallagher, *Examination of the Qualities of the Ordinand,* p. 72; Cappello, *De Sacramentis,* Vol. II, Pars III, n. 536.

[21] S. C. C., *Pientina seu Ilcinen., Ordinationis,* 8 aug. 1733—*Thesaurus,* VI, 147-152; Gasparri, *op. cit.,* n. 724; Regatillo, *loc. cit.*

for the reception of tonsure, however, they would be valid for the reception of minor orders also. If given for the reception of orders without any restriction, they may be used for the reception of all orders inclusive of the priesthood. While many of the authors teach that letters granted for the reception of tonsure and of minor orders would not be valid for the reception of major orders,[22] Gasparri admitted that it was the custom for many curias, and especially the Roman curia, in such cases not to require new testimonial letter before the reception of major orders, provided, of course, that the candidate had not spent any time in that diocese in the meanwhile in the diocese of the bishop who issued the original testimonial letter.[23] He allowed the custom to be followed whenever the advancement of the candidate to major orders took place after a considerable lapse of time following his departure from the diocese of the bishop issuing the letter. His reason for this was that in such a case the bishop would not be able to remember the candidate sufficiently to testify concerning him. When only a short space of time intervened, he required new letters. In either case if the letters implicitly testified to the candidate's fitness for the reception of major orders, even though explicitly they testified exclusively to his fitness for the reception of minor orders, the letters could be considered satisfactory for the reception of major orders as well. The same would be true today.

Coronata teaches, and quite logically it appears, that testimonial letters which are deemed sufficient for the reception of any one order should be considered sufficient also for the reception of all orders.[24] He bases this teaching on canon 973, § 1, in which the bishop is instructed to confer tonsure and minor orders on only those candidates who intend to continue on to the priesthood, and of whom he can judge even now that they will prove their fitness for the priesthood. Accordingly, when testimonial letters have been issued with simply the lower orders in view, if the bishop judged that the necessary qualifications were present in the candidate for the lower orders,

22 Cappello, *De Sacramentis,* Vol. II, Pars III, n. 539; Regatillo, *loc. cit.*

23 *De Sacra Ordinatione,* n. 720.

24 *De Sacramentis,* II, n. 178. Cf. also Gallagher, *Examination of the Qualities of the Ordinand,* p. 73.

then there is no reason why the same letters should not suffice for the reception of the subdiaconate, even though they were issued expressly for the reception of tonsure or of the minor orders unless the candidate in the meantime, i.e., between the conferral of tonsure and the advancement to subdiaconate again spent six months in that diocese and for that reason required another letter. The whole difficulty will be obviated through the request of a letter that testifies regarding the candidate's fitness for all the orders rather than simply for the order the candidate is about to receive when the request is made.

The formalities to be observed with regard to these letters are the same as those which are employed for any public document. There must appear the signature of the person who issued the letters, an indication of his official capacity, a notation of the date and place of issuance, and the mark of the official seal.

In the Constitution *Speculatores,* Innocent XII expressly ordered the candidate for ordination to request these letters,[25] and strictly speaking that is where the obligation rests, since the candidate is bound to prove his fitness for orders, which proof he can furnish in part through the presentation of the testimonial letters.[26] In practice, however, it is usually the ordinary himself, or the rector of the seminary as his agent, who requests these letters. The examination of the letters pertains to the proper bishop, whether he contemplates ordaining the candidate himself or issuing dimissorial letters for his ordination by another. In practice again, however, he usually delegates the rector of the seminary or some other priest to undertake the examination of these letters and to ascertain their contents, with the obligation of then reporting the results to him.[27]

2. *Who May Grant Testimonial Letters*

For the validity of these letters it is necessary that they be granted by a public official acting in his official capacity. The question there-

[25] § 3—*Fontes,* n. 258.

[26] Many, *De Sacra Ordinatione,* p. 323; Coronata, *De Sacramentis, loc. cit.*

[27] According to Many (*op. cit.,* p. 324) the mandate to do this could be express or tacit.

fore arises, who are the public officials who may issue such letters? The Code indicates that these letters are to be obtained from the local ordinary.[28] Canon 198, § 1, in listing those who are to be understood as included in the term *ordinarius loci,* lists the residential bishop, the abbot or prelate *nullius,* and their vicars general, the Apostolic administrator, the vicar and prefect apostolic, and those who according to law or approved custom succeed any of these in ruling their territories. Hence any of these may issue testimonial letters. Before the Code it was necessary for the vicar general to possess a special mandate before he could do so.[29] The present law, however, makes no such limitation, and therefore the vicar general may do this without such a mandate. The vicar capitular is likewise free to issue these letters, not being limited as he is with regard to issuing dimissorial letters.[30]

There seems to be no reason why this power could not be delegated, e.g., to the seminary rector. Certainly if the Code allows the ordinary to delegate his jurisdictional power, and it does,[31] it seems that he may do the same with regard to this power which is not strictly an act of jurisdiction according to Gasparri,[32] Cappello[33] and Coronata.[34] They argue that testifying to certain facts does not entail an exercise of jurisdictional power, and therefore the granting of testimonial letters is not an act of jurisdiction. Any sub-delegation, however, would seem alien to the mind of the Church in this regard. It seems that the original delegation quite naturally is granted with a view to the qualifications of the one delegated. To allow any sub-delegation would leave the way open to abuses, and to the risk of having an unworthy candidate promoted to orders.

28 Can. 993, 4° "[Promovendus saecularis . . . afferat:] Testimoniales litteras Ordinarii loci in quo promovendus tantum temporis moratus est ut canonicum impedimentum contrahere ibi potuerit."

29 Gasparri, *De Sacra Ordinatione,* n. 710; Cappello, *De Sacramentis,* Vol. II, Pars III, n. 537.

30 Can. 958, § 1, 3°.

31 Can. 199, § 1.

32 *De Sacra Ordinatione,* n. 708.

33 *De Sacramentis, loc. cit.*

34 *De Sacramentis,* II, n. 178.

Certain colleges and seminaries enjoy the privilege of granting testimonial letters through their rector. Such letters have the same value and are entitled to the same consideration as the testimonials granted immediately by the local ordinary.[35] Outside of this case, however, or when the seminary rector has been delegated by the local ordinary to issue such letters, the testimonial letters issued by the rector of the seminary or by the pastor would not have the desired valid effect.[36] In the case of a religious who has obtained an indult of secularization, or who has been dismissed from the institute, and now seeks to be ordained as a secular, it is probable, according to Gasparri,[37] and Coronata,[38] that the religious superior in institutes of regulars may issue testimonial letters for the time which the religious spent in the religious institute, even as a novice, on the grounds that such a superior is really the ordinary of the place in so far as the actual site of the monastery is concerned. To the writer such reasoning seems rather specious.

Since, as was seen above,[39] the granting of these letters is not strictly an act of jurisdiction, it follows that letters issued by an ordinary who happened to be excommunicated, suspended or interdicted would still be valid. How much value, however, the ordaining prelate should attach to these in forming his judgment concerning the candidate's fitness is a matter to be decided by himself.[40] Certainly he would incur no penalty for ordaining on the strength of such letters.

[35] Cappello, *De Sacramentis, loc. cit.;* Coronata, *De Sacramentis, loc. cit.* The privileges in this matter granted before the Code still retain their force in accordance with canon 4. In letters issued by virtue of such a privilege there should be mention of the fact that the letters are granted in virtue of the privilege. The date of grant of this privilege and the name of the person or agency that granted it should likewise receive due mention.

[36] Noldin-Schmitt, *Summa Theologiae Moralis,* III, n. 472; Toso, "Consultationes"—*Jus Pontificium,* V (1925), 40-42.

[37] *De Sacra Ordinatione,* n. 711.

[38] *De Sacramentis,* II, n. 178.

[39] *Supra,* p. 111.

[40] Gasparri, *op. cit.,* n. 708; Cappello, *De Sacramentis,* Vol. II, Pars III, n. 537.

Article II. When are Testimonials Required

1. *For Candidates in General*

Testimonial letters are required from the ordinary of any place in which the candidate has spent a sufficient time to incur a canonical impediment.[41] Unlike the Constitution *Speculatores* of Innocent XII and the Constitution *Apostolicae Sedis* of Pius IX, both of which used similar wording, the Code determines exactly what is to be understood as the period of time sufficient for the incurring of a canonical impediment, viz., six months after the age of puberty.[42] Thus the ordinary candidate will be required to produce a testimonial letter from the ordinary of every place in which, even as a *peregrinus* or as a *vagus,* he has spent six months after his attainment of the age of puberty.

This period of time commences with the candidate's entrance into the diocese in question, and is to be computed according to the norms of canon 34, § 3, 3°.[43] Hence the opening day is not to be computed, and the period of six months is completed with the completion of the day which in the sixth subsequent month bears a date identical with the date of entrance. The starting point of this period is implicitly fixed or set through the factor of the candidate's entrance into the place, and therefore the lapse of the period will not begin with the moment of the candidate's arrival in the place, as Blat asserts.[44] The candidate's stay in the diocese must be morally continuous if it is to give rise to an obligation of obtaining testimonial letters. It is the common opinion that an interruption exceeding one month would sufficiently interrupt the candidate's stay to excuse him from any obligation in this regard.[45]

[41] Can. 993, 4°

[42] Can. 994, § 1. For those who have spent time in military service, cf. *infra*, pp. 118 ff.

[43] Cappello, *De Sacramentis,* Vol. II, Pars III, n. 540.

[44] *De Sacramentis,* n. 372. Cf. can. 34, § 2.

[45] Coronata, *De Sacramentis,* II, n. 179; Regatillo, *Ius Sacramentarium,* II, n. 146. With regard to frequently interrupted stays, as a general rule it was suggested in pre-Code law that, whenever the candidate spent six months

Even when the period of time does not add up to six months, or when the stay had occurred before the candidate reached the age of puberty, the ordaining bishop, if he prudently deems it necessary, may demand testimonial letters covering that period of time.[46] Hence with the rise of any question whether there is an obligation in this regard, either because of a doubt as to the exact length of the stay or because of the length of an interruption in the stay, the bishop, if he has any doubts concerning the candidate's fitness, may request these letters. The bishop would not be obliged in such a case to do so, nor would he be obliged in the case in which the candidate over a period of years has spent a part of each year in a certain diocese, but the period of time thus spent by him has never amounted to six continuous months.[47]

If the candidate has in some diocese spent the period of time that calls for the presentation of a testimonial letter, but it is certain that he did not incur any impediment while there, the letter must still be presented on the principle that laws which are enacted for the averting of a general danger bind even in the case wherein such a danger is not present.[48] Certainly the laws in this matter have been established for the purpose of averting a general danger, viz., the admission of unworthy candidates into the ranks of the priesthood, and therefore even though the ordaining bishop may be certain that the candidate had not incurred any impediment, he must still request testimonial letters for that period. Some authors, however, are inclined to admit that in certain cases, e.g., when the candidate was hospitalized for the whole time, there would be no necessity for

out of any year in a given diocese, then testimonial letters were to be obtained from the ordinary of that diocese. Cf. S. C. C., *Pragen.*, 25 iun. 1904—*Fontes,* n. 4318.

[46] Can. 994, § 1. While the Code here mentions the "ordaining bishop," Vermeersch-Creusen (*Epitome,* II, n. 263) understand this power as belonging also to him who does not ordain personally, but who issues the dimissorial letters for the candidate's ordination by some other prelate. Cf. also Cappello, *De Sacramentis,* Vol. II, Pars III, n. 540.

[47] Coronata, *De Sacramentis, loc. cit.*

[48] Can. 21: "Leges latae ad praecavendum periculum generale, urgent, etiamsi in casu peculiari periculum non adsit."

requesting these letters.[49] Cappello regards this opinion as speculatively probable in character, but cautions against following it in practice.[50] This particular caution appears most acceptable to the writer.

What, however, of the candidate who prepares for the priesthood in a seminary situated in another diocese? Must be obtain from the bishop of that diocese testimonial letters covering the time spent in the seminary? In the pre-Code law the matter was by no means clearly defined. Even the Sacred Congregation of the Council wavered in its decisions.[51] Upon request the bishops of Austria were given permission by the Holy Office to ordain candidates in such cases on the strength of the testimonial letter of the rector of the seminary. This faculty was granted for a period of ten years, and could be invoked only when there was grave difficulty in obtaining the letters from the bishop of the diocese.[52] In spite of this insistence upon these letters, Many related that it was the practice in Paris, and, so it was said, in Rome, not to request testimonial letters from the bishop in such cases.[53]

Among the post-Code authors, Regatillo seems to be the only one who treats this question specifically.[54] He argues that the Code's insistence upon testimonial letters from the rector of the seminary and the importance placed upon such testimony by the Instruction *Quam ingens* has given greater juridic force to the practice related by Many. It is his opinion that when the candidate has not spent six months in that diocese as non-resident at the seminary there is no need to request testimonial letters from the bishop of that diocese.

As a basis for this opinion he lists several arguments. His first argument is this: to request testimonial letters in such a case would be a useless undertaking, since the bishop would know nothing of

[49] Cf. Coronata, *De Sacramentis, loc. cit.*

[50] *De Sacramentis,* Vol. II, Pars III, n. 540.

[51] Cf. S. C. C., *in Parentina et Polen.,* 14 iul. 1894—*ASS,* XXVII (1894), 159-162, which gives an account of the various decisions handed down on the question.

[52] 28 oct. 1887—*Analecta Ecclesiastica,* IV (1896), 206-207. Cf. *supra,* pp. 43-46.

[53] *De Sacra Ordinatione,* p. 323.

[54] *Ius Sacramentarium,* II, n. 146.

the candidate outside of what he could learn from the seminary rector, and the ordaining prelate has already been made aware of such information in the rector's own testimonial. Next he remarks that it is the practice at the Spanish College in Rome that the rector alone furnishes the testimonials. He relates the contents of a letter written to him by a certain bishop in 1939. According to this bishop, the rector of the Spanish College asserted that the Spanish bishops did not require testimonial letters from the Vicar of Rome in order to issue dimissorial letters for the candidates who were studying at the College. Instead, they were contented with the information supplied in the rector's testimonial. The bishop then added that as often as he had sought such letters from the curia of the Vicariate of the City of Rome they were given only with reluctance, if at all.

Accordingly, at Rome it was not thought necessary for the Vicar to issue the testimonial in such a case. Therefore, so Regatillo concludes, the interpretation as set forth by him is safe in practice, and may be followed especially when it has already given rise to a customary procedure, or when the seminary is exempt from episcopal jurisdiction, and it is not necessary to supply for the lack of this letter with any other document. If the candidate had spent six months outside the seminary, then Regatillo agrees that a testimonial letter should be requested from the bishop of the diocese.

The fact that a law has become useless in a particular case does not exempt its subjects from the obligation of that law, since it is for the common good, and not for the private good of any particular person that law exists.[55] Therefore, even granted that in the case under consideration a testimonial letter from the bishop would be useless, the obligation imposed by the law nevertheless continues. As to the practice of the Spanish College, it cannot be said that this constitutes a pattern for the universal Church. The tacit approval to which Regatillo refers comes from the Vicariate of the City of Rome, and not from any of the Congregations of the Roman Curia. Hence one cannot regard that approval as proceeding from the Holy See,[56] and hence also one cannot consider the practice as an approved

[55] Cicognani, *Commentarium,* I, 343.

[56] Can. 7.

custom which may be followed by the entire Church. It may very well be that this approval is occasioned by conditions peculiar to the city of Rome.[57]

In forming any judgment regarding this opinion one should likewise consider the relation between the pre-Code law and the present law. The latest decision on the matter prior to the Code held these letters to be necessary in such cases, even though the argument which adverted to their uselessness was offered by the petitioners.[58] Now, whenever there is any reasonable doubt whether the latter law lacks accord with the earlier, then harmony and agreement are to be presumed,[59] and therefore in the present case testimonial letters should be requested from the local ordinary for the time spent by the candidate in a seminary located in his diocese. As to the validity of an already existing custom in the matter, the judgment regarding that must depend upon whether the prescriptions of the Code with regard to custom as a source of law[60] are or are not fulfilled.

What of the case of the religious who after his novitiate leaves the religious institute and thereupon seeks ordination as a secular? When the novitiate was spent in the candidate's own diocese there is no problem, since the testimonial letters which are here under consideration would not be required. However, when the time which was passed in the novitiate was spent in another diocese, the question arises as to who shall issue the testimonial letters which cover that period of time. As has been seen above, certain authors[61] allowed the superior of exempt religious to issue the letters for such a candidate, and did not require in addition letters from the bishop of the see. For non-exempt religious they agreed that the letters would have to be issued by the local ordinary if they are to have any value. To the writer it seems that the latter would be the preferable course of procedure in the case of all religious. There seems, however, to be suffi-

[57] Another possible explanation of the practice might be that this college may be among those which enjoy the privilege of issuing testimonial letters, through the rector, for the time spent there. Cf. *supra*, p. 112.

[58] S. C. S. Off., 28 oct. 1887—*Analecta Ecclesiastica*, IV (1896), 206-207.

[59] Can. 6, 4°.

[60] Cans. 25-27.

[61] Cf. *supra*, p. 112.

cient probability on the side of the authors who regard the testimonial of the exempt superior, as acceptable to warrant for a bishop all escape from the penalty enacted in canon 2373, 2°, in the event that he relied solely upon the religious superior's testimonial when he ordained his own subject.

If after the letters have been granted by the local ordinary the candidate should again spend a period of six morally continuous months in that diocese, a new testimonial letter would have to be obtained before the conferral of orders.[62] The Code in establishing this requirement uses the phrase *rursus moratus est* with regard to the candidate's stay. Does this imply that the Code presupposes an interruption in that stay before new letters become necessary? As Blat points out, this will usually be the case, but it is not necessarily presupposed by the Code.[63] Therefore, whenever the candidate spends such a period of time in any diocese after the issuance of a testimonial letter by the ordinary of the diocese, whether the new stay be continuous with the period already covered by the letters, or whether it be separated from it by a lapse of time, a new letter covering this new stay will be required before the candidate is admitted to orders.

2. *For Those in Military Service*

For those candidates who had seen military service there were special requirements in the pre-Code law. The time for which testimonial letters were to be demanded in such cases was set at three months, rather than six months, as was the case with other candidates.[64] This requirement applied only to clerics who had been in the armed forces, and not to lay persons who later sought admission to the clerical state. Many was of the opinion, more-

[62] Can. 994, § 3.

[63] *De Sacramentis,* n. 372: ". . . sed dicitur 'rursus' proprie relate ad testimonium obtentum etiam continua cum commoratione de qua sunt illae . . ." Cf. Gallagher (*Examination of the Qualities of the Ordinand,* p. 81) who cites Blat as teaching that such an interruption is presupposed by the Code.

[64] S. C. C., *Firmana,* 9 sept. 1893—*Fontes,* n. 4288.

over, that the decisions of the Sacred Congregation of the Council in this matter did not constitute an authentic interpretation of the universal law of the Church.[65]

The Code, in canon 994, § 1, has incorporated this requirement in the universal law. In doing so, however, it has made one important change. Whereas it was generally understood that the pre-Code law applied only to those who were clerics during the period of their military service, the Code makes no such distinction. It establishes the pre-Code ruling in this matter as a requirement with reference to all military personnel alike.[66] This change can be seen clearly in the general wording of the Code in this matter as compared with the restrictive wording of the earlier law. The Code uses the phrase *pro militibus* while the pre-Code legislation employed the phrase *pro clericis ordinandis iam militiae addictis*.[67]

Hence a candidate who has served in any branch of the armed forces must obtain testimonial letters from the bishop of every diocese in which he has spent three continuous months or more as a member of the armed forces.[68] Civilians who may accompany the armed services in such capacities as Red Cross workers, reporters, etc., strictly do not fall under the classification of soldiers, and therefore would not be bound by the provisions of this canon. It would be wise, nevertheless, for the bishop in such cases to request testimonial letters even for periods of less than six months.

What is to be done in the following case? A soldier spends two months in the army in a certain diocese. With the cessation of hostilities he is discharged from the service, but then remains in that diocese as a civilian for another three months. He has spent five months there in all, but he has not spent the time postulated by the Code either for soldiers or for civilians. Coronata is of the opinion that such a candidate would not be bound to obtain testimonial let-

[65] *De Sacra Ordinatione,* p. 313. Cf. *supra,* pp. 47-48.

[66] Coronata, *De Sacramentis,* II, n. 179; Augustine, *Commentary,* IV, 518.

[67] S. C. C., *Urgellen.,* 26 ian. 1895—*Fontes,* n. 4293.

[68] In the United States the Coast Guard during peace time is an arm of the Treasury Department. Nevertheless, in the light of the purpose of the law, it seems that its members should certainly be included under the "*milites*" mentioned in canon 994, § 1.

ters from the bishop of that diocese.[69] In strict accordance with the letter of the law this opinion seems perfectly justified. As with the civilians referred to above, however, there is nothing to prevent the bishop from requesting testimonial letters for such candidates. The making of such a request is in fact to be advised most strongly.

Article III. Suppletory Oath

It is quite evident that in many cases the bishop who is asked to grant testimonial letters in favor of some candidate who has spent six months in his diocese, or three months if enrolled in the military service during that time, will not have gained knowledge of the candidate sufficiently to testify one way or the other regarding his freedom from canonical impediments. This is especially true with regard to those who were in military service, but it is also true with regard to all alike in our large and populous dioceses of today. The problem was presented to the Sacred Congregation of the Council. The solution which was given indicated that with the permission of the Holy See the candidate be allowed to take a suppletory oath for the asserting of his freedom from all canonical impediments.[70]

The Code has, in part, canonized this decision of the Sacred Congregation of the Council.[71] It is said "in part" for there is no longer any need of a special indult to authorize the bishop to follow this procedure.[72] Nor is the use of this suppletory oath restricted so as to favor exclusively those who were soldiers, as had been provided in the original decision. Whenever, therefore, the local ordinary replies that he does not know the candidate sufficiently either personally or through others, the bishop may have recourse to the use of a suppletory oath furnished by the candidate.

In canon 994, § 2, the Code allows the suppletory oath to be used also in another eventuality not considered in the pre-Code law, viz., in the case in which the candidate has spent the postulated

[69] *De Sacramentis,* II, n. 179.

[70] S. C. C., *Urgellen.,* 26 ian. 1895—*Fontes,* n. 4293.

[71] Can. 994, § 2.

[72] Coronata, *De Sacramentis,* II, n. 180.

time in so many dioceses that it is impossible or very difficult to obtain testimonial letters from the ordinary of each and every diocese. The mere fact of having lived in a great many places does not excuse one from seeking testimonial letters from the ordinaries of those places. There must be the added element of impossibility or great difficulty. Each case then will have to be judged on its own merits by the ordinary.[73]

The impossibility which the Code presupposes as present before the bishop may have recourse to the use of the suppletory oath is moral rather than physical.[74] While the canon explicitly considers this impossibility only in connection with the case wherein the candidate has lived in many places,[75] there seems to be no reason why the same method for obtaining proof of the candidate's freedom from canonical impediments could not be employed in the case in which the candidate has lived in only one diocese, but from which it is impossible or very difficult to secure the proper testimonial letters.

It is important to note that canon 994, § 2, in making provision for the use of this oath, uses the word *saltem*, thus signifying that the utilization of other proofs for establishing the candidate's fitness are by no means excluded.[76] Rather, according to Cappello, these are in fact called for, and only when all other means have become unavailable or impracticable may the bishop have recourse to the use of this oath.[77]

[73] Gallagher, *Examination of the Qualities of the Ordinand,* p. 81. Many (*De Sacra Ordinatione,* p. 325), when writing in 1905 had even then allowed the use of the oath in such cases.

[74] Coronata, *De Sacramentis, loc. cit.* An example furnished by this author is the interruption in the means of communication as a result of war or other causes.

[75] Can. 994, 2: ". . . aut si promovendus per tot dioceses vagatus sit ut impossibile vel nimis difficile evadat omnes litteras testimoniales exquirere, . . ."

[76] ". . . provideat Ordinarius saltem per iuramentum suppletorium a promovendo praestandum."

[77] *De Sacramentis,* Vol. II, Pars III, n. 540: "Vox *'saltem'* aperte significat alias probationes et informationes minime excludi, imo desiderari, adeo ut nonnisi, illis deficientibus, locus sit iuramento suppletorio."

In this regard what is to be said with reference to the ex-soldier, who as a candidate for ordination falls under the provisions of this canon? His situation is somewhat different from that of the ordinary candidate, in that during his time in military service he was subject to a personal ordinary as well as to the ordinary of the place in which he was stationed. Must he then obtain letters from the military vicar as well as from the local ordinary? Prior to the Code it was declared necessary for candidates who had served in the Spanish army to obtain such letters from the Patriarch of the Indies, the military vicar for the armed forces of that country.[78] Testimonials from the military vicar were likewise considered necessary in France, even after the Code, even though no reference was made to any official decree or decision in proof of such a specific requirement.[79]

The Code does not mention this ordinary at all. Larraona, when writing with regard to testimonial letters as needed by a candidate prior to his entrance into the novitiate, contends that it is not necessary to seek testimonial letters from the military ordinary, on the grounds namely that he is simply a personal ordinary, whereas the Code specifies the local ordinary as the agency for the issuance of these letters.[80] In a footnote to his article he refers to the decision of the Congregation for the Status of Regulars mentioned above, and says that it is quite evident that in the present connection this docu-

[78] S. C. super Statu Regularium, 5 nov. 1852—*Fontes,* n. 4380. Cf. also S. C. C., 5 apr. 1897—*Analecta Ecclesiastica,* IX (1901), 253, for the same country. The Decree *"De Clericis a Militia Redeuntibus"* (S. C. Consist., 25 oct. 1918—*AAS,* X [1918], 480-485) required that persons returning to the seminary after a period of military service present testimonial letters from the military ordinary regarding their lives in the army, but expressed no similar demand concerning letters prior to the reception of orders.

[79] Boudinhon, "Consultationes"—*Le Canoniste Contemporain* (45 vols., Paris, 1878-1922), XLV (1922), 476.

[80] "Commentarium Codicis"—*Commentarium pro Religiosis et Missionariis* (Romae, 1935—; ab anno 1920: *Commentarium pro Religiosis*), XIX (1938), 154-160. This *Commentarium* will be cited *CpR* for the issues from 1920 to 1934 inclusively, and *CpRM* for the issues since 1935.

ment was not cited in the footnotes to the Code inasmuch as the enacted requirement was of a purely particular character occasioned by the special status of the ancient Patriarch of the Indies.[81] Consequently, he argues, it would not be necessary to obtain such letters from the military vicar under the present law, nor would letters from such an ordinary excuse from the obligation of requesting testimonial letters from the local ordinary. What he says here with reference to a candidate's entrance into the novitiate applies equally, he contends, with reference to a candidate's admission to orders.

Granted that under canon 993, 4°, and canon 994, § 1, there is no obligation to request testimonial letters from the military ordinary, what of canon 994, § 2, and its use of the word *saltem?* It seems to the writer that under this canon there does exist an obligation to request letters from this ordinary before the candidate's bishop may have exclusive recourse to the use of the suppletory oath. To neglect requesting these letters would be to forego exploring a very valuable source of information concerning the candidate's fitness. It is not only possible but also likely that such an ordinary will, through his chaplains, know more concerning the candidate, than would the local ordinary. The Code provides that when the ordinary letters cannot be obtained, the bishop should supply for this defect at least through a suppletory oath on the part of the candidate, thus indicating by its words that it is the mind of the legislator that, when other testimony is available, that testimony should be sought. In this case further testimony is available from the military vicar, and therefore it is the mind of the legislator that such should be obtained.

81 In this regard it is interesting to note that in Gasparri's footnotes to the Code under canon 544, § 5, reference is made to the first two sections of this decision, but not to the third section, in which the document adverts to the right and duty of the military ordinary. Reference is made, however, to the third section of another declaration of the Congregation for the Status of Regulars under date of May 29, 1857, which stated that for novices of another order or also for professed religious who had obtained an indult of secularization, testimonial letters were to be sought from the ordinary of the place, and not from the religious superior.—*Fontes,* n. 4382.

Upon the obtaining of such testimony from the military vicar, when letters from the local ordinary cannot be obtained, would the suppletory oath still be necessary if the military vicar replied that the candidate is free from canonical impediments as far as the time spent under his jurisdiction is concerned? Since the law leaves it to the discretion of the ordinary to determine what method he is to use in supplying for the lack of the proper testimonials, the oath being established as the minimum requirement, it does not seem necessary for the bishop to require the oath of the candidate once such testimony has been obtained. It is not denied, however, that the bishop may do so should he deem such a procedure necessary, since it is he who is to judge concerning the candidate's fitness.

What of the sufficiency of the testimonial furnished by the military ordinary when it is possible and not too difficult to obtain testimonial letters from the local ordinaries? Gasparri,[82] Many [83] and Coronata [84] all agree that with reference to the ex-religious who seeks to receive orders as a secular it is probable that the religious superior, if the institute is exempt, may issue testimonial letters for the time spent in the institute. In such a case, they teach, it would not be necessary to request letters from the local ordinary also, since the letters of the religious superior take the place of the letters of the local ordinary. It seems to the writer that the same would not be true with regard to letters issued by the military ordinary, even though in both cases the issuing agency is an ordinary, though not a local ordinary. Gasparri allowed this custom to be followed on the rather dubious grounds that the religious superior in such a case was actually the *ordinarius loci* of the monastery. The same would not be true with regard to the military ordinary. Hence such letters would not of themselves prove sufficient when it is possible and not too difficult to obtain letters from the local ordinaries.

With regard, then, to the statement of Larraona, namely, that it would not be necessary to obtain testimonial letters from the military ordinary the writer feels that a distinction must be made between the situation in which it is possible and fairly convenient

[82] *De Sacra Ordinatione*, n. 711.

[83] *De Sacra Ordinatione*, pp. 321-322.

[84] *De Sacramentis*, II, n. 178.

to obtain letters from the local ordinaries and the situation in which it is impossible or at least very difficult to follow this procedure. With regard to the first set of circumstances he agrees with Larraona that letters from the military ordinary are neither necessary nor sufficient. With regard to the second set of circumstances, however, he maintains that there is an obligation to obtain letters from the military ordinary, and that such testimonials when obtained can supply completely for the lack of the ordinary testimonial letters. As a matter of practice it is suggested that the testimonial letters be requested from both ordinaries when that is possible. When it is impossible or very difficult to obtain them from the local ordinaries, then they should be requested at least from the military ordinary.

It is quite possible that a candidate while serving in the armed forces may be absent from his diocese for a number of years, and yet during that time, in view of the highly mechanized warfare of today, may not spend three continuous months in any one diocese. In such a case, if strictly gauged according to the wording of the law, no testimonial letter would be required for his time in service. It is suggested, however, that in such cases as a precautionary measure the bishop request testimonial letters from the military ordinary, whose information regarding the candidate spans the time of his military service.

The oath, when taken, is to be taken before the ordinary or his delegate. The right of supplying for the lack of letters through this oath belongs only to the proper ordinary of the candidate, whether he is to ordain the candidate personally, or whether he will issue dimissorial letters for his ordination by another bishop.[85] As with all other oaths in the matter of prerequisites for ordination, this oath should be consigned to writing and signed by the ordinand. It is then to be preserved in the archives of the curia together with all the other documents pertaining to the candidate's ordination.

[85] Coronata, *De Sacramentis,* II, n. 180. Cf. can. 994, § 2.

Article IV. Penalties

According to the provisions of the Constitution *Apostolicae Sedis* of Pope Pius IX (1846-1878), a bishop who while lacking the proper testimonial letters ordained a candidate became suspended from the conferral of orders for the space of one year.[86] The Code has canonized this legislation in canon 2373, 2°, according to which a bishop who ordains one of his subjects while he lacks the testimonial letters required by canons 993, 4°, and 994, is suspended from the conferral of orders for one year. The remission of this suspension is reserved to the Holy See.[87]

This penalty is incurred *ipso facto* upon the commission of the delict. It is a vindicative penalty, as can be seen from the fact that a definite time is established for the suspension. If it were a medicinal penalty no such space of time could be established, since in such penalties the delinquent may be absolved as soon as he is truly penitent.[88] As in all matters pertaining in general to orders, the penalty applies equally to the conferral of tonsure as to the conferral of minor or of major orders. The penalty would not be incurred, however, through the wrongful ordination of one who is not the subject of the ordaining bishop.[89] Thus, if a bishop sends a candidate to another bishop with dimissorial letters, the bishop to whom the candidate is sent could without the risk of incurring the penalty proceed to the ordination, even though he knows that the requirements with regard to the testimonial letters have been neglected. In such a case neither the ordaining bishop nor the bishop issuing the dimissorial letters would incur any penalty; not the first, since he is not ordaining one of his own subjects; and not the second, since he is not the ordaining bishop, for the law contemplates solely the ordaining bishop, and then only in the act of ordaining one of

[86] 12 oct. 1869, § V, art. 3—*Fontes,* n. 552.

[87] "Qui subditum proprium, qui alibi tanto tempore moratus sit ut canonicum impedimentum contrahere ibi potuerit, ordinaverint contra praescriptum can. 993, n. 4, 994;"

[88] Can. 2248, § 1, § 2.

[89] Ayrinhac, *Penal Legislation in the New Code of Canon Law* (revised by Lydon, New York: Benziger, 1936), p. 284; Beste, *Introductio in Codicem,* p. 966.

his own subjects. This is in accord with the strict interpretation of the law in this matter, the interpretation namely, which is prescribed whenever there is question of the incurring of penalties.[90]

This penalty applies also in the cases which involve a violation of the law enacted in canon 994, and hence the bishop who in conferring orders on one of his subjects has neglected to obtain the suppletory oath, that is, when the proper testimonial letters could not be obtained, likewise incurs this penalty. Any other bishop who ordained in virtue of dimissorials would not incur the penalty even though he knew that the obtaining of this oath had been neglected. Would a deliberate neglect of the use of other means of proof for the candidate's freedom from impediments, when such proofs are available, subject the ordaining bishop to this penalty? Canon 994, § 2, prescribes that the bishop shall provide for the lack of the testimonials at least through a suppletory oath on the part of the candidate. Since penalties, as has been pointed out, are subject to a strict interpretation, it seems that as long as the bishop employs the oath he escapes the penalty enacted in canon 2373, 2°.

Ignorance of the law or of the penalty alone, even if it be not crass ignorance, would not excuse the ordaining prelate, since the penalty in question is vindicative, not medicinal, in its character.[91] However, ignorance of fact and ignorance of law excuse from the incurring of vindicative penalties if the ignorance is not gravely sinful, because delictual imputability is thus precluded.[92] Hence, as long as the bishop knows that there is a penalty attached to his mode of action the penalty is incurred.

This penalty begins to bind from the moment of the commission of the delict, and consequently it seems that the time of the suspension is to be computed according to the norms of canon 34, § 2. According to this method of computation, the penalty begins to bind from the very moment of the commission of the delict and the

[90] Can. 19. Cf. Beste, *Introductio in Codicem, loc. cit.;* Coronata, *Institutiones,* IV, n. 2159.

[91] Can. 2229, § 3, 1°.

[92] Swoboda, *Ignorance in Relation to the Imputability of Delicts,* (The Catholic University of America Canon Law Studies, n. 143 (Washington, D. C.: The Catholic University of America Press, 1941), p. 204. Cf. can. 2218, § 2.

year is considered to have elapsed at the same hour of the day having a similar date one year later.[93] Gallagher is of the opinion that the time is to be reckoned according to canon 34, § 3, 3°.[94] To follow such opinion, however, would mean either that the penalty while incurred *ipso facto* upon the commission of the delict still would not bind until the following day, which seems untenable, or else that the penalty did bind from the very moment of the delict in which case the bishop would be penalized for one year plus part of another day. Certainly this would not be the benign interpretation prescribed by canon 2219, § 1 in the matter of the inflicting of penalties.[95] It seems therefore that Blat's opinion is the only one that can be followed without involving oneself in a contradiction.

As to the candidate thus illicitly ordained, he too is to be penalized. If he undertakes to receive orders when he lacks the proper testimonials or while he is bound by a censure, by an irregularity, or by some other canonical impediment he is to be punished at the discretion of the ordinary.[96] This is a *ferendae sententiae* penalty, and hence is not incurred *ipso facto* upon the commission of the delict. Canon 2374 uses the word *malitiose,* and therefore any diminution of culpability, either on the part of the intellect or on the part of the will, would excuse the candidate from incurring any liability for the eventual contracting of a canonical penalty.[97] The same kind of penalty is in store for the candidate who knowingly withholds information as to his residence protracted in a certain place for six months. He too is to be punished at the discretion of the bishop.

As a matter of fact the instances in which the candidate will deserve punishment in this regard will be few and far between. This is simply a natural result of the now prevalent system whereby

93 Blat, *Commentarium, De Delictis et Poenis,* V, n. 215.

94 *Examination of the Qualities of the Ordinand,* p. 134. This author says that it is to be computed according to the norms of canon 34, § 3, 2° but explains the computation according to 3° of the same canon.

95 Cf. Cicognani, *Commentarium,* II, 239.

96 Can. 2374.

97 Can. 2229, § 2.

the bishop or his delegate takes it upon himself to obtain all the required documents for the candidate's ordination. A penalty, however, to which the candidate may become liable more often is the one that may be occasioned by the suppletory oath which he takes to supply for the lack of the testimonial letters. Should the candidate affirm under oath what he knows to be false, he would be guilty of perjury, and thus would become subject to punishment within the discretion of the ordinary.[98]

[98] Can. 2323: "Qui blasphemaverit vel periurium extra iudicium commiserit, prudenti Ordinarii arbitrio puniatur, maxime clericus."

CHAPTER VIII

DIMISSORIAL LETTERS

Article I. General Considerations

1. *Nature*

Throughout the centuries, for reasons seen in the historical section of this study, the Church has been most insistent that each candidate for the priesthood be ordained by his own bishop.[1] When this could not be done for some reason, the Church demanded that any other bishop obtain the permission of the candidate's bishop before conferring orders on him.

The Code has restated this law in canon, 955, § 1, declaring that each candidate is to be ordained by his own bishop or upon the issuance of legitimate dimissorial letters by him.[2] These dimissorial letters may be defined as letters by which the proper bishop of the candidate, in view of his jurisdiction, asks or deputes another bishop, whether specially or generally determined, to confer orders upon one of his subjects.[3] Or they may be defined as denoting the permission granted by a competent superior to one of his subjects, to receive ordination from a bishop other than his own.[4] The two definitions merely view the letters from different angles. Upon a final analysis both are seen to stress the same essential note, viz., the permission for a bishop to ordain one who is not his subject.

[1] Cf. *supra*, pp. 1-2.

[2] "Unusquisque a proprio Episcopo ordinetur aut cum legitimis eiusdem litteris dimissoriis."

[3] Wernz-Vidal, *Ius Canonicum*, Tomus IV, Vol. I, n. 199; Coronata, *De Sacramentis*, II, n. 36; Gasparri, *De Sacra Ordinatione*, n. 864; Regatillo, *Ius Sacramentarium*, II, n. 59.

[4] Many, *De Sacra Ordinatione*, p. 150; Vermeersch-Creusen, *Epitome*, II, n. 241; Beste, *Introductio in Codicem*, p. 508; Cappello, *De Sacramentis*, Vol. II, pars III, n. 341; Aertnys-Damen, *Theologia Moralis*, II, n. 571.

An indication of the history of this term is found in the very term itself. Originally these letters signified the dismissal by a bishop of one of his clerical subjects in order that he might receive orders at the hand of another bishop and at the same time be incardinated in the diocese of that bishop.[5] Hence they were really letters of excardination according to our present terminology. Certainly from the twelfth century, however, they assumed the meaning which is attached to them today, viz., a mere permission to ordain another's subject without thereby acquiring any rights over him.[6]

2. *Form and Contents*

Since the essence of these letters is the permission conferred, it follows that while the word letters is used by the Code, writing is not essential for this purpose.[7] Nevertheless, for the sake of forestalling fraud and other abuses which might easily appear if merely an oral permission were granted for this purpose, it is most strongly advised by all the authors that the permission be given in writing. Coronata sees warrant for the granting of an oral permission only in the case in which the candidate's bishop asks another bishop who is actually present at the time to confer some orders on one of his subjects.[8] If, however, a bishop undertook to confer orders on some candidate after having obtained merely an oral permission, he would not incur the penalties established by the Code for the bishop who ordains without the possession of the proper dimissorials.[9] He should most assuredly, in any case, establish the authenticity of this permission before proceeding to the conferring of orders.

As to the contents of these letters, the essential and all important element is the permission to confer orders upon another's subject. There should, however, be more information contained therein. Thus the name of the bishop, or of some other superior as outlined by the

[5] Cappello, *De Sacramentis, loc. cit.;* cf. *supra,* pp. 6-7.

[6] Cf. *supra,* pp. 17-18.

[7] Gasparri, *De Sacra Ordinatione,* n. 862; Wernz-Vidal, *Ius Canonicum,* Tomus IV, Vol. II, n. 199; Moeder, *Proper Bishop for Ordination,* p. 82.

[8] *De Sacramentis,* II, n. 36.

[9] Can. 2373, 1°.

Code, who issues the letters as well as the name of the bishop to whom the letters are addressed, unless the permission is granted in a general way, e.g., to any bishop in communion with the Holy See, should be given. Next the letters should indicate the candidate in whose favor they are issued. Though there is no express provision for it in the Code, and though the authors fail to discuss the possibility, there seems to be no reason why the letters could not be issued to a class of candidates, provided that the bishop had already approved the candidates in question, and provided also that there was some definite determination as to just which candidates were included. Thus it appears permissible for a bishop who became sick to request a neighboring bishop to ordain all those who are in the deacon class in his seminary, so that he would not have to issue a separate dimissorial letter for each candidate.

The order to be conferred in consequence of the granted permission should also be duly specified. In this connection letters issued for the conferring of orders in general or of all orders are valid for the conferral of major orders, unless the contrary appears from the context of the letters.[10] Testimony regarding the candidate's fitness for orders should also be included. Wernz-Vidal mention in this regard the candidate's parentage, age, knowledge, morals, and his freedom from canonical impediments.[11] Cappello, on the other hand, says that sometimes these letters contain testimony concerning the morals of the candidate, clauses concerning dispensations, etc. He thus apparently indicates that mention of these things is not necessary for the validity of the letters.[12]

It seems to the writer that this latter view is the correct one, since essentially the dimissorial letter implies simply a permission to confer orders. As long as that is duly granted, the letter seems to

[10] Cappello, *De Sacramentis,* Vol. II, pars III, n. 345. The same author states that letters issued for the conferring of a higher order are valid also for the conferring of lower orders which have not yet been received. He notes, however, that this matter is a quite theoretical one, since the letters should contain an attestation of the last order received, and thus the likelihood that some order receive no specific mention is rendered quite remote.

[11] *Ius Canonicum,* Tome IV, Vol. I, n. 199. Cf. also Regatillo, *Ius Sacramentarium,* II, n. 59.

[12] *De Sacramentis,* Vol. II, pars III, n. 341.

have the desired valid force. It is certain, however, that the issuing bishop should be in possession of all the required testimonials before he issues the dimissorial letter.[13] According to the Council of Trent it was necessary that the cause why the proper bishop was unable to ordain should receive mention in the dimissorial letter.[14] This no longer seems necessary under the present law. Finally, as with all public documents, the letter should carry a notation of the place and date of issuance as well as the signature and seal of the grantor.[15] If the letter is granted by the vicar general, in virtue of a special mandate,[16] then mention of the mandate should be made in the dimissorial letter. If the letter is granted by the vicar capitular, there should be a notation of the fulfillment of the conditions placed in canon 958, § 1, 3°, for issuance of this letter by that official.

3. *Duration of Validity for Dimissorial Letters*

Dimissorial letters may be granted with or without a determination as to the time for which the letters shall be valid. Thus, for example, the bishop may grant dimissorial letters for the conferral of orders within three months. If the ordination were deferred beyond that time, the letters would no longer be valid. The validity of the ordinations conferred in virtue of such invalid letters would, however, in no way be affected, unless the orders were conferred by vicars or prefects apostolic, who are not bishops, by prelates or abbots *nullius* or by other priests by virtue of special indult.[17]

[13] Can. 960, § 1. Yet Coronata seemingly allows the granting of the letter apart from the simultaneous possession of the testimonials of the bishop in whose territory the candidate had lived for a period of time sufficient for the contracting of a canonical impediment, for, in a footnote to the specimen of a dimissorial letter which he gives, this author says that, if the bishop had not obtained these testimonials, then that fact should be declared in the letter, in order that the bishop who is being authorized to confer the orders might obtain them.—*De Sacramentis,* Appendix III, form XIV, nota 1. It is difficult to see how this view can be reconciled with canon 960, § 1.

[14] Conc. Trident., sess. VII, *de ref.*, c. 10.

[15] Moeder, *Proper Bishop for Ordination,* p. 98.

[16] Can. 958, §1, 2°.

[17] Can. 957, § 3. Cf. Coronata, *De Sacramentis,* II, n. 39. The bishop who knowingly ordains despite his lack of possessing dimissorials which still have

When, however, the letters contain no such restrictive clause, the letters are valid indefinitely in so far as the question concerns the granted permission. They are likewise indefinitely valid with reference to what they contain by way of studies, etc. With regard to the testimony concerning the candidate's freedom from impediments, the validity of the letters is definitely limited. In this matter the letter is valid for the time for which it testifies, not, however, for the future. Thus if the ordination should be deferred for a period of time, it would have to be determined whether during this period the candidate had spent a sufficient time in any diocese to contract a canonical impediment. If this is found to be true, a new testimonial letter covering that period would have to be secured before the conferral of the orders with reference to which the dimissorial letters had lent due authorization.[18] If this time were spent in the diocese of the bishop who is authorized to ordain, then he would be the one to gather the necessary information to enable him to testify in the matter.[19]

Once legitimately granted, the dimissorial letters do not cease to be valid with the death of the grantor, or with his removal or resignation from office,[20] even though the death or removal or resignation took place before the execution of the letters. Thus letters granted by a vicar capitular in accordance with the provisions of canon 958, § 1, 3°, do not cease to be valid when the newly appointed bishop takes possession of his see.[21] The reason for this lies in the fact that the grant of a dimissorial letter is considered to be a favor, and a favor once granted does not cease with the death of the grantor or with the cessation of his tenure in office.[22]

valid force incurs the penalty which canon 2373, 1° enacts for a bishop who ordains a non-subject without being authorized by any dimissorials at all.

18 Coronata, *De Sacramentis, loc. cit.*

19 Can. 960, § 3.

20 Can. 963.

21 Cappello, *De Sacramentis,* Vol. II, pars III, n. 345. Many (*De Sacra Ordinatione,* p. 167) held that if the ordination were to take place in the diocese of the deceased bishop, with dimissorials from that bishop, the ordaining bishop would be bound to obtain the consent of the vicar capitular for the ordination of the candidate.

22 Cappello, *De Sacramentis, loc. cit.* Cf. cans. 61; 70; 73; 207, § 1.

The authorization conferred by the dimissorial letter may be revoked or limited by the grantor or his successor.[23] Thus a vicar capitular may, after his election, revoke or limit the dimissorial letters granted by the bishop before the expiration of his tenure of office. By the same token a bishop upon taking possession of his see may revoke or limit the letters granted by the vicar capitular during his tenure in office. The letters may be limited through the insertion of a condition, e.g., by making their validity conditional upon the candidate's fitness as determined by the bishop who is authorized to ordain, or by restricting to one certain bishop the right to ordain when previously they had been addressed to every bishop in communion with the Holy See, or by retrenching the time for which they will have valid force, or in any other way.[24] For the revocation or the limitation to take effect, whether done by the grantor or by his successor, it is necessary that it be made known both to the candidate and to the bishop to whom the letter was addressed.[25] When the letters are addressed to every Catholic bishop, it seems that a notification of the candidate will suffice to effect the revocation or the limitation.

According to Gasparri, before the Code not only the grantor and his successor in office, but also the superior of the grantor had this right, e.g., the bishop with regard to letters which the vicar general had granted in virtue of a special mandate.[26] Among post-Code authors Cappello seems to be the only one who concedes such a right to the superior.[27] In so doing he gives as an example the Roman Pontiff. The Code does not make any provision in this matter with reference to the superior of the grantor.[28] Accordingly it does not seem that this superior any longer enjoys this right.

[23] Can. 963.

[24] Coronata, *De Sacramentis,* II, n. 39.

[25] Gasparri, *De Sacra Ordinatione,* n. 888; Coronata, *De Sacramentis, loc. cit.*

[26] *Loc. cit.*

[27] *De Sacramentis,* Vol. II, pars III, n. 345.

[28] Can. 963: "Litterae dimissoriae possunt ab ipso concedente vel ab eius successore limitari aut revocari, . . ."

Cappello's example of the Roman Pontiff can readily be explained in virtue of the pope's supreme jurisdiction over the universal Church, a jurisdiction not enjoyed by any other superior.[29]

A final way in which these letters may cease to be valid is through the renunciation of them on the part of the candidate. The opinion of the authors varies on this point, but Gasparri [30] and Cappello [31] both hold as correct the opinion which affirms this as a method by which dimissorial letters lose their validity. For such an act to have any effect, however, it is necessary that it be made known to the grantor and accepted by him. The acceptance or the refusal of the candidate's renunciation of the dimissorials rests likewise within the competence of the successor of the grantor.[32] Therefore in the final analysis the validity and effect of these letters is dependent solely upon the will of the competent superior.

4. *When Dimissorial Letters are Required*

As often as a candidate for ordination is to be ordained by a bishop who is not the proper bishop for ordination as far as he is concerned, it will be necessary to obtain dimissorial letters from that bishop.[33] This procedure will be necessary even for the conferral of the first clerical tonsure according to a ruling of the Commission for the Interpretation of the Code in answer to the question whether, in virtue of the fact that through the reception of first tonsure a cleric is incardinated in the diocese for which he is promoted,[34] a bishop may confer tonsure on the subject of another bishop without requesting dimissorial letters from the subject's proper bishop.[35]

[29] Coronata, (*De Sacramentis,* II, n. 39), Wernz-Vidal (*Ius Canonicum,* Tomus IV, Vol. I, n. 200) and Regatillo (*Ius Sacramentarium,* II, n. 59) do not list the superior among those who enjoy this right.

[30] *De Sacra Ordinatione,* n. 888.

[31] *De Sacramentis,* Vol. II, pars II, n. 345.

[32] Cf. can. 72, § 1.

[33] Can. 955, § 1.

[34] Can. 111, § 2.

[35] Commissio Pontificia Interpretationis (C. P. I.), 17 febr. 1930—*AAS,* XXII (1930), 195.

Thus in the following case dimissorial letters would be required. A candidate with a domicile in diocese A enters the diocesan seminary to prepare for the priesthood in that diocese. Between the time he enters the seminary and the time he is to be advanced to tonsure, however, his family moves to diocese B, and there establishes a domicile. Therefore when the time arrives for promotion to tonsure the candidate being a minor no longer has a domicile in diocese A, since he cannot establish a domicile of his own the while he is a minor. Accordingly the bishop of diocese A would have to obtain dimissorial letters from the bishop of diocese B, even though the candidate is being ordained for diocese A.[36] If in view of his capacity to do so he actually established a domicile of his own in diocese A, this procedure would not be necessary.[37] In any event it would not be necessary to procure dimissorial letters before the conferral of the succeeding orders, according to a private response of the Commission for the Interpretation of the Code.[38]

Are dimissorial letters required when an auxiliary bishop ordains in the diocese of the bishop to whom he has been named auxiliary? Mothon is the only author found to treat the question.[39] He teaches that while canonists disagree on the question he is of the opinion that it is more conformable with the provisions of canon 955, § 1, to require dimissorial letters in such a case. As a matter of fact the question is quite theoretical. Should the auxiliary bishop be at the same time the vicar general, which is often true, and also be endowed with a special mandate to issue dimissorial letters, he would require no such letters to ordain, since the Code provides that he who is entitled to grant dimissorial letters for the reception of an order may himself confer that order, provided of course that he has the necessary power of orders.[40] In the case in which he does not possess

[36] Such a candidate would not have to take the oath prescribed in canon 956, § 2, prior to the issuance of the dimissorial letters, since he is being promoted for another diocese.

[37] D'Angelo, "De Prima Tonsura—Consultatio"—*Apollinaris,* I (1928), 181-182.

[38] C. P. I., 7 dec. 1931—reported by Bouscaren, *Canon Law Digest,* II, 51.

[39] *Institutions Canoniques* (3 vols., Lille-Bruges; Desclée, DeBrower, 1924), art. 2049, nota, 9.

[40] Can. 959.

such a mandate he will confer orders usually only at the request of the ordinary, and this can certainly be construed as permission to ordain, which constitutes the essential element in dimissorial letters. In practice, then, according to this opinion the only time he would require such letters would be when he proposes to confer orders without the previously manifested knowledge of the residential bishop.

The privilege enjoyed by the students of certain seminaries and colleges, whereby dimissorial letters were not required even though they were being ordained by bishops other than their own, although left intact by the Code, has since been expressly revoked by a decree of the Sacred Congregation of the Consistory.[41] Thus, apart from students attending the College of the Sacred Congregation for the Propagation of the Faith, or seminaries and colleges dependent upon that Congregation, if priests are there educated for the missions and if the granted privilege in this matter has not been revoked by means of the mentioned decree, every candidate who receives ordination from a bishop other than his proper bishop must obtain dimissorial letters.[42]

As for the use of presumed permission in this matter, Cappello says that of itself it remains completely precluded.[43] He contends that only in certain extraordinary circumstances could there be verified the case in which, because of the urgent and grave necessity of the diocese, it would be permissible for a bishop to proceed to the conferral of orders on another's subject with merely the presumed permission of the proper bishop or of the Holy See.

[41] S. C. Consist., 6 nov. 1920—*AAS,* XII (1920), 259.

[42] Coronata (*De Sacramentis,* II, n. 36, footnote 4, p. 41) acknowledges that certain privileges granted to vicars and prefects apostolic because of extraordinary circumstances are still valid for the present if these conditions are verified. He gives as an example the indult granted by the Sacred Congregation for the Propagation of the Faith on January 13, 1665, namely, of promoting without dimissorial letters candidates who have had to flee their countries because of war. Cf. *Collectanea,* n. 159; also Cappello, *De Sacramentis,* Vol. II, pars III, n. 341.

[43] *De Sacramentis,* Vol. II, pars III, n. 345.

5. *To Whom Dimissorial Letters May Be Sent*

Dimissorial letters may be addressed to a certain specified bishop, or in a general way to every bishop in union with the Holy See.[44] Even when the dimissorials were issued to a certain specified bishop, Gasparri allowed the candidate to approach a different bishop if the letters were so granted as a favor to the candidate.[45] Permission granted to "any and every Catholic bishop having a clergy and people" may not be used by a titular bishop. If granted, however, "to any and every bishop in communion with the Apostolic See" it may be used by any bishop, titular or residential, and also by a vicar or prefect apostolic, provided he has episcopal consecration.[46]

The only restriction placed by the Code in this regard is that such letters should not be sent to a bishop whose rite differs from that of the ordinand, unless he has received an apostolic indult for ordaining candidates of a rite other than his own. Were a Latin bishop to send his oriental subject to an oriental bishop of the same rite, no indult would be required.[47] By a different rite there is to be understood any other rite which consists of its own liturgy and ecclesiastical discipline, e.g., an oriental rite as contrasted with the Latin rite, and not a further variety of the same rite, e.g., the Ambrosian rite in the Latin Church.[48]

[44] Can. 961: "Litterae dimissoriae mitti possunt ab Episcopo proprio, etiam Cardinali Episcopo suburbicario. ad quemlibet Episcopum, communionem cum Sede Apostolica habentem, excepto tantum, citra apostolicum indultum, Episcopo ritus diversi a ritu promovendi." Before the Code the bishops of the six suburbicarian sees had to address their dimissorial letters to the Cardinal Vicar of Rome.—Alexander VII, const. *Apostolica solicitudo,* 7 aug. 1662, § 2—*Fontes,* n. 239; *Bullarium,* XVII, 52-53.

[45] *De Sacra Ordinatione,* n. 879; Coronata, *De Sacramentis,* II, n. 38; St. Alphonsus, *Theologia Moralis,* Lib. VI, n. 788, nota 11. It is the writer's opinion that this may still be followed on the basis of canon 68.

[46] Gasparri held that this latter form should be used only rarely and exclusively for some very grave cause.—*loc. cit.*

[47] Cappello, *De Sacramentis,* Vol. II, pars III, n. 343; Diederichs, *The Jurisdiction of the Latin Ordinaries over Their Oriental Subjects,* The Catholic University of America Canon Law Studies, n. 229 (Washington, D. C.: The Catholic University of America Press, 1946), p. 103.

[48] Cappello, *De Sacramentis, loc. cit.* An exception in this regard is that in favor of the Antiochean Patriarch of the Maronites, who enjoys the privilege

6. *Denial of Dimissorial Letters*

It is clear that dimissorial letters are absolutely necessary for the licit ordination of a candidate by a bishop other than his own. What is to be done, however, when the proper bishop refuses to grant such letters? Before giving an answer to this question one must necessarily determine whether the bishop has the right to deny these letters when they are requested.

If the bishop has a reasonable and just cause, even though this cause is known to him only *ex informata conscientia,* he may certainly refuse to grant this permission.[49] If, however, the bishop judges the candidate worthy for orders, and the candidate on his part has a just cause for residing in another diocese and cannot defer the ordination, then the bishop may not refuse these letters. Should he do so, the candidate is nevertheless not thereby authorized to seek ordination in the absence of dimissorial letters. He must have recourse to the Holy See, which, when the facts warrant it, will either command the bishop to issue the letters, or itself give permission for the candidate to receive ordination.[50]

Article II. Who May Issue Dimissorial Letters

1. *The Proper Bishop*

To be valid, dimissorial letters must be granted by one who is legally entitled to perform this function. The first person so entitled by the Code is the proper bishop of the candidate, to whom the ordination primarily pertains.[51] The bishop may do this as soon

of sending his subjects either to a bishop of the Latin rite or to a bishop of any other oriental rite. Cf. Council of Mount Lebanon (1736), Pars II, Cap. XIV, nn. 21-28—*Collectio Lacensis,* II, 237-239.

[49] Coronata, *De Sacramentis,* II, n. 39; Cappello, *De Sacramentis, ibid.,* n. 345.

[50] Gasparri gave in detail an instance in which the Holy See itself granted the permission in such a case.—*De Sacra Ordinatione,* n. 889. Cf. *supra,* p. 54.

[51] Can. 958, § 1, 1°. The writer does not intend to enter here upon a discussion of the question of the proper bishop for ordination and dimissorial letters. For a treatment of this question the reader is referred to Moeder, *The*

as he has canonically taken possession of his see, even though he has not yet been consecrated.[52] This is an exercise of jurisdiction which does not require the presence of the episcopal character. Were he to issue such letters after his appointment but before he has canonically taken possession of the see, they would be invalid.

The metropolitan may issue dimissorials before the reception of the pallium, although he may not personally ordain the candidates for whom he may issue the dimissorials.[53] Moreover, although there is no express provision for it in the Code, yet it is certainly true that the Roman Pontiff in view of his supreme jurisdiction over the universal Church may grant such letter for any candidate, or dispense from the law in this regard.

The concession of dimissorial letters is an act of jurisdiction which is to be performed as an absolutely free gratuity.[54] Letters granted by one who is deprived of that jurisdiction, e.g., if given by an excommunicated or suspended ordinary when a declaratory or a condemnatory sentence has intervened, would be of no value.[55] This is true not only of the proper bishop, but also of any other public person entitled by the Code to grant these letters.

2. *The Vicar General*

The vicar general of the diocese may also issue these letters, but only when he possesses a special mandate from the bishop.[56] This is one of the limitations set upon the powers of the vicar general.[57]

Proper Bishop for Ordination and Dimissorial Letters, and McBride, *Incardination and Excardination of Seculars,* pp. 302-370.

[52] Cf. can. 334, §§ 2, 3.

[53] Coronata, *De Sacramentis,* II, n. 39; Moeder, *Proper Bishop for Ordination,* p. 85.

[54] Wernz-Vidal, *Ius Canonicum,* Tome IV, pars I, n. 200.

[55] Cans. 2264, 2284.

[56] Can. 958, § 1, 2°.

[57] Cf. can. 368. Whether this means that the vicar general when acting without such a mandate would act invalidly or merely illicitly is a greatly disputed question. For a concise treatment of the problem the reader is referred to Roelker, "The Vicar General and the Special Mandate"—*The Jurist,* II (1942), 346-362. There seems to be sufficient probability on the side of those who hold that such an action would be valid but illicit.

Before the Code the mandate could be given even tacitly, while for cases in which the bishop was absent from the diocese the law itself gave the vicar general the necessary power.[58] In the present law, according to which an express mandate is required, the mandate may be given either orally or in writing. Likewise it may be given for a special case or it may be granted for many cases, e.g., for the time of the absence of the bishop.[59]

What if the bishop upon appointing his vicar general, gives to the latter a special mandate which covers all the cases in which the law requires a special mandate for the vicar general to act? Chelodi [60] conceded the validity of such a mandate but noted that such a procedure did not correspond to the mind of the Code in this regard.[61] Nevertheless it seems that such a mandate would be sufficient for the issuance of dimissorial letters by the vicar general.

3. *The Vicar Capitular or Administrator*

With the consent of the chapter the vicar capitular may grant dimissorial letters after the see has been vacant for one year.[62] In accordance with the norms of canon 105, 1°, the vicar capitular who acts without this consent, whether by neglecting to ask for it or by acting contrary to the mind of the chapter, issues the dimissorials invalidly. The duration of the year in question begins with the time of the death of the bishop or of his removal, resignation, or transferral, and not with the time of the election of the vicar capitular. Since the determining factors do not necessarily coincide in point of time with the start of a day, the year's lapse is to be computed according to the norms of canon 34, § 3, 3°. Thus the day of the bishop's death, removal, resignation, or transferral is not counted as a part of the ensuing year. It is the following day that marks the first day of that year, so that the year will have lapsed completely

[58] Gasparri, *De Sacra Ordinatione,* n. 867. Cf. *supra,* p. 20.

[59] Coronata, *De Sacramentis,* II, n. 37.

[60] *Ius Canonicum de Personis,* p. 312.

[61] Vermeersch-Creusen, (*Epitome,* I, 479) likewise admitted that such a mandate would be valid. One is led to question what would be special about such a mandate.

[62] Can. 958, § 1, 3°.

with the close of the day that marks the anniversary. When, as in the United States, an administrator takes the place of the vicar capitular during the vacancy of the see, he too is empowered to issue these letters. In this case the consent would have to come from the diocesan consultors.[63] Even during the course of this year the vicar capitular or diocesan administrator may also grant dimissorials, but only to those who are pressed with the reception of orders in view of a benefice which has been or is due to be conferred upon them, or in view of some certain office for which provision must be made without delay in consideration of the necessity which exists in the diocese.[64] An example of the former would be the case of a deacon who has been elected, presented, or nominated to a benefice which requires in the holder the priestly order.[65] In the latter case there would have to be a true necessity on the part of the diocese; a mere utility would not suffice as a justifying reason for the issuing of the dimissorials.[66]

Many [67] and Gasparri,[68] both writing before the Code, held that the vicar capitular could issue dimissorial letters for the reception of tonsure during the first year of the vacancy of the see, even though there was no question of a necessitated incumbency in a benefice or of a necessity on the part of the diocese. They held this position on the grounds that tonsure was not an order, and that the law applied only to dimissorial letters for the reception of orders. This argument is no longer valid in view of canon 950, which states that tonsure, is included under the term "orders" whenever this word occurs in the Code.[69] It is difficult to see how in accordance with

[63] Can. 427. Cf. Woywod, *Practical Commentary,* I, 501.

[64] Can. 958, § 1, 3°.

[65] Coronata (*De Sacramentis,* II, n. 37) says that this condition would be verified when suitable priests are scarce because of war, revolution, etc.

[66] Cappello, *De Sacramentis,* Vol. II, pars III, n. 432. Regatillo gives as an example the office of the diocesan judge (*officialis*)—*Ius Sacramentarium,* II, n. 59.

[67] *De Sacra Ordinatione,* p. 154.

[68] *De Sacra Ordinatione,* n. 869.

[69] Coronata, *De Sacramentis,* II, n. 37; Moeder, *Proper Bishop for Ordination,* pp. 86-87.

the norms of this canon a vicar capitular could issue dimissorial letters for promotion to tonsure or even to minor orders within a year after the see has become vacant, since such clerics seldom hold benefices and ordinarily cannot supply for the needs of a diocese, and hence can hardly be termed *"arctati."* [70]

Also before the Code the cathedral chapter itself, or in countries such as the United States the diocesan consultors, could issue these letters prior to the election of the vicar capitular.[71] Under the present law no such right is given to the chapter during this period. Moreover, it is difficult to see how the conditions which are required for the issuance of the letters in the year following the end of tenure in office by the bishop could be verified in the eight days intervening between the vacancy of the see and the election of the vicar capitular or the administrator.[72]

In any event, the vicar capitular is instructed by the Code not to grant dimissorial letters to any candidate who had been rejected by the bishop.[73] This is not commanded under pain of nullity, however, and hence, should the vicar capitular or the administrator nevertheless issue dimissorial letters, the letters would certainly be valid.[74]

4. *The Lesser Prelates*

The vicar and the perfect apostolic, and also the abbot and the prelate *nullius* are empowered by the Code to grant dimissorial letters.[75] They may do so even though they are not bishops, and furthermore even with regard to major orders. This is a departure from the pre-Code law, for according to the Council of Trent prelates inferior to bishops were not allowed to grant such letters even for

[70] Moeder, *loc. cit.*

[71] Conc. Trident., sess. VII, *de ref.*, c. 10. Cf. Gasparri, *De Sacra Ordinatione*, n. 871.

[72] Can. 432, § 1. Cf. Coronata, *De Sacramentis, loc. cit.;* Wernz-Vidal, *Ius Canonicum*, Tomus IV, Vol. I, n. 200.

[73] Can. 958, § 2.

[74] Cappello, *De Sacramentis*, Vol. II, pars III, n. 342; cf. Augustine, *Commentary*, IV, 428.

[75] Can. 958, § 1, 4°.

minor orders.[76] This right belonged to the bishop of the diocese in which the territory of the prelate was situated, or to the nearest bishop.[77]

Those who rule the vicariate or prefecture apostolic during its vacancy enjoy the same power in this matter as the vicar or prefect. No limitation is placed upon them as it is placed upon a vicar capitular or a diocesan administrator.[78] The same is true of the pro-prefect and the pro-vicar who rules the territory while the jurisdiction of the vicar or prefect is impeded.[79]

Article III. Penalties

The bishop who ordains the subject of another bishop without possessing dimissorial letters from that bishop is by that very act suspended from the conferral of orders for one year.[80] The remission of this suspension is reserved to the Holy See. There is applicable here whatever has been said in the preceding chapter concerning the computation of the penalty's duration and the effect of ignorance in reference to the incurring of the penalty which results from the unauthorized act of conferring orders when the requisite testimonials have not been obtained.[81]

The vicar capitular who contrary to the prescriptions of canon 958, § 1, 3°, as outlined above, issues dimissorial letters for ordina-

[76] Conc. Trident., sess. XXIII, *de ref.*, c. 10.

[77] Cf. S. C. Ep. et Reg., *Regien.*, 11 apr. 1766—*Analecta Iuris Pontificii*, XII (1873), 103.

[78] C. P. I., 20 iul. 1929—*AAS*, XXI (1929), 573.

[79] Cans. 309, § 1, and 429, § 1.

[80] Can. 2373, 1°.

[81] Cf. *supra*, pp. 127-128. It is difficult to understand why Coronata (*Institutiones*, IV, n. 2158) should say that it is only probable that a bishop who ordained another's subject with merely oral permission would not incur this penalty, when in his work on the sacraments (*De Sacramentis*, II, n. 36) he says that the oral granting of permission would fulfill the requirements of canon 955, § 1, and the penalty enacted in can. 2373, 1°, is incurred through the failure to observe the requirements of canon 955, § 1. It would seem that as a result of his stand in the latter work he should teach that the bishop so acting could certainly escape the penalty.

tion by that very act incurs a suspension *a divinis.*[82] This is a medicinal penalty, unlike the penalty inflicted upon bishops who confer orders when they lack the needed dimissorial letters, and hence the vicar may be absolved as soon as he shows himself repentent.[83] The absolution from this penalty is not reserved in any way; hence any confessor with proper jurisdiction could absolve. Though canon 2409 refers expressly to the vicar capitular, it is quite clear that its enactment applies also to the administrator in those places in which he takes the place of the vicar capitular.[84]

Prior to the Code it was disputed whether this penalty was incurred simply through the issuance of the dimissorials, or whether it was necessary that the ordination authorized in the letters actually have taken place. Now, however, it is clear that the mere granting of the letters suffices for the incurring of the penalty regardless of whether any ordination has or has not followed.[85]

As to the ordinand, if he should maliciously receive orders though no proper dimissorials or only false dimissorials have been issued, he is by that very act suspended from the exercise of the orders so received.[86] False dimissorials are those which are issued by some person other than the one to whom they are attributed, or, if they were issued by the one to whom they are attributed, have been falsified or substantially changed since their issuance, or contain false attestations, or finally are granted by one who is not entitled to do so.[87]

The penalty in question is a medicinal penalty, as can be gathered from the fact that no time limit is set upon the suspension,[88] and consequently the delinquent may be absolved as soon as he shows himself repentent.[89] The use of the word *malitiose* by the canon indicates that full knowledge and deliberation are postulated, and

[82] Can. 2409.

[83] Can. 2241, § 1.

[84] Coronata, *Institutiones,* IV, n. 2229.

[85] Coronata, *Institutiones, loc. cit.*

[86] Can. 2374.

[87] Coronata, *Institutiones,* IV, n. 2163; Augustine, *Commentary,* VIII, 451.

[88] Cf. can. 2298, 2°; Coronata, *Institutiones,* IV, n. 1799.

[89] Can. 2241, § 1.

therefore any diminution of imputability whether on the part of the intellect or on the part of the will would excuse the ordinand from the penalty.[90] It is Ayrinhac's opinion that the ordinand's reception of tonsure in the absence of the needed dimissorials cannot beget any penalty of suspension, since tonsure does not confer any powers from which one could be suspended.[91] Such an opinion seems hardly correct, however, since the effects of a suspension from a certain order involve not only the prohibition of all acts of that order, but also the prohibition to confer that order, to receive any higher order, or to exercise any higher order should it have been received in spite of the prohibition.[92] Hence there do exist penal effects even for those who have thus wrongfully receive tonsure. Furthermore, it is to be remembered that according to canon 950 the word *ordo* comprises also the reception of tonsure. Accordingly it seems that a person who has wrongfully received tonsure, in violation of the law which forbids him to receive it when the due dimissorials have not been issued, incurs the suspension mentioned in canon 2374.

[90] Can. 2229, § 2.

[91] *Penal Legislation,* p. 285.

[92] Can. 2279, § 2, 5°. Cf. Coronata, *Institutiones,* IV, n. 2167.

CHAPTER IX

THE ORDINATION OF RELIGIOUS

WITH regard to the ordination of religious as compared with the ordination of seculars there are some important differences with reference to the documents required prior to ordination. It remains here to point out these differences. Before being admitted to the novitiate the candidate must present certain documents, many of which the Code demands of candidates for the secular priesthood prior to the reception of orders. Thus the candidate for the novitiate must present proof of baptism, proof of confirmation, testimonial letters from the bishop of his place of origin, and testimonial letters from the ordinary of any diocese in which he had stayed one morally continuous year subsequent to the attainment of his fourteenth year.[1]

It is not the intention of the writer to enter here upon a discussion of the documents which are required of the young man who desires to enter the novitiate. Rather, he wishes to point out, with regard to the documents which are more directly concerned with the ordination of religious candidates, the differences which exist between the law as established for them and the law as established for candidates for the secular priesthood. Before proceeding to that, however, the writer deems it necessary to set forth some definitions of terms which will be used frequently in the course of the discussion.

In the first place, just what is meant by a religious? A religious, in the strict sense of the word—and that is the sense in which it will be used here unless the contrary is noted—is a member of a society approved by legitimate ecclesiastical authority, and as such a member tends towards evangelical perfection according to the laws proper to that society by his profession of public vows, whether perpetual or temporary, the latter renewable after the lapse of a fixed

[1] Can. 544, §§ 1, 2.

period of time.[2] Hence members of a society who live in common without the profession of vows, or whose taking of vows does not imply a profession of public vows, do not fall under the classification of religious as that term is here used.[3] For these, in the matter of receiving orders, the law as established for candidates for the secular priesthood is the guiding norm. Any special prescriptions which the Holy See has enacted must of course be held in due regard.[4]

With regard to those who actually do fall under the classification of religious a further distinction must be made between exempt and non-exempt religious. The former belong to an institute, whether of solemn or of simple vows, which is not subject to the local ordinary.[5] The latter are those who belong to an institute which remains subject to the local ordinary.

Article I. Documents Common to the Ordination of the Exempt and the Non-Exempt

1. *The Petition*

Corresponding to the Instruction *Quam ingens*[6] with reference to the ordination of candidates for the secular priesthood is the Instruction issued by the Sacred Congregation of Religious on December 1, 1931, entitled *Quantum Religiones,* regarding the promotion of candidates for the religious priesthood.[7] According to Maroto,[8] this Instruction was sent not only to the superiors of in-

[2] Can. 488, 1°. Cf. Creusen-Ellis, *Religious Men and Women in the Code* (4. English ed., Milwaukee: Bruce, 1940), p. 8; Coronata, *Institutiones,* I, n. 501. A public vow is one which is accepted in the name of the Church by a legitimate ecclesiastical superior—can. 1308, § 1.

[3] Cf. can. 673, § 1.

[4] Can. 678.

[5] Can. 488, 2°. All religious orders of clerics are exempt. In addition some clerical congregations are also exempt by privilege, e.g., the Redemptorists, Jesuits, Passionists, and Salesians.—Creusen-Ellis, *Religious Men and Women in the Code,* p. 9.

[6] 27 dec. 1930—*AAS,* XXIII (1931), 120-127.

[7] *AAS,* XXIV (1932), 74-81. A translation of this important document may be found in Bouscaren, *Canon Law Digest,* I, 473-482.

[8] "Annotationes"—*CpR,* XIII (1932), 175-180.

stitutes of religious strictly so-called, but also to the superiors of those institutes of men who do not take any public vows. Hence the regulations established therein became a guiding norm also for these latter institutes, in accordance with canon 678 [9] which makes due provision for any special prescriptions established by the Holy See.

According to the Instruction each candidate before the profession of temporary vows shall present to the superior a written petition, in which he shall expressly state his vocation to the religious and clerical state, and at the same time announce his firm resolve to give himself forever to service in the ranks of the clergy in the regular life.[10] Thus, unlike the corresponding requirement for secular candidates, the content of the petition presented by the religious is definitely determined in the Instruction, although it does not prescribe the exact words to be used.[11] A further difference is seen in that the petition presented by the religious is to be directed to his superior, whereas the petition presented by the secular candidate is to be directed to his ordinary. The petition and declaration which are required by the Instruction are to be preserved in the archives.[12]

While only one petition is required by the Instruction, Coronata is of the opinion that the ordinary or the major superior may require another explicit petition on the part of the candidate, since very often some years intervene between the presentation of the petition and the promotion to orders in consequence of the fact that the petition is to be presented before the religious makes his temporary profession.[13]

9 "In iis quae ad studiorum rationem et ad suscipiendos ordines pertinent, sodales iisdem legibus tenentur ac saeculares clerici, salvis peculiaribus praescriptionibus a Sancta Sede datis."

10 Instr. *Quantum Religiones,* n. 14—*AAS,* XXIV (1932), 80. Cf. canon 992.

11 Cf. Vermeersch—"Annotationes"—*Periodica,* XXI (1932), 188-193.

12 Instr. *Quantum Religiones, loc. cit.*

13 *De Sacramentis,* II, p. 342, footnote 3. He also gives a sample of the form which may be used for this purpose.—Appendix III, I, b.

Following the receipt of the petition the superior shall make an investigation into the candidate's life, morals, character, studies, etc., calling upon the candidate's spiritual prefect, not to be confused with his confessor, for help in this matter, as well as interviewing the candidate personally to make sure that he is freely and consciously seeking orders in the religious state. A proper record of the making of these inquiries should be drawn up and kept in the archives.[14]

2. *Declaration of Freedom*

As with the candidates for the secular priesthood, the candidate for the religious priesthood prior to his promotion to the subdiaconate must make a declaration under oath to attest his freedom in embracing that order and his understanding of the obligations attached thereto.[15] Unlike the declaration to be made by the secular candidate, this declaration need be made but once, viz., before the reception of the subdiaconate. Moreover, it suffices for the candidate merely to sign a printed form of the declaration, since that is all that is demanded by the language of the Instruction.[16] The form which this declaration is to take is included in the actual text of the Instruction, unlike the form which in connection with the Instruction for secular candidates was added as an appendix. The oath is to be taken before the religious superior, who shall in turn attest to the fulfillment of this and of all the other requirements of the Instruction in his testimonial or dimissorial letters.[17]

[14] Instr. *Quantum Religiones, loc. cit.*

[15] *Ibid.*, n. 17—*AAS,* XXIV (1932), 80-81. The Instruction also outlines the investigations which are to precede promotion to major orders, which correspond very much to those ordered for secular candidates.

[16] Cf. Maroto, "Annotationes"—*CpR,* XIII (1932), 175-180. The language of the two Instructions clearly indicates this difference. The Instruction *Quam ingens* (*AAS,* XXIII [1931], 125) uses the words *"hic scribere debebit sua manu declarationem,"* while the Instruction *Quantum Religiones* (*AAS,* XXIV [1932], 80) uses the words *"manu propria candidati subscriptam."*

[17] Instr. *Quantum Religiones,* n. 19—*AAS,* XXIV (1932), 81.

3. *Profession of Faith and Oath Against Modernism*

Like the candidate for the secular priesthood, the religious prior to his promotion to the subdiaconate must make the profession of faith and take the prescribed anti-Modernistic oath. According to a decision of the Sacred Consistorial Congregation these must be taken before the bishop who is to confer the orders, and not before the religious superior.[18]

The decision made no distinction between exempt and non-exempt religious, and therefore, it must be concluded, even in the case of exempt religious the profession and oath are to be made before the bishop who is to confer orders. Vermeersch [19] interpreted this decision as meaning the bishop in whose diocese the orders were conferred whether the bishop of that diocese personally conferred the orders or whether he gave permission to some other bishop to confer the orders. There does not seem to be any reason, however, why the bishop could not delegate the religious superior, exempt or non-exempt, for this purpose. In either case, whether the bishop receives them personally or through his delegate, the document attesting to the fulfillment of these requirements is to be preserved in the archives of the ordaining prelate.[20]

Article II. Documents Peculiar to the Ordination of the Non-Exempt

1. *Testimonial of the Religious Superior*

Candidates for ordination in an institute which is not exempt from the jurisdiction of the local ordinary are governed in general by the law as established for seculars.[21] Hence such candidates must present all the documents required of a secular candidate. These documents are listed in canon 993. Consideration has been given

[18] S. C. Consist., 17 dec. 1910—*AAS,* III (1911), 25. Cf. Coronata, *Institutiones,* II, 970.

[19] "Annotationes"—*Periodica,* V (1913), 272.

[20] S. C. Consist., 25 oct. 1910—*AAS,* II (1910), 856-857. Cf. *supra,* pp. 102-104.

[21] Can. 964, 4°.

to them previously. In addition to all these documents a testimonial also from their religious superior is to be presented.[22] This requirement has no application for such candidates who belong to clerical societies in which the members do not take public vows, for such societies do not come under the heading of religious institutes as understood in the Code.[23] The major superior mentioned in canon 993, 5° may be either the superior general (*supremus moderator*), the provincial superior, the vicar of either of them, or any other superior who has power and authority equivalent to that of a provincial.[24] In this latter classification are included the vicar general of the institute, the one who is empowered with canonical visitatorial competence and the vice-provincial.[25]

The testimonial letters here in question are not to be confused with the dimissorial letters issued by the major superiors of exempt religious institutes and also of non-exempt religious institutes whose major superiors enjoy special privileges by indult in the matter of issuing dimissorial letters for their subjects' reception of orders.[26] At the same time it must be borne in mind that the requiring of these testimonial letters points to an additional demand which the Code imposes with reference to candidates in religious institutes, and does not supplant the demand for all the other required documents, as does, for instance, the dimissorial letter which is furnished by the religious superior in accordance with the ruling enacted in canon 995, § 1.[27]

In view of attentuating circumstances the testimonial letter may attest to the presence of such documents as the baptismal certificate,

[22] Can. 993, 5°.

[23] Can. 673, § 1.

[24] Can. 488, 8°.

[25] Creusen-Ellis, *Religious Men and Women in the Code,* p. 16.

[26] Can. 995, § 1. Blat seems to confuse the two, for in describing the contents of the testimonial letter he uses almost the exact wording of canon 995, § 1, which deals with the religious superior's granting of the dimissorial letter.—*De Sacramentis,* n. 371.

[27] Cf. can 995, § 2. Blat (*loc. cit.*) seems to imply that there is no additional need of testimonials particularly with regard to the further testimonial letters required from the local ordinary. Cf. "Ex Privata Jurisprudentia"—*Ius Pontificium,* IX (1929), 203.

the confirmation certificate, duly furnished testimonial letters, etc., in the files of the religious house in the same way in which the rector of the seminary may attest to the presence of such documents in the files of the seminary. Such a testimonial letter seems to satisfy the requirement for the presentation of the various documents designated in the law.[28]

The Code does not specify what is to be the content of the testimonial letter furnished by the major superior. It seems quite clear, however, that it should attest to the profession of the candidate in the religious institute, since such a candidate may not be promoted to any orders as long as his status is that of a novice,[29] and that it should furthermore attest to the perpetual profession made by the religious, since such a candidate may not be promoted to major orders as long as his status is that of a religious in temporary profession.[30] In the case of religious institutes in which perpetual vows are not pronounced, major orders are nevertheless not to be conferred before the completion of three years of temporary vows.[31]

Furthermore, the letter should attest to the fact that the candidate is actually attached to a religious house which is under the jurisdiction of the superior issuing the letter. It should also contain an estimate of the candidate's fitness, in the judgment of the superior, for the reception of orders. Hence it should speak of his life, character, morals, etc. According to some authors it should also attest to the completion of the required studies on the part of the candidate.[32] In the opinion of the writer, the latter does not seem necessary, unless the testimonial of studies as required by canon 993, 2°, is to be combined with the testimonial of the religious superior. If the candidate has made his profession in an

[28] Cf. *supra*, p. 67. Gallagher (*Examination of the Qualities of the Ordinand*, pp. 109-110) seems inconsistent in denying this right to the religious superior while granting it to the rector of the seminary.—*Ibid.*, p. 55.

[29] Can. 567, § 2.

[30] Can. 964, 4°.

[31] Instr. *Quantum Religiones*, n. 15—*AAS*, XXIV (1932), 80.

[32] Woywod, "Testimonial Letters before Ordination"—*The Homiletic and Pastoral Review* (New York, 1900—), XXIII (1922-1923), 375-382 (cited *HPR*); Blat, *De Sacramentis*, n. 373.

institute whose members take only temporary vows, then there should also be some mention of the publication of the candidate's name in his parish church.[33] Finally, the letter should likewise contain some statement of the title on which the candidate is to receive his ordination.

How often need such a testimonial be presented? The Code does not specify whether it is to be presented merely before tonsure or also before each separate ordination. But, as with the other documents listed in canon 993, it seems that it is to be presented before each advancement in orders on the part of such a candidate, since with reference to his ordination he is subject to the law which obliges seculars. Obviously it would not be necessary to mention such things as the candidate's presentation of his baptismal certificate or certificate of confirmation, since the candidate's earlier presentation of these documents when he received tonsure continues to evince for these documents the same probative force once for all.

2. *Testimonial of the Local Ordinary*

Prior to his entrance into the novitiate the candidate is required to present testimonial letters from the ordinary of his place of origin as well as from the ordinary of any place in which he had spent one morally continuous year after the attainment of his fourteenth year.[34] When the candidate seeks promotion to orders, may such letters be accepted as satisfying the requirement of canon 993, 4°? Contrary to the opinion of Blat, who favors these letters as acceptable for this purpose,[35] it must be held that they do not respond to what the law demands. As has been seen,[36] it is absolutely necessary in the matter of testimonial letters for ordination that the letters be issued expressly for the reception of orders. Thus letters issued for the purpose of a candidate's entry in the novitiate would not be acceptable unless the bishop, in foreseeing the candi-

[33] Can. 998.

[34] Can. 544, § 2.

[35] *De Sacramentis,* n. 371.

[36] *Supra,* p. 108.

date's future ordination, inserted some clause with regard to the candidate's present fitness for orders and his freedom from canonical impediments thereto.[37]

Moreover, canons 544, § 2, and 994, § 1, point to a divergent duration of time in a candidate's continued residence in a given place as a factor that calls for the presentation of testimonial letters. With reference to a candidate's entry in the novitiate that period of time is designated as a morally continuous year; with relation, however, to a candidate's ordination the period of time is determined as the lapse of six months, or, in the case of soldiers, of three months. Thus there may be a demand for more testimonial letters on the part of a candidate for ordination than on the part of one who seeks to enter a religious novitiate. But the testimonial letters which cover these periods of time need to be presented only once, namely, before the candidate's promotion to tonsure. If, at a later time the candidate had become reduced to the lay state but thereupon was readmitted to clerical status, testimonial letters covering the period of his secularization would be required in accordance with canon 993, 4°.[38]

What, now, is to be said regarding the time spent in the religious institute? Is a testimonial letter from the bishop of the diocese in which the house is situated necessary in the supposition that the candidate has spent six morally continuous months in that house? The case is somewhat similar to that in which a secular candidate for orders has spent a similar amount of time in the seminary. With reference to this latter case it was decided that a testimonial letter from the local ordinary is necessary.[39] For the same reason it seems that the religious candidate must obtain such a letter from the ordinary in whose diocese the house is situated.

A further indication of this requirement, not too clearly expressed, may be found in Gasparri [40] and Coronata.[41] Both of these

[37] Gallagher, *Examination of the Qualities of the Ordinand,* p. 103.

[38] Woywod, "Testimonial Letters Before Ordination"—*HPR,* XXIII (1922-1923), 378.

[39] *Supra,* pp. 115-117.

[40] *De Sacra Ordinatione,* n. 711.

[41] *De Sacramentis,* II, n. 178.

authors visualized the case of a secularized religious who sought promotion to orders in the secular priesthood. They taught that a letter from the major superior of an exempt religious institute satisfied the requirements regarding the presentation of testimonial letters covering the candidate's stay in the religious institute. But they contended that the same was not true if the letter was issued by the superior of a non-exempt institute. Thus it seems that these authors considered a letter from the local ordinary as necessary for covering that period of time, since they exclusively recognized the exempt religious superior's letter as satisfying the law in its demand for the presentation of acceptable testimonials. There does not seem to be any reason, however, why the local ordinary could not delegate the major superior of a non-exempt religious institute to issue this letter.

3. *Dimissorial Letters*

According to canon 964, 4°, members of non-exempt religious institutes in the matter of the proper bishop of ordination are ruled by the law that is established for seculars. That law demands that each candidate is to receive his ordination from his own bishop or from some other bishop who has become duly authorized through dimissorial letters to confer the ordination.[42]

With regard to the proper bishop for the ordination of members of non-exempt religious institutes, the writer does not intend to enter here upon a discussion of that somewhat lengthy problem. Suffice it to say that members of these institutes are governed by the same prescriptions as those established by the Code for the ordination of candidates for the secular priesthood. Thus the proper bishop of ordination is the bishop of the diocese in which the candidate has his domicile. However, since professed religious are not obliged to take the oath prescribed for those whose place of domicile does not coincide with their place of origin,[43] the bishop of the place in which the candidate has his domicile, whether or not that place is at the same time the diocese of his origin, is the candidate's proper bishop for ordination.

[42] Can. 955, § 1.
[43] Can. 956.

Coronata [44] teaches that since it is quite difficult for professed religious to establish a domicile,[45] a quasi—domicile on the part of such a candidate would suffice to constitute a bishop as the proper bishop for ordination.[46] As far as the letters themselves are concerned, there apply the same rules as have been outlined above with regard to dimissorial letters for secular candidates.

Article III. Documents Required By Exempt Religious

Included under the term exempt religious, as used here, are not only those religious who are exempt by reason of the law itself, but also those who are exempt by special privilege as well as those whose superiors in non-exempt religious institutes have by means of a special indult been empowered to grant dimissorial letters for their subjects as candidates for ordination.

These candidates are not subject to the law of canon 993 in its listing of the documents that are to be presented prior to ordination. For them all that is required is a dimissorial letter issued by the major superior of their institute.[47] Unlike the testimonial letter which the major superior of non-exempt religious is to furnish, this letter is by the law of the Code to evince a specifically designated content.[48] It should attest to the fact that the candidate has made his profession, at least a temporary one, for his promotion to tonsure or the minor orders, and a solemn or perpetual one, for his promotion to major orders.[49] It should also testify to the fact that the religious candidate is formally attached to a house which is

[44] *De Sacramentis,* II, n. 46.

[45] Cf. Coronata, *Institutiones,* I, n. 128.

[46] For a fuller discussion of the problems involved here the reader is referred to Fanfani, *De Iure Religiosorum ad Normam Codicis Iuris Canonici* (2. ed., Taurini-Romae: Marietti, 1925), pp. 307, 320; Woywod, *Practical Commentary,* I, 505-506; McBride, *Incardination and Excardination,* p. 344; Moeder, *Proper Bishop for Ordination,* pp. 107-108; Schaaf, "Episcopus Proprius Ordinationis Religiosorum"—*ER,* XC (1934), 508.

[47] Can. 964, 2°.

[48] Can. 995, § 2.

[49] Cans. 995, § 1; 964, §§ 3, 4.

situated in the diocese of the bishop to whom the letters are directed, and which is at the same time subject to the superior issuing the letter.

Testimony regarding studies must also be included in the letter. In this matter it seems that religious are governed by the same requirements as secular candidates,[50] and that the more stringent requirements which were established for religious prior to the Code[51] have been abrogated.[52] Included also must be testimony that the candidate has successfully passed the examination in orders which is required by canon 996, § 1.[53] Lastly, canon 995, § 1 states that the letter is to contain testimony regarding the fulfillment of all the other demands made by the law.[54] The provision calls for the giving of testimony concerning the performance of the spiritual exercises required prior to the reception of orders,[55] the fulfillment of the requirements established by the Instruction *Quantum Religiones*, the identification of the source of exemption, the selection of a canonical title of ordination, and finally the compliance with the law regarding the mandatory profession of faith and the oath against Modernism. If, however, with regard to these latter considerations the superior simply states that the requirements of the Code and of the Constitutions have all been duly fulfilled, such a comprehensive statement certainly seems to satisfy the requirements of the law as enacted in canon 995, § 1.[56] Once such a dimissorial letter has been received, the bishop may proceed to the ordination of the candidate without any further documents.[57]

As to the actual form of the letter Moeder[58] indicates the following elements which should appear therein: date of issuance, name

[50] Can. 976, §§ 1, 2. Cf. *supra*, pp. 76-79, 94-96.

[51] S. C. de Rel., 7 sept. 1909—*AAS*, I (1909), 701-704. Cf. *supra*, pp. 50-51.

[52] Coronata, *De Sacramentis*, II, n. 181.

[53] "Quilibet promovendus sive saecularis sive religiosus debet praevium ac diligens examen subire circa ipsum ordinem suscipiendum."

[54] ". . . deque aliis iure requisitis."

[55] Can. 1001, § 4.

[56] Gallagher, *Examination of the Qualities of the Ordinand*, p. 116; Goyeneche, S., "Consultationes"—*CpR*, VIII (1927), 376-379.

[57] Can. 995, § 2.

[58] *Proper Bishop for Ordination*, pp. 122-123.

of grantor—full name and title—, designation of bishop who is to ordain, mention of orders for which the letter is issued, testimony of the grantor to the fitness of the candidate, attestation of the religious profession of the candidate, name of monastery to which he is attached, statement of exemption, and finally the signature of the grantor and the seal of the institute.

To whom are these letters to be directed? Some religious institutes enjoy the privilege of sending candidates to any bishop in communion with the Holy See. This is not the general rule, however, for the religious superior is definitely limited by the law in the matter of who is to ordain such candidates.[59] The religious superior may direct his dimissorial letter only to the bishop of the diocese in which is situated the house to which the ordinand is attached. Only when that bishop is absent, or gives his permission, or is of a different rite, or, though present in the diocese, does not intend to hold ordinations at the next regularly appointed time, or finally the see is vacant and the one who is ruling it is not a bishop in orders, may the letters be directed to any other bishop.[60]

When any one of these conditions is fulfilled, so that the candidate may be sent to some other bishop for ordination, there is required an authentic attestation of this fact from the episcopal curia.[61] This attestation should be made by the vicar general, chancellor, or secretary to the bishop,[62] and, according to Augustine,[63] should bear the diocesan seal. The letters may then be directed to any bishop in communion with the Holy See,[64] provided that he be of the same rite as the ordinand, unless there is a special indult to the con-

59 Can. 965: "Episcopus ad quem Superior religiosus litteras dimissorias mittere debet, est Episcopus dioecesis, in qua sita est domus religiosa, ad cuius familiam pertinet ordinandus."

60 Can. 966, § 1.

61 Can. 966, § 2.

62 Benedictus XIV, const. *Impositi nobis,* 27 febr. 1747, § 12—*Fontes,* n. 376; Wernz-Vidal, *Ius Canonicum,* Tomus IV, Vol. I, n. 197; Coronata, *De Sacramentis,* II, n. 45.

63 *Commentary,* IV, 441-442.

64 Can. 961.

trary, except in the case in which the proper bishop freely gave permission for the candidate to be ordained by some other bishop and in so doing designated that bishop.

Superiors are warned in this matter not to send their candidates fraudulently to a religious house in another diocese or purposely to defer the time of ordination to a time when they know that the bishop will be away, or, if present, will not be having ordinations at that time.[65]

As long as the proper attestation regarding the fulfillment of the provision of canon 966, § 1, has not been furnished by a duly accredited curial official, any bishop who even though he has received the dimissorial letter of the major religious superior, ordains the latter's subject when he belongs to a religious house which is situated outside the territory of the ordaining prelate, thereby incurs a suspension which bars him from the conferring of orders for a year and the remission of this suspension is reserved to the Holy See.[66] As far as the ordaining prelate is concerned, he does not fall a prey to the enacted penalty as long as he relies upon the attestation presented by a duly accredited curial official, even though the religious superior had acted fraudulently, with a view to having the attestation furnished in the case. This conclusion appears imperative in the light of the principle which calls for a strict interpretation in all penal matters.[67] This strictness of interpretation in turn implies that with reference to all alleged offenders the law assumes the benign attitude of exculpating rather than of incriminating such persons.[68]

On the other hand, if contrary to the prescriptions of canons 965-967 a religious superior presumes to send his subjects to a bishop other than the local episcopal ordinary for their ordination, he thereby becomes suspended from the celebration of Mass for one month.[69]

[65] Can. 967.

[66] Can. 2373, 4°.

[67] Can. 19.

[68] Can. 2219, § 1.

[69] Can. 2410.

APPENDIX I

SCHEMA OF DOCUMENTS REQUIRED FOR THE RECEPTION OF ORDERS [1]

	Tonsure	Half-Minors	Full-Minors	Subdiaconate	Diaconate	Priesthood
Petition for Orders—*Quam ingens* & Can. 992	x[2]			x		
Pastor's Investigation—*Quam ingens* & Can. 1000, § 1	x			x		
Testimony regarding Baptism—Can. 993, 1°	x					
Testimony regarding Confirmation—Can. 993, 1°	x					
Testimony regarding the Last Order Conferred—Can. 993, 1°		x	x	x	x	x
Testimony regarding Studies—Can. 976	x			x	x	x
Testimony regarding the Examination in Orders—Can. 996, § 1	x	x	x	x	x	x
Testimonial of the Rector—Can. 993, 3°	x	x	x	x	x	x
Testimonial Letter from Major Religious Superior—Can. 993, 4°	x	x	x	x	x	x
Testimony regarding Performance of the Spiritual Exercises—Can. 1001	x	x	x	x	x	x
Testimonial Letters—Can. 993, 4°	x	x	x	x	x	x
Oath regarding Intended Retention of Domicile—Can. 956	x					
Testimony regarding the Publication of the Banns—Can. 998				x	x	x
Oath of Service to Diocese—Can. 981, § 1				x		
Declaration of Freedom—*Quam ingens*				x[3]	x	x
Profession of Faith—Can. 1406, 7°				x		
Oath against Modernism—*Sacrorum Antistitum*				x		

Dispensation from Lack of Requisite Age—Can. 975				x	x	x
Dispensation from Interstices—Can. 978				x	x	x
Dispensation from Impediment Arising from non-Catholic Parentage—Can. 987, 1°	x					
Dispensation from Banns—Can. 998, § 1				x	x	x
Other Dispensations (*in specie*)	x	x	x	x	x	x
Dimissorial Letters—Can. 955	x[4]	x	x	x	x	x
Notification of Church of Baptism—Can. 1011				x		

1 "x" indicates for which order the document is required.

2 According to the Instruction *Quantum Religiones,* religious are to present the petition prior to the profession of temporary vows.

3 According to the Instruction *Quantum Religiones* this declaration on the part of religious candidates is necessary only once, prior to subdiaconate.

4 Dimissorial letters sent by a religious superior to a bishop other than the local bishop should be accompanied by an attestation from the curia of the local bishop in accordance with canon 966 § 2.

APPENDIX II

MODEL FORMS

1. Petition for Tonsure and Minor Orders

I, the undersigned ...., of the diocese of ...., feeling myself called by God to the clerical state, freely, and moved thereto by no consideration other than the promotion of the glory of God in the service of the Church and the salvation of my own soul, intending ultimately to embrace the Sacred Order of Priesthood, do hereby petition His Excellency, ..., the Bishop of the diocese of ...., that I may be admitted to tonsure and minor orders.

....
(Date)

....
(Signature)

2. Petition for Major Orders

I, the undersigned .... of the diocese of ...., having duly received tonsure and minor orders, freely, and moved thereto by no consideration other than the promotion of the glory of God in the service of the Church and my own salvation, do hereby present my petition to His Excellency, ..., the Bishop of the diocese of ...., for advancement to the Sacred Order of ....

....
(Date)

....
(Signature)

3. Confidential Investigation to be Conducted by Pastor in accordance with the Instruction *Quam ingens*

I, the undersigned .... pastor of the Church of ...., do hereby testify that the answers herein set down are true to the best of my knowledge and belief.

In the first place I declare that Mr. ...., a student at .... Seminary, has been known to me for the period from .... 19...... to .... 19......

1. Is he faithful and devoted to his exercises of piety: namely, meditation, Mass, visits to the Blessed Sacrament, and recitation of the Rosary?............
2. Does he devoutly frequent the Sacraments of Penance and the Holy Eucharist? ....
3. Is he diligent and religious in the service of the sanctuary? ....
4. Does he teach Christian Doctrine? If so, did he perform his work diligently? ....
5. Does he manifest a desire and earnestness to promote the worship of God, to care for souls, and does he show a zealous inclination for exercising sacred functions? ....
6. Has he a special interest in any particular studies, and with what diligence does he follow this interest? ....
7. Has he been given to reading profane books and papers which foster sentiments against faith or morals? ....
8. During his holidays does he dress in a manner befitting a seminarian? ....
9. Has he associated with persons of doubtful reputation? ....
10. Has he conducted himself with persons of the other sex in such a way as to cause scandal or criticism or suspicion? ....
11. Does he seek recreation in places unbecoming to his state in life? ....
12. Is he always proper in speech? .... Or does he use language unbecoming a seminarian? ....
13. Has he laid himself open to any blame in respect to his morals or to his submission to the doctrines and precepts of the Church? ....

14. How does he conduct himself in the company of boys and young men? .... With members of the other sex? ....
15. Does he show any leaning towards a life of ease; towards worldly pleasures ....
16. Has he shown any inclination to indulge in intoxicants? ....
17. Does he manifest the virtue of charity? Does he render proper submission and deference to his superiors? ....
18. What is the public opinion concerning his vocation? ....
19. What is the opinion of your Reverend Assistants? ....
20. Are there indications of any infirmity in the family? In particular, are there any signs of mental disease or moral depravity in the family? ....
21. Are his parents or others urging him to enter the priesthood? ....

Additional remarks: ....

Name ....

L.S. Parish ....

at ....

Date ....

4. Testimony of Studies Required for Each Order according to canon 993, 2°

Ego infrascriptus Rector Seminarii .... coram Domino testor ....huius Seminarii alumnum e Dioecesi .... studia a canone 976 ad susceptionem .... ordinis requisita rite peregisse.

Datum ex Aedibus Seminarii apud ....

Die ...., mensis ...., anni 19............

L. S.

....

Rector

5. Testimony of Examination in Orders according to canon 996, § 1

Ego infrascriptus Rector Seminarii ....
coram Domino testor ....huius Seminarii alumnum e Dioecesi ....
diligens circa ordines ....ab ipso suscipiendos examen feliciter subiisse.

Datum ex Aedibus Seminarii apud ....

Die ...., mensis ...., anni 19...........

L. S.

....

Rector

6. Testimonial of Rector regarding the Performance of the Investigations required by the Instruction *Quam ingens*

Ego infrascriptus Rector Seminarii .... acceptis litteris quibus mihi commissum est munus faciendi inquisitionem de idoneitate, qualitatibus et vocatione ad statum clericalem candidati .... mandato mihi commisso adimplendo statim manus apposui. Ad illud autem rite obeundum praefectos et magistros eiusdem candidati prius singulariter et deinde collegialiter convocatos audivi circa signa vocationis sacerdotalis, propositis iisdem interrogatoriis iuxta modulos a Sacra Congregatione de Sacramentis definitos.

Ex his autem inquisitionibus, quae allegantur, satis constat candidatum .... vere esse idoneum ad statum sacerdotalem et signa praebuisse vocationis, videlicet: pietatem, modestiam, castitatem, ad sacras functiones propensionem, profectum in studiis sacris, bonos mores.

Quae cum ita sint, persuasum habeo ipsum candidatum .... ad statum clericalem idoneum esse et vera vocatione sacerdotali donatum, ita ut promoveri possit.

In quorum fidem subscribo.

....

Rector

Die ...., mensis ...., anni ....

L. S.

7. Testimonial of Rector [1]

Excellentia Vestra:

Ego, infrascriptus Rector Seminarii .... testor de sequentibus necessariis ad promotionem .... ad ordinem subdiaconatus:

1. Me, qua delegatum vestrum, petitionem inclusam candidati recepisse.
2. Candidatum feliciter peregisse studia per canonem 976 requisita.
3. Candidatum comprobatum esse a Rectore et Facultate huius Seminarii.
4. Candidatum obtinuisse litteras testimoniales requisitas.
5. Praescriptiones Instructionis *Quam ingens* quoad investigationes de idoneitate candidati peractas esse.
6. Candidatum feliciter subiisse examen de ordine subdiaconatus suscipiendo.
7. Candidatum emisisse requisitam, quam includo, Professionem Fidei.
8. Candidatum emisisse declarationem quam includo juratam de libertate etc. ad normas Instructionis *Quam ingens.*
9. Candidatum praestitisse iusiurandum quod includo anti-modernisticum.
10. Publicationes peractas esse secundum normam per canonem 998 praescriptam.
11. Candidatum peregisse (vel peracturum esse) exercitia spiritualia in hoc Seminario per sex integros dies.

Datum ex Aedibus Seminarii ....

Die ...., mensis ...., anni ....

L. S.

....

Rector

[1] This is a form which may be found useful especially for candidates studying in a seminary in another diocese.

8. Testimony regarding Performance of the Spiritual Exercises

Ego infrascriptus Rector Seminarii .... coram Domino testor .... alumnum eiusdem Seminarii de Dioecesi ...., a die .... mensis ...., ad diem .... mensis .... anni 19 ...., Spiritualibus Exercitiis per .... integros dies iuxta normas statutas vacasse prout ad ordinem .... suscipiendum canone 1001 praescribitur.

Datum ex Aedibus Seminarii ....

Die ...., mensis ...., anni 19 ....

L. S.

....

Rector

9. Testimonial Letter

Praesentibus litteris testamur dilectum filium nostrum ...., dum intra limites nostrae iurisdictionis moras habuit, vitam duxisse morum honestate et religione commendabilem, et nullum, in quantum nobis constat, contraxisse impedimentum quominus ad militiam clericalem suscipiendam admitti possit.

Datum .... ex Aedibus .... sub manu sigilloque Nostro die .... mensis .... A. D. 19...........

L. S.

....

Episcopus...............................

10. Oath of Intended Retention of Domicile[2]

Ego infrascriptus .... in Dioecesi .... natus, sed domicilium meum nunc in Dioecesi .... habens, animum meum in hac eadem Dioecesi perpetuo manendi his litteris declaro.

Sic voveo ac iuro, sic me Deus adiuvet, et haec Sancta Evangelia quae manibus meis tango.

Die ...., mensis ...., anni 19...........

....

(Signature)

11. Testimony regarding the Publications of the Banns

Reverend and dear Father:

This is to inform you that Mr. ...., a seminarian from your parish, is to be promoted to the sacred order of .... on .... 19........... In accordance with canon 998 of the Code of Canon Law would you kindly make the required announcement in your church and return the form below in attestation that you have done so?

Sincerely yours in Christ,

....

Rector

This is to certify that I, the undersigned .... pastor of .... Church, in accordance with canon 998 have made the required announcement of the forthcoming promotion of Mr. ...., to the sacred

[2] If this oath is taken before the rector as delegate of the ordinary, then some mention of that delegation should be incorporated together with the signature of the delegate, as for example:

Rite coram me delegato emissum.

....

Rector

order of ...., and know of no reason why he should not be advanced.
Date ...., 19 ....
L. S.

....
Pastor

12. Oath of Service to Diocese

Ego .... candidatus ad ordinem subdiaconatus titulo servitii dioecesis suscipiendi, ad normam iuris spondeo ac iuro me Dioecesi .... perpetuo inserviturum, sub Ordinarii praedictae Dioecesis pro tempore Auctoritate.

Sic me Deus adiuvet, et haec sancta Dei Evangelia quae manibus tango.

....
(Signature)

Die ...., mensis ...., anni ....

13. Declaration to be made before the Reception of Major Orders according to the norms of the Instruction *Quam ingens*

I, the undersigned ...., having presented to the Bishop my petition for the reception of the subdiaconate (diaconate, or priesthood), now at the approach of Sacred Ordination, having diligently weighed the matter before God, do hereby testify under oath, first that I am not compelled to the reception of this Sacred Order by any coercion or force, or by any fear, but do spontaneously desire it and of my own full and free will wish to receive it, as I am convinced and feel that I am really called by God.

I profess that I know fully all the obligations and other consequences which this Sacred Order entails, which of my own will I desire and purpose to receive, and I resolve to observe them all, with the help of God, most diligently during the entire course of my life.

In particular I declare that I clearly understand all that the law of celibacy implies, and I firmly resolve that, with God's help, I will willingly fulfill it and keep it in its entirety until death.

Finally, in all sincerity, I promise that I will most obediently observe, according to the Sacred Canons, all that my superiors command me and ecclesiastical discipline requires, and that I am prepared to set a good example both in word and deed, in order that I may be rewarded by God for the undertaking of so great an office.

So I promise, vow, and swear, so help me God and these His Holy Gospels which I touch with my hands.

Date ....

....
(Signature of candidate)

14. Dimissorial Letter

A.

Dilecto Nobis in Christo .... acolytho, nostri Seminarii maioris alumno salutem in Domino, qui est vera salus.

Ut ab Excellentissimo Domino .... Episcopo .... ad ordinem subdiaconatus, ad titulum servitii dioecesis a Nobis recognitum et approbatum promoveri possis et valeas, statutis a iure temporibus, et servatis temporum interstitiis, licentiam et facultatem concedimus et impertimur.

Insimul autem testamur, te de legitimo matrimonio natum, prima clericali tonsura insignitum, ad quattuor ordines minores rite promotum, in aetate legitima constitutum, utpote natum die .... mensis .... anni ...., in propria paroeciali ecclesia .... ad normam iuris proclamationes factae fuisse, praevia inquisitione ad normam *Instructionis* Sacrae Congregationis de Disciplina Sacramentorum 27 Decembris 1930 idoneum repertum fuisse, et signa clericalis et sacerdotalis vocationis indubia praebuisse, ac bonis moribus vitaeque integritate aliisque requisitis ornatum esse, atque nulla irregularitate aut canonico impedimento, quod sciamus, ligatum esse.

Testamur pariter te in exeunte tertio cursus theologici anno studiis sacris incumbere in nostro Seminario maiori, et propositum habere ad sacrum presbyteratum ascendendi, necnon declarationem propria manu conscriptam et coram Nobis iureiurando firmatam circa tuam libertatem in amplectendo statu sacerdotali, itemque circa tuam scientiam de obligationibus assumendis tamquam ordinibus sacris annexis, praesertim de caelibatu et castitate servanda, ad normam *Instructionis* citatae emississe.

Testamur etiam te coram Nobis circa ordinem suscipiendum et circa alios tractatus theologicos examini subiectum fuisse et satis edoctum repertum fuisse.

Denique testamur has nostras litteras valere etiam pro tempore quo extra nostram dioecesim moratus es, cum pro tali tempore necessarias litteras testimoniales ipsi obtinuerimus ad normam iuris.

Praecipimus autem tibi ut exercitiis spiritualibus integris diebus sex saltem vaces, de quibus rite peractis testimonium Episcopo ordinanti exhibebis.

In quorum fidem.

Datum .... ex Aedibus .... sub signo Nostro die ...., mensis ....,
anni 19...........
L. S.

....
(Ordinarius loci)

....
Cancellarius

B.

Dilecto nobis in Christo Dno ....
.... Seminarii .... alumno, salutem et benedictionem in Domino.

Cum ob rationes nobis apprime notas, sacram ordinationem a nobismetipsis suscipere non possis, per has Litteras Dimissoriales, habitis testimoniis quae iure exiguntur, tibi licentiam et facultatem concedimus, ut coram Exmo ac Rmo Dno .... Episcopo ...., aut quolibet alio Antistite gratiam et communionem cum Sede Apostolica habente sacrasque ordinationes rite celebrante, te sistas; et Eum rogamus ut pro pastorali sua benignitate te ad .... promovere dignetur.

Datum .... ex aedibus Curiae hac die .... mensis .... anno ....

....

Episcopus

L. S.

....

Cancellarius

15. Petition to be made by Candidates in Religious Institutes

I, the undersigned .... a novice in the Order or Congregation of .... in the Province of .... feeling myself called by God to the religious and clerical state, and moved thereto by no consideration other than the desire to serve God in that state, do hereby petition my Superior, the Very Reverend .... that I may be admitted to the profession of temporary vows and to the clerical state, intending ultimately to embrace the Sacred Order of Priesthood.

....

(Date)

....

(Signature)

16. Testimonial of the Major Religious Superior

Praesentibus litteris nostrum alumnum .... ad domum nostram .... in dioecesi .... sitam pertinentem, qui professionem emisit votorum simplicium temporariorum (vel perpetuorum) praesentamus ut ad primam tonsuram et ordines minores promoveatur, testamur eundem iampridem dum adhuc in novitiatu versaretur ante emissam religiosam professionem et iterum paucis abhinc diebus, ad normam Instructionis *Quantum Religiones* nobis supplices preces porrexisse quibus declaravit se ad statum religiosum clericalem vocari et simul postulavit ut ad primam tonsuram et ordines minores promoveretur. Nos autem, acceptis eius precibus, ad normam eiusdem *Instructionis* inquisitionem de idoneitate, qualitatibus et vocatione religiosa faciendam curavimus ex qua inquisitione satis constat alumnum .... vere esse idoneum ad statum religiosum et clericalem et signa praebuisse vocationis nec ulla irregularitate nec canonico impedimento ligatum esse.

Testamur proinde eundem candidatum ex matrimonio legitimo natum, Baptismate renatum, sacro chrismate confirmatum, in legitima aetate constitutum tunc in cursu theologico nostri conventus .... studiis sacris incumbere et propositum habere ad presbyteratum ascendendi.

Testamur etiam nos candidato .... ex praecepto ad normam iuris imposuisse ut per tres integros dies ante ordinationem exercitiis spiritualibus vacet.

In quorum fidem subscribo.

....

Superior maior

Die ...., mensis ...., anni ....

L. S.

17. Declaration to be made by Candidates in Religious Institutes prior to the Reception of Subdiaconate

I, the undersigned, ... a member of the Order or Congregation of ...., in presenting to my superiors this petition for the reception of the order of the subdiaconate having diligently considered the matter before God, do hereby testify under oath:

1. That I am moved to the reception of this order by no compulsion, force, or fear, but do spontaneously desire it and of my own full and free will desire to embrace it together with the obligations that are attached to it.

2. I profess that I know fully all the obligations which this sacred order entails. I freely embrace them and with God's help, I resolve to observe them diligently during the entire course of my life.

3. I declare that I clearly understand all that is commanded by the vow of chastity and the law of celibacy, and I firmly resolve that, with God's help, I will observe them in their integrity until the end of my life.

4. Finally, in all sincerity, I promise that I will always most obediently observe, according to the Sacred Canons, all that my superiors command me according to ecclesiastical discipline, and that I am prepared to give others a good example both in word and deed, in order that by undertaking this great office I may receive the reward that God has promised. So I testify and swear upon these Sacred Gospels which I touch with my hand.

Date ....

....

(Signature of candidate)

CONCLUSIONS

1. Prior to the Council of Trent the only document required by universal law was a dimissorial letter on the part of the candidate when he received ordination from a bishop other than his own.

2. The Council of Trent, and even more so the Constitution *Speculatores*, made testimonials necessary on the part of all candidates.

3. Documents as required by the Code prior to ordination are intended by the legislator to help the bishop in passing upon the fitness of the candidate. Hence the candidate has the obligation of obtaining these, although generally the task is performed by the seminary rector.

4. One petition suffices for tonsure and minor orders. For major orders, however, a separate petition is required for each order.

5. In the absence of the ordinary testimony regarding the reception of baptism, the provisions of canon 779, i.e., the testimony of one qualified witness or the oath of the candidate, may be invoked. The same is true with regard to the oath of the candidate in the absence of the ordinary testimony regarding the reception of orders.

6. An attestation concerning the candidate's studies is required for tonsure and each of the major orders, but not for the minor orders.

7. A testimonial from the rector of the seminary attesting to the candidate's general fitness is required before tonsure and each of the orders. However, when two minor orders are to be conferred together, one such testimonial will suffice.

8. An attestation to the performance of the required spiritual exercises must be presented before each ordination, except in the case in which two minor orders are being conferred on the same day; in that event one such testimonial will suffice for both orders.

9. A dispensation from the simple impediment arising from the non-Catholic status of one of the parents, when granted for the reception of tonsure and the minor orders, may be used also for the reception of the major orders.

10. The candidate may not be permitted to take the oath of an intended retention of domicile before he has attained his majority.

11. Proof of the announcement of the impending ordination must be presented before the reception of each major order, all contrary custom notwithstanding.

12. In keeping with the purpose of the Instruction *Quam ingens,* the declaration of his free acceptance and full knowledge of the obligations entailed in the reception of Sacred Orders should be made before each major order in the candidate's own tongue, and written in the candidate's own hand.

13. An attestation of the fulfillment of the law with regard to the profession of faith and the rendering of the oath against Modernism must be presented before the subdiaconate.

14. While the testimonial letter mentioned in canon 993, 4°, concerns primarily the canonical impediments strictly so called there is no reason why the letter should not also testify regarding the candidate's moral fitness, especially when there is something reprehensible in the candidate's conduct or character, though it be not strictly an impediment.

15. The testimonial letter must be issued expressly for the reception of orders if it is to be of any value.

16. Testimonial letters deemed acceptable by the bishop for one order may be used for all orders, even though they are issued for one order only.

17. The ordinary may delegate to the seminary rector the issuance of testimonial letters for the time spent in the seminary.

18. The six months and the three months mentioned in canon 994, § 1, refer to a period of time which is morally continuous.

19. Even when there is moral certainty that the candidate has not incurred any impediment, the testimonial letter designated in canon 993, 4°, is still required. Thus for the time spent in a seminary in another diocese testimonial letters are required from the bishop of that diocese in addition to the testimonial of the rector.

20. As to those who have been in military service, when letters from the ordinaries in whose diocese the candidate has spent three morally continuous months are impossible or very difficult to obtain,

the ordinary is obliged to obtain a testimonial from the military ordinary, if there be one, before having recourse to the suppletory oath. If such a letter is obtained, the oath is not necessary.

21. The penalty enacted in canon 2373, 2°, applies only to a bishop who actually ordains one of his own subjects in violation of canon 993, 4°, or canon 994.

22. With regard to ex-soldiers, the bishop who neglects to obtain the testimonial letter from the military ordinary, but has recourse to the suppletory oath escapes the penalty enacted in canon 2373, 2°, for this canon in its nature of a penal law is subject to a strict interpretation.

23. The essential element of a dimissorial letter is the conferral of permission to ordain another's subject. However, it is not the only element.

24. Before the issuance of a dimissorial letter the bishop must have all the required documents.

25. In and of themselves dimissorial letters are valid indefinitely, subject of course to the provisions of canon 963.

26. In the event that some bishop other than the proper bishop is the ordaining prelate, dimissorial letters are required even for the conferral of the first tonsure.

27. The suspension incurred through the reception of orders in the lack of proper dimissorial letters applies to tonsure as well as to orders strictly so called.

28. The Instruction *Quantum Religiones* applies to societies living in common without vows as well as to religious strictly so called.

29. The declaration of his free acceptance and knowledge of the obligations entailed in the reception of sacred orders need only be signed by the candidate who is a religious and this only before the subdiaconate.

30. The profession of faith and the oath against Modernism are to be pronounced before the bishop who is the ordaining prelate, and not before the religious superior in his capacity of superior, but the latter may be delegated as an agent for the bishop.

31. The candidates in non-exempt institutes must in addition to all the documents required by the secular candidate, present a testimonial from their major religious superior.

32. Testimonial letters obtained for entry in the novitiate are not acceptable ordinarily for the reception of orders.

BIBLIOGRAPHY

Sources

Acta Apostolica Sedis, Commentarium Officiale, Romae, 1909—.

Acta et Decreta Sacrorum Conciliorum Recentiorum, Collectio Lacensis, 7 vols., Friburgi Brisgoviae, 1879-1890.

Acta Sanctae Sedis, 41 vols., Romae, 1865-1908.

Bruns, H., *Canones Apostolorum et Conciliorum Saeculorum IV-VII,* 2 vols., Berolini, 1839.

Bouscaren, T. Lincoln, *Canon Law Digest,* 2 vols., Milwaukee: Bruce, 1934-1943.

Bullarum Diplomatum et Privilegiorum Sanctorum Pontificum Taurinensis Editio, 24 vols. et Appendix, Augustae Taurinorum, 1857-1872.

Codex Iuris Canonici Pii X Pontificis Maximi iussu digestus Benedicti XV auctoritate promulgatus, Romae: Typis Polyglottis Vaticanis, 1917. Reimpressio, 1934.

Codicis Iuris Canonici Fontes, cura Emi Petri Card. Gasparri editi, 9 vols., Romae (postea Civitate Vaticana): Typis Polyglottis Vaticanis, 1923-1939. (Vols. VII-IX ed. cura et studio Emi Iustiniani Card. Serédi.)

Collectanea in Usum Secretariae Sacrae Congregationis Episcoporum et Regularium, cura A. Bizzarri, 2. ed., Romae, 1885.

Collectanea S. Congregationis de Propaganda Fide, 2 vols., Romae: Typographia Polyglotta, S. C. de Propaganda Fide, 1907.

Collectanea S. Congregationis de Propaganda Fide seu Decreta, Instructiones, Rescripta pro Apostolicis Missionibus ex Tabulario eiusdem Sacrae Congregationis Deprompta, Romae, 1893.

Concilii Plenarii Baltimorensis II, in Ecclesia Metropolitana Baltimorensi, a die VII ad diem XXI Octobris A. D. MDCCCLXVI, Habiti, et a Sede Apostolica Recogniti, Acta et Decreta, Baltimorae: John Murphy, 1894.

Concilium Tridentinum, Diariorum, Actorum, Epistularum, Tractatuum Nova Collectio, ed. Societas Goerresiana, 13 vols., Friburgi Brisgoviae: B. Herder, 1901-1938.

Continuatio Bullarii Romani Benedicti XIV, 3 vols. in 4, Prati, 1845-1847.

Corpus Iuris Canonici, editio Lipsiensis secunda post Aemilii Richteri curas instruxit Aemilius Friedburg, 2 vols., Lipsiae, 1879-1881.

Corpus Scriptorum Ecclesiasticorum Latinorum, Editum Consilio et Impensis Academiae Litterarum Caesariae Vindobonensis (*Corpus Vindobonense*), Vindobonae, 1866—.

Decreta Concilii Plenarii Baltimorensis Tertii A. D. MDCCCLXXXIV, Baltimorae: Typis Joannis Murphy et Sociorum, 1894.

Decretales D. Gregorii IX una cum Glossis Restitutae, Romae, 1582.

Decretum Gratiani emendatum et notationibus illustratum una cum Glossis Gregorii XIII Pont. Max. iussu editum, 2 vols., Romae, 1582.

Jaffé, P., *Regesta Pontificum Romanorum ab condita Ecclesia ad annum post Christum natum MCXCVIII,* 2. ed. correctam et auctam auspiciis Gulielmi Wattenbach curaverunt F. Kaltenbrunner, P. Ewald, S. Löwenfeld, 2 vols. in 1, Lipsiae, 1885-1888.

Liber Sextus Decretalium D. Bonifatii Papae VIII suae integritati una cum Clementinis et Extravagantibus earumque Glossis restitutis, Romae, 1582.

Mansi, I. D., *Sacrorum Conciliorum Nova et Amplissima Collectio,* 53 vols. in 60, Parisiis, Arnhem, Lipsiae, 1901-1927.

Monumenta Germaniae Historica, Gregorii I Papae Registrum Epistolarum, 4 vols., ed. L. M. Hartmann post Pauli Ewaldi obitum, Berolini, 1887-1899.

———, *Legum Sectio III, Concilia Aevi Karolini,* 2 vols., ed. A. Werminghoff, Hannoverae et Lipsiae, 1906-1908.

Pallottini, Salvator, *Collectio omnium conclusionum et resolutionum quae in causis propositis apud Sacram Congregationem Cardinalium S. Concilii Tridentini Interpretum prodierunt ab eius institutione anno MDLXIV ad annum MDCCCLX, distinctis titulis alphabetico ordine per materias digesta,* 17 vols., Romae, 1868-1893.

Potthast, A., *Regesta Pontificum Romanorum inde ab anno post Christum natum 1198 ad annum 1304,* 2 vols., Berolini, 1874-1875.

Schroeder, H., *Canons and Decrees of the Council of Trent,* St. Louis: B. Herder, 1941.

Thesaurus Resolutionum Sacrae Congregationis Concilii, 167 vols., Romae, 1718-1908.

AUTHORS

Aertnys, J.-Damen C., *Theologia Moralis,* 14. ed., 2 vols., Taurini: Marietti, 1944.

Augustine, Charles, *A Commentary on the New Code of Canon Law,* 8 vols., Vol. IV, 1921; Vol. VII, 1921; Vol. VIII, 1922; St. Louis: B. Herder.

Ayrinhac, H., *Penal Legislation in the New Code of Canon Law,* revised by P. Lydon, New York: Benziger, 1936.

Ballerini, A.-Palmieri, D., *Opus Theologicum Morale,* 3. ed., 7 vols., Prati, 1898-1901.

Barbosa, A., *Collectanea Doctorum in Varia Concilii Tridentini Decreta et Canones,* Lugduni, 1657.

———, *De Officio et Potestate Episcopi,* 2 vols., Lugduni, 1656.

———, *Juris Ecclesiastici Universi Libri Tres,* Lugduni, 1660.

Baronius, C., Annales Ecclesiastici, 37 vols., Vols. I-XXVIII, Barri-Ducis, 1864-1875; Vols. XXIX-XXXVII, Parisiis, 1876-1883.

Beste, U., *Introductio in Codicem,* 2. ed., Collegeville, Minn.: St. John's Abbey Press, 1944.

Blat, A., *Commentarium Textus Codicis Iuris Canonici,* 5 vols. in 6, Romae: Collegio Angelico, 1919-1927.

Bouix, D., *Tractatus de Episcopo,* 2 vols., Parisiis, 1859.

Canavan, W., *The Profession of Faith,* The Catholic University of America Canon Law Studies, n. 151, Washington, D. C.: The Catholic University of America Press, 1942.

Cappello, F., *Summa Iuris Canonici,* 3 vols., Romae: apud aedes Universitatis Gregorianae, 1938-1940. Vol. I, 3. ed., 1938; Vol. II, 3. ed., 1939; Vol. III, 2. ed., 1940.

———, *Tractatus Canonico-Moralis de Sacramentis,* 3 vols. in 6, Taurinorum Augustae: Marietti, 1935-1945. Vol. I, 4. ed., 1945; Vol. II, Pars III, 1935; Vol. III, Pars I et II, 4. ed., 1939.

Chelodi, J., *Ius de Personis,* 3. ed. cura Ciprotti, Vicenza: Società Anonima Tipografica; Trento: Libreria Moderna Editrice, 1942.

Cicognani, A., *Commentarium ad Librum Primum Codicis Iuris Canonici,* recognitum et auctum a Dino Staffa, 2 vols., Romae: Ex Officina Typographica Romana "Buona Stampa," 1939-1942.

Claeys-Bouuaert, F., *De Canonica Cleri Saecularis Obedientia,* Lovanii, 1904.

Claeys-Bouuaert, F.-Simenon, G., *Manuale Iuris Canonici,* 3 vols., Vols. I and III, 3. ed., Gamdae et Leodii: apud Auctores in Seminariis Gandavensi et Leodiensi, 1930-1931.

Coronata, M. Conte a, *Institutiones Iuris Canonici, De Sacramentis,* 3 vols., Taurini-Romae: Marietti, 1943-1946.

———, *Institutiones Iuris Canonici,* 2. ed., 5 vols., Taurini-Romae: Marietti, 1936-1946. (Vol. 5, 1. ed.).

Costello, J., *Domicile and Quasi-Domicile,* The Catholic University of America Canon Law Studies, n. 60, Washington, D. C.: The Catholic University of America, 1930.

Creusen, J.-Ellis, A., *Religious Men and Women in the Code,* 4. English ed., Milwaukee: Bruce, 1940.

Davis, H., *Moral and Pastoral Theology,* 4. ed., 4 vols., New York: Sheed and Ward, 1943.

Diederichs, M., *The Jurisdiction of the Latin Ordinaries Over Their Oriental Subjects,* The Catholic University of America Canon Law Studies, n. 229, Washington, D. C.: The Catholic University of America Press, 1946.

Devoti, J., *Institutionum Canonicarum Libri IV,* 2 vols., Romae, 1830.

Fagnanus, P., *Commentaria in Libros Decretalium,* 5 vols. in 3, Venetiis, 1697.

Fanfani, L., *De Iure Religiosorum ad Normam Codicis Iuris Canonici,* 2. ed., Taurini-Romae: Marietti, 1925.

Ferraris, L., *Prompta Bibliotheca Canonica, Iuridica, Moralis, Theologica, necnon Ascetica, Polemica, Rubricistica, Historica,* ed. novissima, 9 vols., Romae, 1885-1899.

Gallagher, T., *The Examination of the Qualities of the Ordinand,* The Catholic University of America Canon Law Studies, n. 195, Washington, D. C.: The Catholic University of America Press, 1944.

Gams, Series Episcoporum Ecclesiae Catholicae, Ratisbonae, 1873.

Gasparri, P., *Tractatus Canonicus de Sacra Ordinatione,* 2 vols., Parisiis et Lugduni, 1894.

Genicot, E., *Theologiae Moralis Institutiones,* 4. ed., 2 vols., Lovanii, 1902.

Hallier, F., *De Sacris Electionibus et Ordinationibus ex Antiquo et Novo Ecclesiae Usu* (in J. P. Migne, *Theologiae Cursus Completus,* Vol. XXIV), Parisiis, 1860.

Hefele, C.-LeClercq, H., *Histoire des Conciles,* 10 vols. in 19, Paris: Letouzey et Ané, 1907-1938.

Hickey, J., *Irregularities and Simple Impediments in the New Code of Canon Law,* The Catholic University of America Canon Law Studies, n. 7, Washington, D. C.: The Catholic University of America, 1920.

Hinschius, P., *Decretales Pseudo-Isidorianae et Capitula Angilramni,* Lipsiae, 1863.

———, *System des katholischen Kirchenrechts,* 4 vols., Berlin, 1869-1888.

Honorante, R., *Praxis Secretariae Tribunalis Cardinalis Urbis Vicarii,* 2. ed., Romae, 1762.

Huguenin, L., *Constitutionis* Apostolicae Sedis *Brevis Explanatio,* Parisiis, 1877.

Ioannes Andreae, *In VI Libros Decretalium Novella Commentaria,* 6 vols. in 5, Venetiis, 1581.

Jordanus, Pax, *Opera Omnia,* 3 vols., Coloniae Allobrogum et Lugduni, 1729.

Liguori, Alphonsus S., *Theologia Moralis,* ed. nova, cura Gaudé, 4 vols., Romae: Typis Polyglottis Vaticanis, 1905-1912.

Lucidi, A., *De Visitatione Sacrorum Liminum,* 3. ed. (aucta per Iosephum Schneider), 3 vols., Romae, 1883.

Lupus, C., *Opera Omnia Canonica,* 12 vols., Venetiis, 1727.

McBride, J., *Incardination and Excardination of Seculars,* The Catholic University of America Canon Law Studies, n. 145, Washington, D. C.: The Catholic University of America Press, 1941.

Many, S., *Praelectiones de Sacra Ordinatione,* Parisiis, 1905.

Merkelbach, B., *Summa Theologiae Moralis,* 3. ed., 3 vols., Parisiis: Desclée, de Brouwer et Soc., 1938-1939.

Migne, J. P., *Patrologiae Cursus Completus, Series Latina,* 221 vols., Parisiis, 1844-1864.

———, *Theologiae Cursus Completus,* 28 vols., Parisiis, 1863-1866. Vol. XXIV, *De Sacris Electionibus et Ordinationibus,* auctore Francisco Hallier, Parisiis, 1860.

Moeder, J., *The Proper Bishop for Ordination and Dimissorial Letters,* The Catholic University of America Canon Law Studies, n. 95, Washington, D. C.: The Catholic University of America, 1935.

Monacelli, F., *Formularium Legale Practicum Fori Ecclesiastici,* 3. ed., 4 vols. in 3, Romae, 1844.

Mothon, J., *Institutions Canoniques,* 3 vols., Lille-Bruges: Desclée, De Brouwer, 1924.

Noldin, H.-Schmitt, A., *Summa Theologiae Moralis,* 3 vols., Oeniponte-Lipsiae: Rauch, 1939-1940. Vol. I, 27 ed., 1940; Vol. II, 26. ed., 1939; Vol. III, 26. ed., 1940.

O'Rourke, J., *Parish Registers,* The Catholic University of America Canon Law Studies, n. 88, Washington, D. C.: The Catholic University of America, 1934.

Passerini, P., *Commentaria in Primum Librum Sextum Decretalium,* 2 vols., Venetiis, 1698.

Pennacchi, J., *Commentaria in Constitutionem* Apostolicae Sedis, 2 vols., Romae, 1883.

Petra, V., *Commentaria ad Constitutiones Apostolicas, seu Bullas Singulas Summorum Pontificum,* 5 vols. in 2, Venetiis, 1729.

Pirhing, E., *Jus Canonicum in V Libros Decretalium distributum,* 5 vols., Dilingae, 1674-1678.

Regatillo, E., *Ius Sacramentarium,* 2 vols., Santander: Sal Terrae, 1945-1946.

Reiffenstuel, A., *Jus Canonicum Universum,* 5 vols., Parisiis, 1864-1868.

Santi, F., *Praelectiones Iuris Canonici,* 4. ed. cura M. Leitner, 5 vols. in 3, Ratisbonae, 1903-1905.

Schmalzgrueber, F., *Jus Ecclesiasticum Universum,* 5 vols. in 12, Romae, 1843-1845.

Schroeder, H., *Disciplinary Decrees of the General Councils,* St. Louis: B. Herder, 1937.

Sipos, S., *Enchiridion Iuris Canonici,* Pecs: Ex Typographia "Haladas H. T.," 1926.

Sullivan, E., *Proof of the Reception of the Sacraments,* The Catholic University of America Canon Law Studies, n. 209, Washington, D. C.: The Catholic University of America Press, 1944.

Swoboda, I., *Ignorance in Relation to the Imputability of Delicts,* The Catholic University of America Canon Law Studies, n. 143, Washington, D. C.: The Catholic University of America Press, 1941.

Téphany, J., *Constitution* Apostolicae Sedis: *Commentaire,* Tours, 1883.

Thomas Aquinas, S., *Summa Theologica,* 22. ed., 6 vols., Taurini-Romae: Marietti, 1939.

Thomassinus, L., *Vetus et Nova Ecclesiae Disciplina circa Beneficia et Beneficiarios,* 10 vols., Moguntiaci, 1787.

Van Espen, Z., *Commentarium in Canones Juris Veteris ac Novi et in Jus Novissimum,* Lovanii, 1753.

———, *Jus Ecclesiasticum Universum,* 10 vols., Lovanii et reperitur Lugduni, 1778.

Van Hove, A., *Commentarium Lovaniense in Codicem Iuris Canonici,* Vol. I, Tom. I (*Prologomena ad Codicem Iuris Canonici*), 2. ed., Mechliniae-Romae: H. Dessain, 1945.

Vermeersch, A.-Creusen, J., *Epitome Iuris Canonici,* 6. ed., 3 vols., Mechliniae-Romae: H. Dessain, 1937-1946.

Vogelpohl, H., *The Simple Impediments to Holy Orders,* The Catholic University of America Canon Law Studies, n. 224, Washington, D. C.: The Catholic University of America Press, 1945.

Wanenmacher, F., *Canonical Evidence in Marriage Cases,* Philadelphia: Dolphin Press, 1935.

Wernz, F., *Ius Decretalium,* 3. ed., 6 vols., Prati, 1913-1915.

Wernz, F.-Vidal, P., *Ius Canonicum,* 7 toms. in 8 vols., Romae: apud aedes Universitatis Gregorianae, 1923-1938. Tom. IV, Pars I, 1934; Tom. IV, Pars II, 1935.

Willett, R., *The Probative Value of Documents in Ecclesiastical Trials,* The Catholic University of America Canon Law Studies, n. 171, Washington, D. C.: The Catholic University of America Press, 1942.

Woywod, S., *A Practical Commentary on the Code of Canon Law,* 2 vols., 8. printing, revised by C. Smith, New York: Wagner, 1944.

Articles

Anonymous, "De studiis requisitis ante ordinationem"—*Periodica,* XII (1923), (9)-(10).

———, "Ex Privata Jurisprudentia"—*Ius Pontificium,* IX (1929), 203.

Boudinhon, A., "Consultationes"—*Le Canoniste Contemporain,* XLV (1922), 476.

D'Angelo, S., "De Prima Tonsura—Consultatio"—*Apollinaris,* I (1928), 181-182.

Goyeneche, S., "Consultationes"—*CpR,* VIII (1927), 376-379.

Hannan, J., "Ordinations at Christmas"—*The Jurist,* I (1941), 153-154.

———, "Ex-Seminarian and Novice"—*The Jurist,* II (1942), 380-382.

Larraona, A., "Animadversiones"—*Apollinaris,* IV (1931), 207-210.

———, "Commentarium Codicis"—*CpRM,* XIX (1938), 154-160.

Maroto, P., "Annotationes"—*CpR,* XIII (1932), 175-180.

Mahoney, E. J., "The Tonsure and Incardination"—*ER,* LXXXII (1930), 394-406.

Roelker, E., "The Vicar General and the Special Mandate"—*The Jurist,* II (1942), 346-362.

Schaaf, V., "Episcopus Proprius Ordinationis Religiosorum"—*ER,* XV (1934), 490-501.

Toso, A., "Consultationes"—*Jus Pontificium,* V (1925), 40-42.

Vermeersch, A., "Annotationes"—*Periodica,* V (1913), 272; XXI (1932), 188-193.

Woywod, S., "Testimonial Letters Before Ordination"—*HPR,* XXIII (1922-1923), 375-378.

PERIODICALS

American Ecclesiastical Review, The (1905-1943 *The Ecclesiastical Review*), Philadelphia, 1889-1943; Baltimore, 1944—.

Analecta Ecclesiastica, Romae, 1893-1911.

Analecta Iuris Pontificii, Romae, 1855-1869; Parisiis, 1872-1891.

Apollinaris, Romae, 1928—.

Commentarium pro Religiosis, Romae, 1920-1934; ab anno 1935: *Commentarium pro Religiosis et Missionariis.*

Homiletic and Pastoral Review, The, New York, 1900—.

Jurist, The, Washington, D. C., 1941—.

Jus Pontificium, Romae, 1920-1940.

Le Canoniste Contemporain, Paris, 1878-1922.

Periodica de Re Canonica et Morali Utili praesertim Religiosis et Missionariis. Brugis, 1905—; ab anno 1927; *Periodica de Re Canonica, Morali, Liturgica.*

ABBREVIATIONS

AAS—*Acta Apostolicae Sedis.*
AER—*The American Ecclesiastical Review.*
ASS—*Acta Sanctae Sedis.*
Bruns—*Canones Apostolorum et Conciliorum Saeculorum IV-VII.*
Bullarium—*Bullarum Diplomatum et Privilegiorum Sanctorum Pontificum Taurinensis Editio.*
c.—canon seu caput (iuris antiqui).
cc.—canones seu capita (iuris antiqui).
can.—canon (novi Codicis).
cans.—canones (novi Codicis).
Collectanea—*Collectanea S. Congregationis de Propaganda Fide.*
CSEL—*Corpus Scriptorum Ecclesiasticorum Latinorum.*
C.P.I.—*Commissio Pontificia Interpretationis.*
CpR(M)—*Commentarium pro Religiosis* (*et Missionariis*).
ER—*The Ecclesiastical Review.*
Fontes—*Codicis Iuris Canonici Fontes.*
Mansi—*Sacrorum Conciliorum Nova et Amplissima Collectio.*
MGH, Conc.—*Monumenta Germaniae Historica,* Legum Sectio III, *Concilia Aevi Karolini.*
MPL—Migne, *Patrologia Latina.*
MTC—Migne, *Theologiae Cursus Completus.*
Periodica—*Periodica de Re Canonica, Morali, Liturgica.*
Pallottini—*Collectio omnium conclusionum et resolutionum quae in causis propositis apud Sacram Congregationem Cardinalium S. Concilii Tridentini Interpretum prodierunt 1564-1860.*
Quam ingens—S. C. de Sacr., instr., 27 dec. 1930.
Quantum Religiones—S. C. de Rel., instr., 1 dec. 1931.
S. C. C.—Sacra Congregatio Concilii.
S. C. de Prop. Fide—Sacra Congregatio de Propaganda Fide.
S. C. de Rel.—Sacra Congregatio de Religiosis.
S. C. de Sacr.—Sacra Congregatio de Sacramentis.
S. C. Consist.—Sacra Congregatio Consistorialis.
S. C. Ep. et Reg.—Sacra Congregatio Episcoporum et Regularium.
S. C. S. Off.—Sacra Congregatio Sancti Officii.
Thesaurus—*Thesaurus Resolutionum Sacrae Congregationis Concilii.*

ALPHABETICAL INDEX

BIOGRAPHICAL NOTE

Joseph James Quinn was born in Brooklyn, New York, on May 9, 1920. He attended St. Raymond's Parochial School in Bronx, New York, and Cathedral College—the preparatory Seminary of the Archdiocese of New York—from which institution he received the degree of Bachelor of Arts. In September, 1939, he entered St. Joseph's Seminary, Dunwoodie, Yonkers, N. Y., and was ordained to the priesthood on January 27, 1945. He thereupon enrolled in the School of Canon Law at the Catholic University of America, and completed work for the degree of Bachelor of Canon Law in February, 1946, receiving the degree at the commencement exercises in June, 1946. He completed his work for the Licentiate in Canon Law in February, 1947, receiving the degree at the commencement exercises in June, 1947.

CANON LAW STUDIES *

1. FRERIKS, REV. CELESTINE A., C.PP.S., J.C.D., Religious Congregations in Their External Relations, 121 pp., 1916.
2. GALLIHER, REV. DANIEL M., O.P., J.C.D., Canonical Elections, 117 pp., 1917.
3. BORKOWSKI, REV. AURELIUS L., O.F.M., J.C.D., De Confraternitatibus Ecclesiasticis, 136 pp., 1918.
4. CASTILLO, REV. CAYO, J.C.D., Disertacion Historico-Canonica sobre la Potestad del Cabildo en Sede Vacante o Impedida del Vicario Capitular, 99 pp., 1919 (1918).
5. KUBELBECK, REV. WILLIAM J., S.T.B., J.C.D., The Sacred Penitentiaria and Its Relation to Faculties of Ordinaries and Priests, 129 pp., 1918.
6. PETROVITS, REV. JOSEPH, J.C., S.T.D., J.C.D., The New Church Law on Matrimony, X-461 pp., 1919.
7. HICKEY, REV. JOHN J., S.T.B., J.C.D., Irregularities and Simple Impediments in the New Code of Canon Law, 100 pp., 1920.
8. KLEKOTKA, REV. PETER J., S.T.B., J.C.D., Diocesan Consultors, 179 pp., 1920.
9. WANENMACHER, REV. FRANCIS, J.C.D., The Evidence in Ecclesiastical Procedure Affecting the Marriage Bond, 1920 (Printed 1935).
10. GOLDEN, REV. HENRY FRANCIS, J.C.D., Parochial Benefices in the New Code, IV-119 pp., 1921 (Printed 1925).
11. KOUDELKA, REV. CHARLES J., J.C.D., Pastors, Their Rights and Duties According to the New Code of Canon Law, 211 pp., 1921.
12. MELO, REV. ANTONIUS, O.F.M., J.C.D., De Exemptione Regularium, X-188 pp., 1921.
13. SCHAAF, REV. VALENTINE THEODORE, O.F.M., S.T.B., J.C.D., The Cloister, X-180 pp., 1921.
14. BURKE, REV. THOMAS JOSEPH, S.T.D., J.C.D., Competence in Ecclesiastical Tribunals, IV-117 pp., 1922.
15. LEECH, REV. GEORGE LEO, J.C.D., A Comparative Study of the Constitution "Apostolicae Sedis" and the "Codex Juris Canonici," 179 pp., 1922.
16. MOTRY, REV. HUBERT LOUIS, S.T.D., J.C.D., Diocesan Faculties According to the Code of Canon Law, II-167 pp., 1922.
17. MURPHY, REV. GEORGE LAWRENCE, J.C.D., Delinquencies and Penalties in the Administration and the Reception of the Sacraments, IV-121 pp., 1923.
18. O'REILLY, REV. JOHN ANTHONY, S.T.B., J.C.D., Ecclesiastical Sepulture in the New Code of Canon Law, II-129 pp., 1923.

* All published numbers of this series are available from the Catholic University of America Press, 621 Michigan Ave., N.E., Washington 17, D. C., except the following: nn. 1-114 inclusive, 116, 118, 120, 122, 123, 136, 162 and 198.

19. Michalicka, Rev. Wenceslas Cyrill, O.S.B., J.C.D., Judicial Procedure in Dismissal of Clerical Exempt Religious, 107 pp., 1923.
20. Dargin, Rev. Edward Vincent, S.T.B., J.C.D., Reserved Cases According to the Code of Canon Law, IV-103 pp., 1924.
21. Godfrey, Rev. John A., S.T.B., J.C.D., The Right of Patronage According to the Code of Canon Law, 153 pp., 1924.
22. Hagedorn, Rev. Francis Edward, J.C.D., General Legislation on Indulgences, II-154 pp., 1924.
23. King, Rev. James Ignatius, J.C.D., The Administration of the Sacraments to Dying Non-Catholics, V-141 pp., 1924.
24. Winslow, Rev. Francis Joseph, O.F.M., J.C.D., Vicars and Prefects Apostolic, IV-149 pp., 1924.
25. Correa, Rev. Jose Servelion, S.T.L., J.C.D., La Potestad Legislativa de la Iglesia Catolica, IV-127 pp., 1925.
26. Dugan, Rev. Henry Francis, A.M., J.C.D., The Judiciary Department of the Diocesan Curia, 87 pp., 1925.
27. Keller, Rev. Charles Frederick, S.T.B., J.C.D., Mass Stipends, 167 pp., 1925.
28. Paschang, Rev. John Linus, J.C.D., The Sacramentals According to the Code of Canon Law, 129 pp., 1925.
29. Piontek, Rev. Cyrillus, O.F.M., S.T.B., J.C.D., De Indulto Exclaustrationis necnon Saecularizationis, XIII-289 pp., 1925.
30. Kearney, Rev. Richard Joseph, S.T.B., J.C.D., Sponsors at Baptism According to the Code of Canon Law, IV-127 pp., 1925.
31. Bartlett, Rev. Chester Joseph, A.M., LL.B., J.C.D., The Tenure of Parochial Property in the United States of America, V-108 pp., 1926.
32. Kilker, Rev. Adrian Jerome, J.C.D., Extreme Unction, V-425 pp., 1926.
33. McCormick, Rev. Robert Emmett, J.C.D., Confessors of Religious, VIII-266 pp., 1926.
34. Miller, Rev. Newton Thomas, J.C.D., Founded Masses According to the Code of Canon Law, VII-93 pp., 1926.
35. Roelker, Rev. Edward G., S.T.D., J.C.D., Principles of Privilege According to the Code of Canon Law, XI-166 pp., 1926.
36. Bakalarczyk, Rev. Richardus, M.I.C., J.U.D., De Novitiatu, VIII-208 pp., 1927.
37. Pizzuti, Rev. Lawrence, O.F.M., J.U.L., De Parochis Religiosis, 1927. (Not Printed.)
38. Bliley, Rev. Nicholas Martin, O.S.B., J.C.D., Altars According to the Code of Canon Law, XIX-132 pp., 1927.
39. Brown, Mr. Brendan Francis, A.B., LL.M., J.U.D., The Canonical Juristic Personality with Special Reference to its Status in the United States of America, V-212 pp., 1927.
40. Cavanaugh, Rev. William Thomas, C.P., J.U.D., The Reservation of the Blessed Sacrament, VIII-101 pp., 1927.

41. DOHENY, REV. WILLIAM J., C.S.C., A.B., J.C.D., Church Property: Modes of Acquisition, X-118 pp., 1927.
42. FELDHAUS, REV. ALOYSIUS H., C.PP.S., J.C.D., Oratories, IX-141 pp., 1927.
43. KELLY, REV. JAMES PATRICK, A.B., J.C.D., The Jurisdiction of the Simple Confessor, X-208 pp., 1927.
44. NEUBERGER, REV. NICHOLAS J., J.C.D., Canon 6 or the Relation of the Codex Juris Canonici to the Preceding Legislation, V-95 pp., 1927.
45. O'KEEFE, REV. GERALD MICHAEL, J.C.D., Matrimonial Dispensations, Powers of Bishops, Priests, and Confessors, VIII-232 pp., 1927.
46. QUIGLEY, REV. JOSEPH A. M., A.B., J.C.D., Condemned Societies, 139 pp., 1927.
47. ZAPLOTNIK, REV. JOHANNES LEO, J.C.D., De Vicariis Foraneis, X-142 pp., 1927.
48. DUSKIE, REV. JOHN ALOYSIUS, A.B., J.C.D., The Canonical Status of the Orientals in the United States, VIII-196 pp., 1928.
49. HYLAND, REV. FRANCIS EDWARD, J.C.D., Excommunication, Its Nature, Historical Development and Effects, VIII-181 pp., 1928.
50. REINMANN, REV. GERALD JOSEPH, O.M.C., J.C.D., The Third Order Secular of Saint Francis, 201 pp., 1928.
51. SCHENK, REV. FRANCIS J., J.C.D., The Matrimonial Impediments of Mixed Religion and Disparity of Cult, XVI-318 pp., 1929.
52. COADY, REV. JOHN JOSEPH, S.T.D., J.U.D., A.M., The Appointment of Pastors, VIII-150 pp., 1929.
53. KAY, REV. THOMAS HENRY, J.C.D., Competence in Matrimonial Procedure, VIII-164 pp., 1929.
54. TURNER, REV. SIDNEY JOSEPH, C.P., J.U.D., The Vow of Poverty, XLIX-217 pp., 1929.
55. KEARNEY, REV. RAYMOND A., A.B., S.T.D., J.C.D., The Principles of Delegation, VII-149 pp., 1929.
56. CONRAN, REV. EDWARD JAMES, A.B., J.C.D., The Interdict, V-163 pp., 1930.
57. O'NEILL, REV. WILLIAM H., J.C.D., Papal Rescripts of Favor, VII-218 pp., 1930.
58. BASTNAGEL, REV. CLEMENT VINCENT, J.U.D., The Appointment of Parochial Adjutants and Assistants, XV-257 pp., 1930.
59. FERRY, REV. WILLIAM A., A.B., J.C.D., Stole Fees, V-136 pp., 1930.
60. COSTELLO, REV. JOHN MICHAEL, A.B., J.C.D., Domicile and Quasi-Domicile, VII-201 pp., 1930.
61. KREMER, REV. MICHAEL NICHOLAS, A.B., S.T.B., J.C.D., Church Support in the United States, VI-136 pp., 1930.
62. ANGULO, REV. LUIS, C.M., J.C.D., Legislation de la Iglesia sobre la intencion en la application de la Santa Misa, VII-104 pp., 1931.
63. FREY, REV. WOLFGANG NORBERT, O.S.B., A.B., J.C.D., The Act of Religious Profession, VIII-174 pp., 1931.

64. ROBERTS, REV. JAMES BRENDAN, A.B., J.C.D., The Banns of Marriage, XIV-140 pp., 1931.

65. RYDER, REV. RAYMOND ALOYSIUS, A.B., J.C.D., Simony, IX-151 pp., 1931.

66. CAMPAGNA, REV. ANGELO, PH.D., J.U.D., Il Vicario Generale del Vescovo, VII-205 pp., 1931.

67. COX, REV. JOSEPH GODFREY, A.B., J.C.D., The Administration of Seminaries, VI-124 pp., 1931.

68. GREGORY, REV. DONALD J., J.U.D., The Pauline Privilege, XV-165 pp., 1931.

69. DONOHUE, REV. JOHN F., J.C.D., The Impediment of Crime, VII-110 pp., 1931.

70. DOOLEY, REV. EUGENE A., O.M.I., J.C.D., Church Law on Sacred Relics, IX-143 pp., 1931.

71. ORTH, REV. CLEMENT RAYMOND, O.M.C., J.C.D., The Approbation of Religious Institutes, 171 pp., 1931.

72. PERNICONE, REV. JOSEPH M., A.B., J.C.D., The Ecclesiastical Prohibition of Books, XII-267 pp., 1932.

73. CLINTON, REV. CONNELL, A.B., J.C.D., The Paschal Precept, IX-108 pp., 1932.

74. DONNELLY, REV. FRANCIS B., A.M., S.T.L., J.C.D., The Diocesan Synod, VIII-125 pp., 1932.

75. TORRENTE, REV. CAMILO, C.M.F., J.C.D., Las Procesiones Sagradas, V-145 pp., 1932.

76. MURPHY, REV. EDWIN J., C.PP.S., J.C.D., Suspension Ex Informata Conscientia, XI-122 pp., 1932.

77. MACKENZIE, REV. ERIC F., A.M., S.T.L., J.C.D., The Delict of Heresy in its Commission, Penalization, Absolution, VII-124 pp., 1932.

78. LYONS, REV. AVITUS E., S.T.B., J.C.D., The Collegiate Tribunal of First Instance, XI-147 pp., 1932.

79. CONNOLLY, REV. THOMAS A., J.C.D., Appeals, XI-195, pp., 1932.

80. SANGMEISTER, REV. JOSEPH V., A.B., J.C.D., Force and Fear as Precluding Matrimonial Consent, V-211 pp., 1932.

81. JAEGER, REV. LEO A., A.B., J.C.D., The Administration of Vacant and Quasi-Vacant Episcopal Sees in the United States, IX-229 pp., 1932.

82. RIMLINGER, REV. HERBERT T., J.C.D., Error Invalidating Matrimonial Consent, VII-79 pp., 1932.

83. BARRETT, REV. JOHN D. M., S.S., J.C.D., A Comparative Study of the Councils of Baltimore and the Code of Canon Law, IX-223 pp., 1932.

84. CARBERRY, REV. JOHN J., PH.D., S.T.D., J.C.D., The Juridical Form of Marriage, X-177 pp., 1934.

85. DOLAN, REV. JOHN L., A.B., J.C.D., The Defensor Vinculi, XII-157 pp., 1934.

86. HANNAN, REV. JEROME D., A.M., S.T.D., LL.B., J.C.D., The Canon Law of Wills, IX-517 pp., 1934.

87. Lemieux, Rev. Delise A., A.M., J.C.D., The Sentence in Ecclesiastical Procedure, IX-131 pp., 1934.
88. O'Rourke, Rev. James J., A.B., J.C.D., Parish Registers, VII-109 pp., 1934.
89. Timlin, Rev. Bartholomew, O.F.M., A.M., J.C.D., Conditional Matrimonial Consent, X-381 pp., 1934.
90. Wahl, Rev. Francis X., A.B., J.C.D., The Matrimonial Impediments of Consanguinity and Affinity, VI-125 pp., 1934.
91. White, Rev. Robert J., A.B., LL.B., S.T.B., J.C.D., Canonical Ante-Nuptial Promises and the Civil Law, VI-152 pp., 1934.
92. Herrera, Rev. Antonio Parra, O.C.D., J.C.D., Legislacion Ecclesiastica sobra el Ayuno y la Abstinencia, XI-191 pp., 1935.
93. Kennedy, Rev. Edwin J., J.C.D., The Special Matrimonial Process in Cases of Evident Nullity, X-165 pp., 1935.
94. Manning, Rev. John J., A.B., J.C.D., Presumption of Law in Matrimonial Procedure, XI-111 pp., 1935.
95. Moeder, Rev. John M., J.C.D., The Proper Bishop for Ordination and Dismissorial Letters, VII-135 pp., 1935.
96. O'Mara, Rev. William A., A.B., J.C.D., Canonical Causes for Matrimonial Dispensations, IX-155 pp., 1935.
97. Reilly, Rev. Peter, J.C.D., Residence of Pastors, IX-81 pp., 1935.
98. Smith, Rev. Mariner T., O.P., S.T.Lr., J.C.D., The Penal Law for Religious, VIII-169 pp., 1935.
99. Whalen, Rev. Donald W., A.M., J.C.D., The Value of Testimonial Evidence in Matrimonial Procedure, XIII-297 pp., 1935.
100. Cleary, Rev. Joseph F., J.C.D., Canonical Limitations on the Alienation of Church Property, VIII-141 pp., 1936.
101. Glynn, Rev. John C., J.C.D., The Promoter of Justice, XX-337 pp., 1936.
102. Brennan, Rev. James H., S.S., M.A., S.T.B., J.C.D., The Simple Convalidation of Marriage, VI-135 pp., 1937.
103. Brunini, Rev. Joseph Bernard, J.C.D., The Clerical Obligations of Canons 139 and 142, X-121 pp., 1937.
104. Connor, Rev. Maurice, A.B., J.C.D., The Administrative Removal of Pastors, VIII-159 pp., 1937.
105. Guilfoyle, Rev. Merlin Joseph, J.C.D., Custom, XI-144 pp., 1937.
106. Hughes, Rev. James Austin, A.B., A.M., J.C.D., Witnesses in Criminal Trials of Clerics, IX-140 pp., 1937.
107. Jansen, Rev. Raymond J., A.B., S.T.L., J.C.D., Canonical Provisions for Catechetical Instruction, VII-153 pp., 1937.
108. Kealy, Rev. John James, A.B., J.C.D., The Introductory Libellus in Church Court Procedure, XI-121 pp., 1937.
109. McManus, Rev. James Edward, C.SS.R., J.C.D., The Administration of Temporal Goods in Religious Institutes, XVI-196 pp., 1937.

110. Moriarty, Rev. Eugene James, J.C.D., Oaths in Ecclesiastical Courts, X-115 pp., 1937.
111. Rainer, Rev. Eligius George, C.SS.R., J.C.D., Suspension of Clerics, XVII-249 pp., 1937.
112. Reilly, Rev. Thomas F., C.SS.R., J.C.D., Visitation of Religious, VI-195 pp., 1938.
113. Moriarty, Rev. Francis E., C.SS.R., J.C.D., The Extraordinary Absolution from Censures, XV-334 pp., 1938.
114. Connolly, Rev. Nicholas P., J.C.D., The Canonical Erection of Parishes, X-132 pp., 1938.
115. Donovan, Rev. James Joseph, J.C.D., The Pastor's Obligation in Prenuptial Investigation, XII-322 pp., 1938.
116. Harrigan, Rev. Robert J., M.A., S.T.B., J.C.D., The Radical Sanation of Invalid Marriages, VIII-208 pp., 1938.
117. Boffa, Rev. Conrad Humbert, J.C.D., Canonical Provisions for Catholic Schools, VII-211 pp., 1939.
118. Parsons, Rev. Anscar John, O.M.Cap., J.C.D., Canonical Elections, XII-236 pp., 1939.
119. Reilly, Rev. Edward Michael, A.B., J.C.D., The General Norms of Dispensation, XII-156 pp., 1939.
120. Ryan, Rev. Gerald Aloysius, A.B., J.C.D., Principles of Episcopal Jurisdiction, XII-172 pp., 1939.
121. Burton, Rev. Francis James, C.S.C., A.B., J.C.D., A Commentary on Canon 1125, X-222 pp., 1940.
122. Miaskiewicz, Rev. Francis Sigismund, J.C.D., Supplied Jurisdiction According to Canon 209, XII-340 pp., 1940.
123. Rice, Rev. Patrick William, A.B., J.C.D., Proof of Death in Prenuptial Investigation, VIII-156 pp., 1940.
124. Anglin, Rev. Thomas Francis, M.S., J.C.D., The Eucharistic Fast, VIII-183 pp., 1941.
125. Coleman, Rev. John Jerome, J.C.D., The Minister of Confirmation, VI-153 pp., 1941.
126. Downs, Rev. John Emmanuel, A.B., J.C.D., The Concept of Clerical Immunity, XI-163 pp., 1941.
127. Esswein, Rev. Anthony Albert, J.C.D., Extrajudicial Penal Powers of Ecclesiastical Superiors, X-144 pp., 1941.
128. Farrell, Rev. Benjamin Francis, M.A., S.T.L., J.C.D., The Rights and Duties of the Local Ordinary Regarding Congregations of Women Religious of Pontifical Approval, V-195 pp., 1941.
129. Feeney, Rev. Thomas John, A.B., S.T.L., J.C.D., Restitutio in Integrum, VI-169 pp., 1941.
130. Findlay, Rev. Stephen William, O.S.B., A.B., J.C.D., Canonical Norms Governing the Deposition and Degradation of Clerics, XVII-279 pp., 1941.

131. GOODWINE, REV. JOHN, A.B., S.T.L., J.C.D., The Right of the Church to Acquire Property, VIII-119 pp., 1941.
132. HESTON, REV. EDWARD LOUIS, C.S.C., Ph.D., S.T.D., J.C.D., The Alienation of Church Property in the United States, XII-222 pp., 1941.
133. HOGAN, REV. JAMES JOHN, A.B., S.T.L., J.C.D., Judicial Advocates and Procurators, XIII-200 pp., 1941.
134. KEALY, REV. THOMAS M., A.B., Litt.B., J.C.D., Dowry of Women Religious, IX-152 pp., 1941.
135. KEENE, REV. MICHAEL JAMES, O.S.B., J.C.D., Religious Ordinaries and Canon 198, V-164 pp., 1942.
136. KERIN, REV. CHARLES A., S.S., M.A., S.T.B., J.C.D., The Privation of Christian Burial, XVI-279 pp., 1941.
137. LOUIS, REV. WILLIAM FRANCIS, M.A., J.C.D., Diocesan Archives, X-101 pp., 1941.
138. MCDEVITT, REV. GILBERT JOSEPH, A.B., J.C.D., Legitimacy and Legitimation, X-247 pp., 1941.
139. MCDONOUGH, REV. THOMAS JOSEPH, A.B., J.C.D., Apostolic Administrators, X-217 pp., 1941.
140. MEIER, REV. CARL ANTHONY, A.B., J.C.D., Penal Administrative Procedure Against Negligent Pastors, XI-240 pp., 1941.
141. SCHMIDT, REV. JOHN ROGG, A.B., J.C.D., The Principles of Authentic Interpretation in Canon 17 of the Code of Canon Law, XII-331 pp., 1941.
142. SLAFKOSKY, REV. ANDREW LEONARD, A.B., J.C.D., The Canonical Episcopal Visitation of the Diocese, X-197 pp., 1941.
143. SWOBODA, REV. INNOCENT ROBERT, O.F.M., J.C.D., Ignorance in Relation to the Imputability of Delicts, IX-271 pp., 1941.
144. DUBÉ, REV. ARTHUR JOSEPH, A.B., J.C.D., The General Principles for the Reckoning of Time in Canon Law, VIII-299 pp., 1941.
145. MCBRIDE, REV. JAMES T., A.B., J.C.D., Incardination and Excardination of Seculars, XX-585 pp., 1941.
146. KRÓL, REV. JOHN T., J.C.D., The Defendant in Ecclesiastical Trials, XII-207 pp., 1942.
147. COMYNS, REV. JOSEPH J., C.SS.R., A.B., J.C.D., Papal and Episcopal Administration of Church Property, XIV-155 pp., 1942.
148. BARRY, REV. GARRETT FRANCIS, O.M.I., J.C.D., Violation of the Cloister, XII-260 pp., 1942.
149. BOLDUC, REV. GATIEN, C.S.V., A.B., S.T.L., J.C.D., Les Études dans les Religions Cléricales, VIII-155 pp., 1942.
150. BOYLE, REV. DAVID JOHN, M.A., J.C.D., The Juridic Effects of Moral Certitude on Pre-Nuptial Guarantees, XII-188 pp., 1942.
151. CANAVAN, REV. WALTER JOSEPH, M.A., Litt.D., J.C.D., The Profession of Faith, XII-143 pp., 1942.
152. DESROCHERS, REV. BRUNO, A.B., Ph.L., S.T.B., J.C.D., Le Premier Concile Plénier de Québec et le Code de Droit Canonique, XIV-186 pp., 1942.

153. Dillon, Rev. Robert Edward, A.B., J.C.D., Common Law Marriage, X-148 pp., 1942.
154. Dodwell, Rev. Edward John, Ph.D., S.T.B., J.C.D., The Time and Place for the Celebration of Marriage, X-156 pp., 1942.
155. Donnellan, Rev. Thomas Andrew, A.B., J.C.D., The Obligation of the Missa pro Populo, VII-131 pp., 1942.
156. Eltz, Rev. Louis Anthony, A.B., J.C.D., Cooperation in Crime, XII-208 pp., 1942.
157. Gass, Rev. Sylvester Francis, M.A., J.C.D., Ecclesiastical Pensions, XI-206 pp., 1942.
158. Guiniven, Rev. John Joseph, C.SS.R., J.C.D., The Precept of Hearing Mass, XIV-188 pp., 1942.
159. Gulczynski, Rev. John Theophilus, J.C.D., The Desecration and Violation of Churches, X-126 pp., 1942.
160. Hammill, Rev. John Leo, M.A., J.C.D., The Obligations of the Traveler According to Canon 14, VIII-204 pp., 1942.
161. Haydt, Rev. John Joseph, A.B., J.C.D., Reserved Benefices, XI-148 pp., 1942.
162. Huser, Rev. Roger John, O.F.M., A.B., J.C.D., The Crime of Abortion in Canon Law, XII-187 pp., 1942.
163. Kearney, Rev. Francis Patrick, A.B., S.T.L., J.C.D., The Principles of Canon 1127, X-162 pp., 1942.
164. Linahen, Rev. Leo James, S.T.L., J.C.D., De Absolutione Complicis in Peccato Turpi, V-114 pp., 1942.
165. McCloskey, Rev. Joseph Aloysius, A.B., J.C.D., The Subject of Ecclesiastical Law According to Canon 12, XVII-246 pp., 1942.
166. O'Neill, Rev. Francis Joseph, C.SS.R., J.C.D., The Dismissal of Religious in Temporary Vows, XIII-220 pp., 1942.
167. Prince, Rev. John Edward, A.B., S.T.B., J.C.D., The Diocesan Chancellor, X-136 pp., 1942.
168. Riesner, Rev. Albert Joseph, C.SS.R., J.C.D., Apostates and Fugitives from Religious Institutes, IX-168 pp., 1942.
169. Stenger, Rev. Joseph Bernard, J.C.D., The Mortgaging of Church Property, 186 pp., 1942.
170. Waldron, Rev. Joseph Francis, A.B., J.C.D., The Minister of Baptism, XII-197 pp., 1942.
171. Willett, Rev. Robert Albert, J.C.D., The Probative Value of Documents in Ecclesiastical Trials, X-124 pp., 1942.
172. Woeber, Rev. Edward Martin, M.A., J.C.D., The Interpellations, XII-161 pp., 1942.
173. Benko, Rev. Matthew Aloysius, O.S.B., M.A., J.C.D., The Abbot *Nullius*, XVI-148 pp., 1943.
174. Christ, Rev. Joseph James, M.A., S.T.L., J.C.D., Dispensation from Vindicative Penalties, XIV-285 pp., 1943.

175. Clancy, Rev. Patrick M. J., O.P., A.B., S.T.Lr., J.C.D., The Local Religious Superior, X-229 pp., 1943.

176. Clarke, Rev. Thomas James, J.C.D., Parish Societies, XII-147 pp., 1943.

177. Connolly, Rev. John Patrick, S.T.L., J.C.D., Synodal Examiners and Parish Priest Consultors, X-223 pp., 1943.

178. Drumm, Rev. William Martin, A.B., J.C.D., Hospital Chaplains, XII-175 pp., 1943.

179. Flanagan, Rev. Bernard Joseph, A.B., S.T.L., J.C.D., The Canonical Erection of Religious Houses, X-147 pp., 1943.

180. Kelleher, Rev. Stephen Joseph, A.B., S.T.B., J.C.D., Discussions with Non-Catholics: Canonical Legislation, X-93 pp., 1943.

181. Lewis, Rev. Gordian, C.P., J.C.D., Chapters in Religious Institutes, XII-169 pp., 1943.

182. Marx, Rev. Adolph, J.C.D., The Declaration of Nullity of Marriages Contracted Outside the Church, X-151 pp., 1943.

183. Matulenas, Rev. Raymond Anthony, O.S.B., A.B., J.C.D., Communication, a Source of Privileges, XII-225 pp., 1943.

184. O'Leary, Rev. Charles Gerard, C.SS.R., J.C.D., Religious Dismissed After Perpetual Profession, X-213 pp., 1943.

185. Power, Rev. Cornelius Michael, J.C.D., The Blessing of Cemeteries, XII-231 pp., 1943.

186. Shuhler, Rev. Ralph Vincent, O.S.A., J.C.D., Privileges of Religious to Absolve and Dispense, XII-195 pp., 1943.

187. Ziolkowski, Rev. Thaddeus Stanislaus, A.B., J.C.D., The Consecration and Blessing of Churches, XII-151 pp., 1943.

188. Heneghan, Rev. John Joseph, S.T.D., J.C.D., The Marriages of Unworthy Catholics: Canons 1065 and 1066, XVI-213 pp., 1944.

189. Carroll, Rev. Coleman Francis, M.A., S.T.L., J.C.L., Charitable Institutions.

190. Ciesluk, Rev. Joseph Edward, Ph.B., S.T.L., J.C.D., National Parishes in the United States, VI-178 pp., 1944.

191. Coburn, Rev. Vincent Paul, A.B., J.C.D., Marriages of Conscience, XII-172 pp., 1944.

192. Connors, Rev. Charles Paul, C.S.Sp., A.B., J.C.D., Extra-Judicial Procurators in the Code of Canon Law, X-94 pp., 1944.

193. Coyle, Rev. Paul Raymond, A.B., J.C.D., Judicial Exceptions, X-142 pp., 1944.

194. Fair, Rev. Bartholomew Francis, A.B., S.T.L., J.C.D., The Impediment of Abduction, XII-122 pp., 1944.

195. Gallagher, Rev. Thomas Raphael, O.P., A.B., S.T.Lr., J.C.D., The Examination of the Qualities of the Ordinand, X-166 pp., 1944.

196. Gannon, Rev. John Mark, S.T.L., J.C.D., The Interstices Required for the Promotion to Orders, XII-100 pp., 1944.

197. Goldsmith, Rev. J. William, B.C.S., S.T.L., J.C.D., The Competence of Church and State Over Marriages—Disputed Points, X-128 pp., 1944.

198. Goodwine, Rev. Joseph Gerard, A.B., S.T.B., J.C.D., The Reception of Converts, XIV-326 pp., 1944.

199. Kowalski, Rev. Romuald Eugene, O.F.M., A.B., J.C.D., Sustenance of Religious Houses of Regulars, X-174 pp., 1944.

200. McCoy, Rev. Alan Edward, O.F.M., J.C.D., Force and Fear in Relation to Delictual Imputability and Penal Responsibility, XII-160 pp., 1944.

201. McDevitt, Rev. Vincent John, Ph.B., S.T.L., J.C.L., Perjury.

202. Martin, Rev. Thomas Owen, Ph.D., S.T.D., J.C.D., Adverse Possession, Prescription and Limitation of Actions: The Canonical "Praescriptio," XX-208 pp., 1944.

203. Miklosovic, Rev. Paul John, A.B., J.C.L., Attempted Marriages and Their Consequent Juridic Effects.

204. Mundy, Rev. Thomas Maurice, A.B., S.T.L., J.C.D., The Union of Parishes, X-164 pp., 1944.

205. O'Dea, Rev. John Coyle, A.B., J.C.D., The Matrimonial Impediment of Nonage, VIII-126 pp., 1944.

206. Olalia, Rev. Alexander Ayson, S.T.L., J.C.D., A Comparative Study of the Christian Constitution of States and the Constitution of the Philippine Commonwealth, XII-136 pp., 1944.

207. Poisson, Rev. Pierre-Marie, C.S.C., A.B., Ph.L., Th.L., J.C.L., Droits Patrimoniaux des Maisons et des Eglises Religieuses.

208. Stadalnikas, Rev. Casimir Joseph, M.I.C., J.C.D., Reservation of Censures, X-141 pp., 1944.

209. Sullivan, Rev. Eugene Henry, S.T.L., J.C.D., Proof of the Reception of the Sacraments, X-165 pp., 1944.

210. Vaughan, Rev. William Edward, J.C.D., Constitutions for Diocesan Courts, X-210 pp., 1944.

211. Paro, Rev. Gino, S.T.D., J.C.L., The Right of Apostolic Legation.

212. Balzer, Rev. Ralph Francis, C.P., J.C.D., The Computation of Time in a Canonical Novitiate, X-227 pp., 1945.

213. Dougherty, Rev. John Whelan, A.B., S.T.L., J.C.D., De Inquisitione Speciali, XII-195 pp., 1945.

214. Dziob, Rev. Michael Walter, J.C.D., The Sacred Congregation for the Oriental Church, XII-181 pp., 1945.

215. Eidenschink, Rev. John Albert, O.S.B., B.A., J.C.D., The Election of Bishops in the Letters of Pope Gregory the Great, VIII-200 pp., 1945.

216. Gill, Rev. Nicholas, C.P., J.C.D., The Spiritual Prefect in Clerical Religious Houses of Study, X-140 pp., 1945.

217. Hynes, Rev. Harry Gerard, S.T.L., J.C.D., The Privileges of Cardinals, XII-183 pp., 1945.

218. McDevitt, Rev. Gerald Vincent, S.T.L., J.C.D., The Renunciation of an Ecclesiastical Office, XIV-179 pp., 1945.

219. Manning, Rev. Joseph Leroy, J.C.D., The Free Conferral of Offices, VII-116 pp., 1945.

220. Meyer, Rev. Louis G., O.S.B., A.B., S.T.B., J.C.D., Alms-gathering by Religious, XII-163 pp., 1945.

221. O'Donnell, Rev. Cletus Francis, M.A., J.C.D., The Marriage of Minors, XII-268 pp., 1945.

222. Prunskis, Rev. Joseph, J.C.D., Comparative Law, Ecclesiastical and Civil, in Lithuanian Concordat, X-161 pp., 1945.

223. Sweeney, Rev. Francis Patrick, C.SS.R., J.C.D., The Reduction of Clerics to the Lay State, X-199 pp., 1945.

224. Vogelpohl, Rev. Henry John, J.C.D., The Simple Impediments to Holy Orders, XVI-190 pp., 1945.

225. Brockhaus, Rev. Thomas Aquinas, O.S.B., J.C.D., Religious who are known as *Conversi*, X-127 pp., 1945.

226. Griese, Rev. Orville Nicholas, S.T.D., J.C.D., The Marriage Contract and the Procreation of Offspring, XVI-224 pp., 1946.

227. Boudreaux, Rev. Warren Louis, J.C.D., The *"ab acatholicis nati"* of Canon 1099, § 2, XII-110 pp., 1946.

228. Bowe, Rev. Thomas Joseph, A.B., J.C.D., Religious Superioresses, VIII-206 pp., 1946.

229. Diederichs, Rev. Michael Ferdinand, S.C.J., J.C.D., The Jurisdiction of the Latin Ordinaries over their Oriental Subjects, XIV-153 pp., 1946.

230. Dingman, Rev. Maurice John, A.B., S.T.L., J.C.L., The Plaintiff in Contentious Trials.

231. Frison, Rev. Basil, C.M.F., M.Mus., J.C.D., The Retroactivity of Law, X-221 pp., 1946.

232. Galvin, Rev. William Anthony, M.A., J.C.D., The Administrative Transfer of Pastors, XII-288 pp., 1946.

233. Goracy, Rev. Joseph C., J.C.L., The Diriment Matrimonial Impediment of Major Orders.

234. Hale, Rev. Joseph Francis, M.A., S.T.L., J.C.L., The Pastor of Burial.

235. Henry, Rev. Joseph Arthur, A.B., J.C.D., The Mass and Holy Communion: Interritual Law, XII-138 pp., 1946.

236. Linenberger, Rev. Herbert, C.PP.S., J.C.L., The False Denunciation of an Innocent Confessor.

237. Lowry, Rev. James Martin, A.B., J.C.D., Dispensation from Private Vows, XII-266 pp., 1946.

238. Lynch, Rev. George Edward, A.B., S.T.L., J.C.D., Coadjutors and Auxiliaries of Bishops, X-107 pp., 1947.

239. Lynch, Rev. Timothy, M.S.SS.T., J.C.D., Contracts between Bishops and Religious Congregations, XIII-232 pp., 1946.

240. McClunn, Rev. Justin David, A.B., S.T.L., J.C.D., Administrative Recourse, VII-142 pp., 1946.

241. Lohmuller, Rev. Martin Nicholas, A.B., J.C.D., The Promulgation of Law, XII-140 pp., 1947.
242. McGrath, Rev. James, A.B., J.C.D., The Privilege of the Canon, XII-156 pp., 1946.
243. Marbach, Rev. Joseph Francis, A.B., J.C.D., Marriage Legislation for the Catholics of the Oriental Rites in the United States and Canada, XIV-314 pp., 1946.
244. Shimkus, Rev. Bernard Aloysius, A.B., J.C.L., The Determination and Transfer of Rite.
245. Smith, Rev. Vincent Michael, A.B., S.T.L., J.C.L., Ignorance Affecting Matrimonial Consent.
246. Wachtrle, Rev. Paul Anthony, A.B., J.C.L., The Baptism of the Children of Non-Catholics.
247. Crotty, Rev. Matthew M., J.C.D., The Recipient of First Holy Communion, X-142 pp., 1947.
248. Eagleton, Rev. George, J.C.L., The Quinquennial Faculties, Formula IV.
249. Gibbons, Rev. Marion L., C.M., LL.B., J.C.D., Domicile of the Wife Unlawfully Separated from Her Husband, XIV-171 pp., 1947.
250. Kelly, Rev. Bernard M., S.T.L., J.C.D., The Functions Reserved to Pastors, XII-141 pp., 1947.
251. Kilcullen, Rev. Thomas J., LL.M., J.C.D., The Collegiate Moral Person as Party Litigant, X-150 pp., 1947.
252. Lafontaine, Rev. Germain Joseph, W.F., J.C.L., Relations Canoniques entre le Missionnaire et Ses Superieurs.
253. Lane, Rev. Loras Thomas, A.B., S.T.L., J.C.L., Matrimonial Procedure in the Ordinary Court of Second Instance.
254. Lover, Rev. James F., C.SS.R., M.A., J.C.D., The Master of Novices, X-168 pp., 1947.
255. McNicholas, Rev. Timothy Joseph, J.C.L., The *Septimae Manus* Witness.
256. Marositz, Rev. Joseph J., M.S.C., J.C.D., Obligations and Privileges of Religious Promoted to the Episcopal or Cardinalitial Dignities, XII-180 pp., 1947.
257. Murphy, Rev. Francis J., A.B., J.C.D., Legislative Powers of the Provincial Council, XII-158 pp., 1947.
258. O'Brien, Rev. Romaeus W., O. Carm., J.C.D., The Provincial Superior in Religious Orders of Men, X-294 pp., 1947.
259. Pfaller, Rev. Benedict A., O.S.B., J.C.L., The *Ipso facto* Effected Dismissal of Religious.
260. Popek, Rev. Alphonse S., M.A., J.C.D., The Rights and Obligations of Metropolitans, XX-460 pp., 1947.
261. Ristuccia, Rev. Bernard Joseph, C.M., J.C.L., Quasi-Religious.
262. Sonntag, Rev. Nathaniel L., O.F.M. Cap., J.C.D., Censorship of Special Classes of Books, XII-147 pp., 1947.
263. Stadler, Rev. Joseph Nicholas, J.C.L., Frequent Holy Communion.

264. SZAL, REV. IGNATIUS JOSEPH, J.C.L., The Communication of Catholics with Schismatics.
265. WAGNER, REV. URBAN S., O.F.M. Conv., J.C.D., Parochial Substitute Vicars and Supplying Priests, X-126 pp., 1947.
266. QUINN, REV. JOSEPH JAMES, A.B., J.C.L., Documents Required for the Reception of Orders.

www.ingramcontent.com/pod-product-compliance
Lightning Source LLC
LaVergne TN
LVHW050242080826
844660LV00012B/579

* 9 7 8 0 8 1 3 2 2 4 4 4 2 *